When Mortals Play God

When Mortals Play God

Eugenics and One Family's Story of Tragedy, Loss, and Perseverance

John Erickson

ROWMAN & LITTLEFIELD
Lanham • Boulder • New York • London

Published by Rowman & Littlefield
An imprint of The Rowman & Littlefield Publishing Group, Inc.
4501 Forbes Boulevard, Suite 200, Lanham, Maryland 20706
www.rowman.com

86-90 Paul Street, London EC2A 4NE

British Library Cataloguing in Publication Information Available

Library of Congress Cataloging-in-Publication Data Is Available

ISBN: 978-1-5381-6669-7 (cloth)
ISBN: 978-1-5381-6670-3 (electronic)

For Millie

Contents

Foreword

I first came across John Erickson's grandmother Rose in a large red and gold leather-bound volume with the words "sterilization cases" embossed on the cover. I was doing research on eugenic sterilization at the Minnesota History Center, and she was listed, along with a thousand others, in a register of sterilization operations performed at the state institution for the "feebleminded" in southern Minnesota. Rose was one of seven women to undergo surgery one Friday in April 1926, a few months after the state's sterilization law went into effect.

I tried to tell the stories of women like Rose in my 2017 book, *Fixing the Poor: Eugenic Sterilization in the Twentieth Century*, but after years of research I could tell only a partial story about sterilization at one point, possibly the lowest point, in people's lives. In *When Mortals Play God*, John Erickson rounds out the story. His vivid portrait of Rose and her family over generations is a powerful exposé of the heartbreaking—and long-lasting—effects of an epic policy failure.

Rose's story may seem shocking today, but it was all too common in 1920s and 1930s America. Thirty-two states passed eugenic sterilization laws between 1907 and 1937. More than 63,000 Americans were sterilized. Minnesota alone sterilized at least 2,350 persons, nearly two-thirds of them women like Rose who carried the label "feebleminded."

The sterilization crusade swept other countries too. Sweden, Norway, Canada, Japan, and of course Nazi Germany, which sterilized an estimated 400,000 people, were among the nations with eugenics laws designed to prevent the reproduction of the "unfit": the so-called mentally defective, insane, criminalistic, epileptic, or morally degenerate. In 1927 the U.S. Supreme Court ruled that compulsory sterilization for eugenic purposes was constitutional. Its notorious decision, *Buck v. Bell*, cemented the state's power to "prevent those who are manifestly unfit from continuing their kind" and authorized the involuntary sterilization of Carrie Buck, a young white woman from Virginia who was branded feebleminded and promiscuous because she was poor and had a baby out of wedlock. And coerced sterilizations persisted long after eugenics ideas were discredited, as recent scandals over forced sterilizations in women's prisons and immigrant detention centers makes clear.

Eugenics, a term the English statistician Francis Galton coined in 1883 from the Greek word for "well-born," was the science of improving the human race through better breeding. Eugenics became popular because it combined the commonsense idea that certain attributes run in families with a scientific (but simplistic) theory of human heredity. Eugenicists posited that personal characteristics like intelligence, criminality, alcoholism, and immorality were biological traits transmitted across generations in a predictable pattern. Just as farmers could improve their livestock through animal breeding, they believed that poverty, crime, and disease could be reduced if people with desirable traits had more children and those with undesirable traits had fewer. Eugenicists wanted the "fittest" families to have more children, but eugenics legislation focused chiefly on ridding society of supposed undesirables. As a result, the least powerful segments of the population—African Americans, indigenous people, immigrants, people with disabilities, and individuals like Rose who were poor, uneducated, and "oversexed"—were disproportionately targeted.

Eugenics is most closely identified with sterilization, but it also involved prohibitions on interracial marriage and the marriage of disabled people, drastic reductions to immigration on racial grounds, and—of particular importance to Rose's family—the compulsory institutionalization, or "eugenic segregation" of those deemed to be feebleminded. The early twentieth century brought a major expansion of custodial state institutions, with many states mandating the compulsory institutionalization of the "feebleminded" during their childbearing years. When Rose was committed to the Minnesota School for the Feeble-Minded in 1924, more than 43,000 people across the United States were similarly confined. For many, sterilization was the price they had to pay to regain their freedom.

If eugenics ideas justified state-mandated sterilizations, in practice, sterilization programs functioned to reduce welfare costs by ensuring that poor, sexually active women did not have more children than they could care for or support. Rose's entire family fell victim to that system: child welfare authorities entered her house, put her in an institution, took away her children, and convinced her mother to consent to her daughter's sterilization. While Rose's family struggled to cope with hardship, calamity, and loss, welfare officials "protected" her children by removing them from their home. The family never saw her youngest son again.

Rose came of age in the flapper era, when young women defied traditional expectations for feminine behavior and asserted their sexual independence. Her story illuminates the cost of that defiance. As a teenager during World

War I, Rose drank and socialized with older men. She was eighteen when her first husband deserted her and their infant son, twenty-one when her second husband left her with two young children, and twenty-three when her third child was born. She was sterilized at twenty-four. To state and county welfare authorities, Rose's sexual immorality was a symptom of her feeblemindedness and the cause of her "broken" home. John shows that there was more to the story. What social workers saw as inherited degeneracy we recognize today as the intergenerational consequences of trauma, loss, hunger, and sexual abuse. A kinder child welfare system might have helped Rose's family stay together. Instead, the family was torn apart. The consequences echo today for the DeChaines as for many others.

Since surgical sterilization prevents reproduction, its impact is often assumed to have ended in one generation. But many sterilized individuals, like Rose, already had children, and they too suffered from the state's eugenics policies. *When Mortals Play God* brings these children of eugenics into focus. Rose's children, like immigrant, black, and indigenous children separated from their families more recently, were casualties of a broken system. The policies and practices that fractured the DeChaine family—from eugenic sterilization and child removal to sealed adoption records—are rarely discussed together. John shows how these practices worked in concert to destabilize one family, revealing the scope of Minnesota's eugenics policy and its impact on one family over generations.

Through dogged detective work over twenty years, John uncovered shocking secrets in his own family—and in the American past. The story he tells is an American story, a story of love and loss, rage and ruination, destitution and despair, but also of fortitude and hope, for the children of eugenics turned eugenics on its head. When we remember, John tells us, we can do better.

Molly Ladd-Taylor
Toronto, Ontario, Canada

Acknowledgments

I want to thank everyone who helped in the compilation of this book, from the clerks at the Crow Wing County Historical Society who provided me with obituaries, property records, and typewritten Works Progress Administration interviews done with various members of the DeChaine family, to the folks who maintain the incredible archive at the Minnesota Historical Society, located inside the Minnesota History Center building in downtown St. Paul. I spent many hours there poring over old city directories, prison records, jail dockets, World War II bonus payment logs, various records from that strange place where my grandmother Rose lived for nearly six years—the Faribault School for the Feeble-Minded—and even health records. It was at the history center where I found my mom's medical records from Gillette Hospital, where she was sent after leaving the St. James Catholic Orphanage in 1928.

Mostly I want to thank the many family members who provided invaluable recollections of events that were sometimes painful. Ernie's daughter Carolyn never once declined to answer a question, even when we strayed into deeply personal and unpleasant territory. Ernie's ex-wife Billie, whom he aimed his gun at in the courtroom, agreed to revisit that period in her life even though she has long since put it behind her. Robert's sister Sheila had trouble breathing yet returned my phone call and reminisced about him as best she could. It was through Sheila that I learned her father's real name was Rudolph, making her parents Santa and Rudolph.

Others, too, provided invaluable insights. I got a bird's-eye view of the St. James orphanage through the eyes of Eugene Saumer, who spent a year there and patiently recalled the sexual abuse he was subjected to as a ten-year-old boy. Saumer was so vivid in his recollections his wife, Bonnie, asked at one point if I was writing a novel. If only.

This book wouldn't have been possible without the help of Breanna Schueller, a development associate at the former Woodland Hills Residential Treatment Center in Duluth, which was housed in the same building where the St. James orphanage once sat. Without my asking, she dug into their files and allowed us to examine records we couldn't have found anywhere else. Watching my mother study those records—compiled nearly ninety years ago and containing significant details of her life and that of her two brothers—is one of the proudest moments of my life. Seeing my wife Lynda embrace my mom in celebration of the amazing find that was gifted to us was also one of those moments that can't ever be erased. My mom has given so much to all of us. It was nice to give something back.

My mom didn't hold back while recounting painful episodes in her childhood. She often referred to "Dad" when I was a kid, and I had no idea what Orvel McClain did to earn that mantle. I was surprised when she told me that he had legally adopted her and even more surprised when she showed me the paperwork: she had been nineteen at the time. Mom told me Orvel was afraid that members of his family would go after their money if he wasn't her legal guardian, but I suspect it had more to do with cementing a bond that had been established years before. He was her father in every sense of the word.

My mom wrote out lengthy answers to the questions I sent her, provided most of the photos that are in this book, and reached out to other family members for additional information. I had to laugh when I reread one of those letters, which included recollections from my mom's cousin that weren't entirely accurate.

"She's a little mixed up," my mom wrote. Now I know where I got my fact-checking gene.

I've tried to parent the way my mom did, although my children would probably say I constantly fall short. I remember one of her practices that I've always admired. I was a temperamental kid who clung to each perceived indignity like a prized possession. And with three older brothers, there were plenty of perceived indignities. Yet no matter how angry I was when I went to bed, my mom always came into my room and said something to make me feel better. She didn't want me carrying that anger into my dreams. I don't know where she learned that trick, but I suspect it didn't come from her own mother.

I hope I've portrayed Rose accurately in this book. I knew nothing of her past when I was a kid and in fact knew little of her drinking. I remember dreading our many visits, but that had more to do with me being a thirteen-year-old kid surrounded by grownups. If she ever had a drink in her hand during those visits, I don't remember it.

My dad didn't let me go to her funeral; he must have thought I was too young. My last memory of her was in her hospital room where I went to see her twice. The first time she was alert and talkative and I assumed she would go home in a day or two. She seemed so healthy I couldn't understand why she was even there. It was during my second visit when I realized that she would never go home. I remember asking my mom why Grandma's stomach was so big.

As I think back, my parents must have shielded me from the worst of Rose's behavior. I experienced nothing like Carolyn did, when she had to lock the bathroom door to protect her and her sister. In fact, most of my memories of Rose were positive ones. She was a complicated person whose hard life and addiction probably led to the harsh treatment of her only daughter. But she was also a tragic figure whose lot in life was punched at a young age. She was locked up as if she'd robbed a bank and her body defiled because she was seen as a danger to society. The state has since apologized for its hatefulness, but unfortunately some things can never be undone.

Rose's behavior was far from exemplary, but she was capable of more than the state gave her credit for. I keep thinking of the well-crafted letters she wrote to the prison on behalf of her son, expressing concern for his well-being. Maybe Orvel, her husband at the time, ghostwrote them, but he couldn't mimic the love she had for her son. She didn't always show my mom that same level of affection, but her letters prove she was capable of being a caring and doting mother. Perhaps with a little help, she was capable of much more.

I am deeply grateful to the many people who provided encouragement and guidance along the way, including my agent, Diane Nine; the author Molly Ladd-Taylor, who graciously agreed to write a foreword for the book and suggested changes that unquestionably made the manuscript better; and Jonathan Sisk and the wonderful group of professionals at Rowman & Littlefield. I can't thank them enough for having faith in this project and helping to bring it home.

Mostly I want to thank my family: my wife Lynda, son Travis, daughter Nicole, and granddaughter Riley—each of you make me better every day—and the various Ericksons, Fagelys, Nelsens, Saucermans, Klocksiens, Nordgrens, Petersens, Gagnes, Martins, Cartiers, Reeds, Makis, and Andersons. Together you show that families are a jigsaw puzzle with unlimited pieces.

And to my many dear friends out there—you know who you are—remember what Eleanor Roosevelt once said: "Many people will walk in and out of your life, but only true friends will leave footprints on your heart."

This story is about one family, but all families have their heroes and tragic figures. Heroes come in many colors and sometimes the most heroic among us are the ones who attract the least attention. Put my mother in a room with one hundred people and she wouldn't stand out.

It is her unique gift that she doesn't have to.

Author's Note

This is a true story. In a few places scenes and dialogue were invented for narrative purposes, but the horrendous treatment of the mentally ill and the impact such treatment had on American families is all too real. It took the state of Minnesota more than eighty years after it passed a eugenic sterilization law to finally own up to its brutal treatment of people with mental health issues and apologize to their families. *Eighty years.* And Minnesota was far from alone. Before World War II largely put an end to the practice of forced sterilizations, more than thirty states adopted laws using human beings in a social engineering experiment designed to cleanse the population of people of low birth and intelligence—in other words, to protect society from its polluted seeds. As the author Edwin Black wrote in his book *War against the Weak*, "Mankind's quest for perfection has always turned dark."[1]

For decades, sterilization was seen as an effective tool against the spread of immoral behavior. There were male patients in these supposedly voluntary operations. (In Minnesota, consent was so easily obtained it could come from a spouse, meaning a husband could have his wife sterilized by claiming she was insane or vice-versa.)[2] But the overwhelming majority of the subjects in Minnesota and elsewhere were women. They were mostly poor, uneducated, and completely unaware of what was happening to them. Some were teenagers. All were given a label that officials believed best summed up what they were: feebleminded. Yet it wasn't the minds of these women that so frightened the hard-core eugenicists. It was their bodies. After all, if their brains were the main concern, why is it that they were almost universally released from incarceration *after* undergoing sterilization?[3] Did the procedure magically make them smarter?

No, it was a woman's ability to conceive life that most frightened judges, politicians, educators, and scientists—in other words, the biggest thinkers of the day. In the frenzy surrounding eugenics, which took the nation by storm during the 1920s and 1930s, it was widely believed that "feebleminded" women had to be sterilized for the sake of future generations. Nothing less than mankind itself was at stake. Little thought was given to the rank cruelty of the policy or even who these women were. All that mattered was the score registered on their IQ test, a highly biased marker used by officials to justify any number of sins, including sterilization.

Eugenics was a solution to what was believed to be a vexing problem: what to do about a burgeoning population that didn't look, act, or think the way society thought they should. Hitler and his ministers eventually took genetic engineering to an extreme, using murder and extermination to speed the transition to their dream of a master race, but the practice of eugenics came of age in the United States—not in Germany—and was fully embraced for decades in Minnesota.[4]

The protagonist of this book, Rose DeChaine, was one of the early subjects of this awful experiment—in essence, a guinea pig.[5]

She wasn't someone to put on a pedestal. She had three children, likely from three different men.[6] She was a prostitute (for a time), a bad mother (for a longer time), and an alcoholic (for most of her life). She was the kind of person who engenders whispers in the beauty shop and headshakes at the dinner table. In a respectable family, she was the black sheep. She wasn't a monster, however. She could be good-natured and even loving at times. She showed deep love for her son and, on occasion, her daughter. No, she wasn't a monster. Yet she was treated like one by a state that often boasts of its progressive pedigree. And in the end, she may not have been the family's biggest victim.

Her life was marked by struggle. She lost four siblings, did three stints in a mental institution, was sterilized (among the first women in Minnesota to undergo the operation under the law passed in 1925), and was separated from her children for long periods. Her youngest son was adopted while she was in the institution, and she never saw him again. Her oldest son—well—it's probably best she didn't live to see the morning of February 13, 1979. That's when Ernie McClain made national headlines when he shot up a courtroom in Portland, Oregon, killing a young woman before putting a gun to his own head.[7]

And it's definitely a relief she wasn't alive seventeen years later when Ernie's son—her grandson—set off a pair of bombs in two crowded restaurants on a Sunday morning and then killed himself in front of a crowd of witnesses there to enjoy their eggs and bacon.[8]

In a life of struggle, being spared those acts of violence should count as a blessing.

Rose wasn't one to tell tales, but it would be remarkable if, with so little safety net available to her, she wasn't a subject of physical, emotional, and sexual abuse at one time or perhaps many times in her life. She disappeared from her family for lengthy stints and was the subject of ridicule and scorn due to her mental handicap. She was desperate for money and severely lacking in esteem. She lived on the streets on occasion. Words like "slut" and "whore" were routinely ascribed to her. By the age of twenty-one, she was the mother of two and had been abandoned by two husbands. Mystery shrouds the father of her third child, a boy she named Robert. He was born eight-and-a-half months after she first entered the Faribault School for the Feeble-Minded, a mental institution in Faribault, Minnesota.[9] Was he conceived before or after she was committed? Was he the product of consensual sex or something else?

And here's a chilling thought: what else happened in that institution, which housed men and women viewed, even by the administrators, as "subhuman"?

The tragedies that occurred in the DeChaine family can't be attributed to any one thing, even if that one thing was as brutally harmful as eugenics turned out to be. Did Ernie McClain take a gun into a courtroom because his mother was sterilized fifty years before? Perhaps not. But childhood experiences matter, and what happened to Rose—the blatant discrimination against her because she was poor, intellectually challenged, or a woman (and perhaps all three)—didn't play out harmlessly for her or those around her. It had a ripple effect that can't be fully quantified. Ernie's demons were his demons, but the cold reality of what he did that day—his blatant disregard for human life, including his own—was a product of a lot of things, some of them nurtured and fed at an early age. Childhood experiences matter, and for Ernie—and others in the family too—those experiences had a tenuous hold.

This is a tragic tale but, strangely, an uplifting one. Because even as the Roses of the world were stripped of their rights and subjected to man's most vile tendencies, others rose up to surpass their assigned stations in life. The intellectuals eventually abandoned eugenics, but it was ordinary folks that really turned it on its head. Far from destroying mankind, they improved it, helping us to form what our founders envisioned when they drafted language about a more perfect union.

Apologies are nice, and it's not nothing that Minnesota's lawmakers put in writing their acknowledgment of the shoddy treatment that mentally ill individuals received at the hands of state institutions during the course of decades.[10] But recognizing what can happen when mortals attempt to play God isn't enough. There's something else we should do, or more specifically, not do. We must never forget.

NOTES

1. Edwin Black, *War against the Weak* (Washington, DC: Dialog Press, 2012), 9.

2. See Molly Ladd-Taylor, *Fixing the Poor: Eugenic Sterilization and Child Welfare in the Twentieth Century* (Baltimore: Johns Hopkins University Press, 2017), 84–88.

3. Ladd-Taylor, *Fixing the Poor*, 124.

4. For the origin of eugenics, see Black, *War against the Weak*, 67.

5. Rose's sterilization is documented in archived records from the now-closed Faribault School for the Feeble-Minded and Epileptics, which can be accessed at the Minnesota Historical Society in St. Paul, Minnesota. For Minnesota sterilization data, see Ladd-Taylor, *Fixing the Poor*, 147.

6. Birth records, Minnesota Department of Health. Also child history records from the St. James Catholic Orphanage in Duluth, Minnesota.

7. Stan Federman, Jim Hill and Leslie L. Zaitz, "Attorney, Gunman Killed before Terrorized Court," *Oregonian*, February 14, 1979.

8. "Bombs Go Off in Two Crowded Coffee Shops; Suspect Commits Suicide," *Associated Press*, November 5, 1996.

9. Child history records, St. James Catholic Orphanage.

10. House file no. 1680, Minnesota House of Representatives, May 15, 2010.

Feebleminded: Any person, minor or adult, other than an insane person, who is so mentally defective as to be incapable of managing himself and his affairs, and to require supervision, control and care for his own or the public welfare. —Minnesota Children's Code, 1917

Prologue

The headline in the *Carlton County Vidette* on October 18, 1918, all but leapt off the page, its thick black ink blaring a message no one wanted to hear: "Awfullest fire horror in state's history!"[1]

Like most of the tragedies you will read about in this book, this one was preventable. The locomotives that crisscrossed Minnesota's Iron Range, home to the richest iron ore deposits in the world, had such poorly maintained chimney screens that the embers of burned coal flew up and then rained down like lit matches, turning the timber-kissed wonderland into a blackened panorama of doom. Wind gusts of seventy-five miles per hour or more added fuel and direction until the small fires that started first here and then there became a monstrous conflagration that was impossible to contain. Houses, barns, schools, and even rivers offered no deterrent. Fifteen hundred square miles were destroyed, 11,000 families displaced, 453 people killed and 52,000 injured, some with head-to-toe burns serving as permanent reminders of nature's strength.[2]

The dimensions of the firestorm are almost impossible to imagine. Ash from burned paper and debris landed in three neighboring states. The haze that blanketed huge parts of Minnesota and Wisconsin was spotted by fleets in the North Atlantic. The town of Cloquet, near where the biggest of the fires originated and home to the Frederick Weyerhaeuser–built sawmill, which was the nation's largest at the time, disappeared almost as if by magician's command.

"It looked as if the whole country was burning up," one farmer exclaimed.

The fire burned so hot remnants of it survived through the next Minnesota winter. Some residents fled to the many lakes in the region only to be tossed like rag dolls from their wind-swept boats. With the entire town of Moose Lake lying in ruins, Mayor Richard Hart walked six miles along the Northern Pacific Railway tracks to the nearest town and telegraphed a message to Minnesota Governor Joseph A. A. Burquist.

We must have food and clothing for three thousand people and three hundred caskels [*sic*] at Moose Lake at once. Entire county burned and people sufnering [*sic*] All coming to Moose Lake for aid[.] We must also have financial aid[.] This appeal is urgent[.]

Some of the towns around Moose Lake never recovered, their names erased from modern maps. Duluth, the city on the hill and nerve center of the region, was more fortunate. There, National Guard and local Home Guard troops worked through the night delivering supplies and moving residents to safety. One of the major rescue efforts occurred at the St. James Catholic Orphanage, where young boys and girls—some with no family life whatsoever—were fed structure and scripture by the stern hand of the Benedictine nuns. Troops trained in firefighting and rescue operations evacuated the orphanage and the nearby tuberculosis hospital, escorting residents and staff to a schoolhouse eight miles away. The orphanage, a citadel of brick and stone, was saved.

Ten years later, eight-year-old Ernie McClain, abandoned by his family and traumatized by the nuns put there to mold kids like him, would wish a different fate for the institution.[3]

NOTES

1. Franklin R. Raiter and Francis M. Carroll, *The Fires of Autumn: The Cloquet-Moose Lake Disaster of 1918* (St. Paul: Minnesota Historical Society Press, 1990), 3.
2. Raiter and Carroll, *The Fires of Autumn*, 4.
3. Child history records, St. James Catholic Orphanage.

1

Brainerd

They were French in a country that had long ago surrendered its flag—but not its soul—to the English.

Generations of the DeChaine family, previously the Miville family, lived this history. Jean Miville dit Deschenes, five generations removed from the family that would come to America, was part of the small-town heroes who repelled the mighty British warships led by Sir William Phips in 1690.[1] Jean's grandson Bernard was among Montcalm's overmatched troops on the Plains of Abraham in 1759. Bernard's grandson Prosper—the last in the line to be born and also die in Canada—saw his countrymen turn back the American invasion in the War of 1812, when no less an authority than Jefferson, the former president, famously dubbed the conquest a "mere matter of marching."[2]

They were a fertile bunch. Several of the DeChaines could number their children in the teens. One had at least fourteen children, another had fifteen. Like so many of their Canadian brethren, the DeChaine women tended to go through pregnancies until God or fatigue willed them to stop.

They were born with the Canadian gene, present in most, to be stubborn. Louise Marineau, who married Prosper's son Antoine, decried even the perfidy of old age, dying just days shy of her 104th birthday.[3] And that wasn't the full substance of her stubbornness. Louise lived in America for sixty-two years, and for sixty-two years she uttered not a single word of English, save for the name of her adopted home state, which she pronounced MIN-A-SOOO-TAH.

They were fiercely French, resisting even the slightest nod toward the British crown. After England took possession of Canada, the DeChaines—the spelling they adopted in America—settled near the French-speaking town of Saint-Paulin, northwest of Trois-Rivières in Quebec's Mauricie region.[4] (Drive 200 miles straight north from Burlington, Vermont, and you'll be there in about three-and-a-half hours.) The area is known for its lush forests, serpentine rivers, and lakes so pristine you can see your toes while wading up to your beltline. And as Britain sought to silence the voices of dissent in its North American possession, the region became known for something else: rebellion. Louis-Joseph Papineau, the former leader of the rebel group most responsible for the English pique, fled to the United States to escape imprisonment after organizing a boycott of British goods. When he returned, much had changed, but not Papineau, who continued his verbal assaults on the English (and anyone else who disagreed with him) while representing the district that includes Mauricie in the Canadian parliament.[5]

Quebec won the right to govern itself long after it had earned it. By then, however, America had survived its own war with England, and Canadians by the thousands were streaming across the border. Few of them spoke English and none could read it, but there was nothing wrong with their ears, and what they heard from those who went first was irresistible. *Come. Come before it's too late.*

Most went east, where America's great cities were opening their arms to the world, but the DeChaines headed in a different direction. Minnesota, still largely untouched by white hands, was fertile ground for the captains of industry, who eyed the state's natural beauty, the splendor of its pinewood vistas, and saw a different shade of green. All that was needed to make these dreams come true was something that was in short supply: workers. Thus, the mantra: *Come. Come before it's too late.*

The railroads and mining companies did the bulk of their headhunting in Europe, flouting the art of truth telling with advertisements of dubious accuracy. ("The assertion that the climate of Minnesota is one of the healthiest in the world may be broadly and confidently made," one such guide stated.)[6] The lumber barons who held sway over Minnesota's outback didn't have to concoct fictions about the weather, however. Their target audience already knew to put on an extra layer or two when braving the winter chill. By the time the DeChaines left for the United States, the woods of Wisconsin, Michigan, New York, and New England were flooded with Canadians, men so proficient in the art of felling trees that they could drive a stake into the ground thirty feet from a tree, which would slice it in half as it fell. Boys started in the camps as young as thirteen, rising at sunrise and quitting only when the day turned black. A timber baron named Joseph Tremblay provided a strong argument for child labor laws when, sometime before his death in 1937, he described what it was like beginning work at a lumber shanty at age twelve in 1861.

> You had to walk seven miles from camp to the depot and portage provisions on foot, with sixty pounds on your back. The rest of the time you were cutting roads and felling trees. Many's the evening I spent on a stump crying.[7]

If the boys didn't spend their evenings crying, they often slept in clothes so wet you could see the steam when they threw off their blankets at the morning bell. As for food, beans were a staple, often served three times a day. The English coined a name for them, perhaps inspired by the lumber camps. They called them "echo plums."

Prosper DeChaine married a Mauricie girl, Celeste Lajoie, in 1832, and they had seven children, including three sons: Pierre, Thomas, and Antoine. All three would join the great Canadian migration to America, each yearning for something better than what they had.[8] And with the railroads revolutionizing transportation the way America's interstate highways would do generations later, something better was achingly within reach. Between 1840 and 1930, more than one million Canadians crossed the border in search of the dream that held so many in its thrall, heeding the summons from the nectar of hope and the promise of America.

Come. Come before it's too late.

Lumbermen like the DeChaines followed the pine, and when the pine ran thin, as the saying went, they moved. Antoine was the last to leave, gathering up his wife, eight children, and aging mother in search of his pot of gold. He found it in a booming small city along the banks of the Mississippi River not far from its source. There the Northern Pacific Railway put a hub along its transcontinental train route to the West and, for a brief time, its headquarters.[9] The NP's president named the town in tribute to his wife, whose maiden name was Brainerd, and its early development served as an antidote to small thinking. When the DeChaines arrived in Brainerd, located some 130 miles north of Minneapolis and St. Paul, the city's train repair shops were expanding and the population was booming, from 1,864 people in 1880 to 7,110 in 1885.[10] The scent of fresh lumber in the air smelled of victory or at least progress. The seventy-five-room, three-story Villard Hotel—named after Henry Villard, the NP's president who, along with President Ulysses S. Grant, tapped the golden spike signaling completion of the Northern Pacific's transcontinental train route—was "the most conspicuous building in Brainerd and handsomest in northern Minnesota," gushed the author in an article in the publication *The Northwest.* Of the gleaming 150-foot-high, three-story train depot/headquarters downtown, the *Brainerd Dispatch* brazenly declared, "We Brainerdites are as proud of it as a little boy with a new knife."

That knife had some seriously rough edges. Brainerd was a place for dreamers, a small town that strove to be big, but with progress came people and with people came trouble. It wasn't just the clickety-clack of tempered steel on hastily assembled tracks above spongy ground that foreshadowed doom. (There were bridge collapses and fatal wrecks from day one.) The town itself was built on an expectation that the good times would last forever, and the bill would never come due. And for the DeChaines—some of them anyway—it always did.

Particularly in its early years, Brainerd earned a reputation as a rough-and-tumble town where one's wits were a fleeting possession. Taverns outnumbered churches three to one and nearly equaled the number of hotels and boardinghouses that accompanied life in a boomtown. Clearly drinking was right there with sleeping as a necessity for living. Bar fights were common as were disputes over pay and living conditions, which for many of the workers meant sleeping in tent cities or railcars idled in the yard. More than 200 workers rioted over working conditions in 1871, resulting in the arrests of twelve of the "ringleaders," as the railroad labeled them. Some of the workers claimed later that they were fingered by NP officials for the sole purpose of swindling them out of the wages they were owed.[11]

The Wild, Wild West show was rapidly getting out of hand, and that summer NP officials summoned help from the federal government to quell the disturbances. An August 1, 1871, *Minneapolis Tribune* editorial described the situation:

> Heretofore, pimps, gamblers, roughs and bullies have held high carnival in the wilderness through which this great highway was being constructed. Peace officers were not to be found, the courts were not in existence, and the revolver and bowie-knife was the judge that adjudicated the simplest disputes. The simple-hearted Scandinavian laborers have been swindled and robbed in every imaginable manner, and these roughs have in many instances not even stopped at murder in their unscrupulous pursuit for gain.

The deputy U.S. marshal brought in to bring peace to the area, Alfred B. Brackett, responded by banning liquor sales in Brainerd, which is a little like prohibiting partying on Bourbon Street. A Civil War veteran, Brackett probably had more success on Killdeer Mountain than in lawless Minnesota, but he did learn a thing or two about marketing, as evidenced by another *Minneapolis Tribune* piece, which declared, "All the gamblers, pimps, bullies and harlots that have been following up the [NP] road . . . are now located in Fargo."

In other words, the vermin were driven clear out of the state.

Whiskey and horrible working conditions weren't the only combustible fuel. Brainerd was built on Ojibwe territory, and tensions between the two cultures ran high. The most famous of these encounters occurred in 1872, when a young white girl named Helen McArthur disappeared from her home and was never heard from again.[12] The sheriff, perhaps feeling the intense heat from a citizenry demanding justice, arrested two Ojibwe men who were said to have boasted of killing a white woman and disposing of her body.

Whether it was true or not didn't really matter. They were in custody and that meant they were guilty. No trial was necessary.

Desperate, the two men made a plea for leniency (or at least for their lives), showing the sheriff bones that could have belonged to a pterodactyl for all he cared. That night 300 townspeople stormed the jail and removed the men from their cell, dragging them to a couple of trees outside. A photograph captures the moment, the two men suspended high above ground, facing each other and locked together in a death pose, their necks stiff and bent back as if seeking eternal wisdom from above. The townsfolk apparently weren't looking for any heavenly guidance; they stared straight into the camera, their dress attesting to the prominence of the occasion.

Most wore suits.

The 1872 hanging in Brainerd occurred in front of the fittingly named Last Turn Saloon. Rumors spread that some 200 Ojibwe, many wearing war paint, were gathering outside of town. Sheriff John Gurrell fired off a telegraph to Minnesota's governor, Horace Austin, with an urgent plea: "Please send troops immediately; town full of Indians and have been ordered to leave . . . but do not."

Alarmed, the governor dispatched three companies of the First National Guard—some seventy men along with the adjutant general—to Brainerd in what was thought to be a seat of war. Instead, it was a seat of quiet. Not only were the Indians not decked out in war paint, they had apparently gathered outside of town to pick blueberries. The newspapers gave the affair a derisive dub: the "Blueberry War."[13]

Brainerd was growing up in a hurry. By the end of 1872, there were five churches in the town, a school, a library, and enough people to support a county fair. There was plenty to do besides frequenting one of the fifteen local taverns. The Brainerd Baseball Club was organized in 1873, and a short time later the "Young Men's Club of Brainerd" came into existence, its stated purpose to "offset influence of the saloon."

The culture of drink in Brainerd was so pervasive (the number of taverns would soon grow to twenty-six) that citizens began demanding reforms. And that's when the real trouble started, as this unnamed citizen described in a March 1872 letter to the editor in the *Brainerd Tribune*:

> I have lived in many parts of the state—during the worst of her troubles, but have never been in a place where there was so much night prowling and shooting as in this little town of Brainerd. It is worse than the Sioux Indian outbreak, for then we knew who our enemies were; while here, we are in danger at all times from a set of half-drunken braggadocios walking the streets and firing pistols at every corner, and I think it's full time something is done.

Brainerd "was flaming with illuminated signs and gambling places indiscriminate, and all of which seemed to be doing a thriving business," the writer H. L. Bridgeman reminisced in a 1922 *St. Paul Pioneer Press* article that looked back on Brainerd's beginnings. Bridgeman wrote that he personally observed one of those indiscriminate gambling places—the Dolly Varden Club—"desirous of seeing all the life of the frontier." The scene he described was right out of Deadwood or Dodge City. In the front room, signs with the words Chuck-a-Luck, High Dice, and Mustang hung over the tables, while higher stakes games were played in a room in the rear. No liquor could be sold in compliance with the conditions of the deed, according to Bridgeman, but "placards in red announced that gentleman will be furnished with refreshments by the proprietor, for which they will please pay in advance."

The writer was skeptical that Brainerd could sustain its early boom: "The town is artificial," he wrote, "the creature and product of the railroad, and the moment the plans of the corporation changes, its life is checked and its growth stopped, as though the Merrimack were taken from Lowell or the fishing banks from Cape Cod."

Bridgeman's comments would prove prophetic. The town was humming along—socially and, it appeared, financially. And then it wasn't. Tight money, high freight rates, and even a grasshopper scourge pulverized the Minnesota economy in the wake of the Panic of 1873. The trains ran slowly, if at all, and tracklaying all but stopped. The Philadelphia House of Jay Cooke, which had financed much of the town's early development, collapsed and creditors began calling for his head.[14] Many in Brainerd did, too, as the city that was built by the railroad was in grave danger of becoming another one of those towns that have a past but no future. Fortunately, it was a momentary blip. Aided by the discovery of gold in the Black Hills, the NP soon resumed its westward expansion. And proving that any publicity is good publicity, the Northern Pacific named its Black Hills–bound junket "The Custer Route."

In 1877 Brainerd celebrated what appeared to be its greatest triumph yet.[15] The NP that year opened a branch line to the city of Sauk Rapids, which gave Brainerd a direct connection with the fast-growing twin cities of Minneapolis and St. Paul. The townsfolk assumed the link would yield untold riches by opening up a corridor between the state's heartland and its major population center. It didn't seem to register with the booster crowd that the exploding transportation network also meant that the railroads would be less reliant in the future on these artificial hubs established based on little more than a surveyor's compass. The following year the Northern Pacific moved its headquarters to St. Paul, essentially ending Brainerd's dreams of becoming a railroad Mecca in the middle of the Minnesota prairie. Later, the NP would bypass Brainerd entirely on its western route from the Twin Cities, further minimizing the city's standing.

But Brainerd was resilient. Almost from the beginning, it would punch above its weight, come crashing down, and then somehow emerge intact. Or at least standing. In the 1880s the town became a major lumber center. Mining burst forth a decade or so later, and by the 1920s this once remote outpost became a sanctuary for recreation (in the summer anyway), its resorts attracting movie stars like Clark Gable and Carole Lombard and other celebrities, like the gangster John Dillinger and the boxer Jack Dempsey. In 1945, the town's well-constructed plans for putting veterans to work was the subject of a *Collier's Weekly* article, which appeared in the publication one page after a short story by J. D. Salinger. In the 1970s and 1980s, Brainerd International Raceway was a big draw on the racing circuit, featuring names like Bobby and Al Unser. Paul Newman set a lap record there in 1977 and won his first professional race at the speedway in 1982. Parts of the movie *Fargo* were filmed there and the Minnesota-born directors, Joel and Ethan Coen, even considered naming the movie *Brainerd*.[16]

Perhaps it was destiny or sheer luck, but the arrival of Antoine and his family in Brainerd coincided with the town's growth as a lumber producer. Pine trees were the gold standard for lumber companies of the day because the trees are tall, thick at the trunk, and light enough to float down rivers. Hardwoods, much valued now, were then the second-class citizens of the forest, largely because they sank in water, making it impossible for the so-called river rats to move the logs to the mills. The "junk" trees—the hardwoods—were mostly cleared and discarded for farmland, a treasure forever lost.

Lumber helped fulfill the American dream. It was used for everything from houses to railroad ties to river dams to fence posts. Lumber barons from their offices in Boston, Philadelphia, Chicago, and Minneapolis invested heavily in Minnesota's seemingly limitless pineries and then established a distribution system that made the harvesting profitable. The railroads made that infinitely easier.

In 1854 a rail line reached the Mississippi River at Rock Island, Illinois, providing a terminus for the East Coast. One sawmill center was developed on the west bank of the Mississippi at Minneapolis (then called St. Anthony), with another further downriver at Winona. The white pine that lined the Rum River from Lake Mille Lacs, the St. Croix delta, and the Mississippi River corridor all brought lumbermen from Canada, the New England states, New York, Pennsylvania, and even Europe and Russia.[17] Some of the greatest family names in Minnesota—the Steeles, the Washburns, the Godfreys, and the Pillsburys—were drawn there by logging. John S. Pillsbury may be best known as a flour manufacturer, but he was a lumberman well before then. John and his brother George were principals in a number of lumber companies, and they also invested heavily in the pinelands around Brainerd.

In 1880, John and George Pillsbury and their nephew Charles built a sawmill and a general store along a tributary to beautiful Gull Lake, northwest
of Brainerd.[18] Their Brainerd interests would become enormously profitable,
but first they had to employ a business principle that still endures today with
public financing of sports stadiums and other expensive projects: if you don't
want to pay for it yourself, make some outlandish claims about jobs and get
the public to pony up the money.

The Pillsburys were the incorporators of a company that promised to
build a rail line from Brainerd to the company's existing rail terminus at the
then-named Gilpatrick Lake (now Lake Margaret) and north from there once
the nearby forests were logged out. In exchange for public financing through
a $100,000 bond offering, the company would also construct a new sawmill
on the banks of the newly created Rice Lake.

Government leaders initially balked and then agreed to let county voters
decide. And decide they did. Intrigued by the prospect of jobs—the *Brainerd
Tribune* said approval of the bond issue would result in "one of the biggest
lumber mills in the country"—the voters made a clear statement. The final
tally was 1,613 in favor of the bonds and only ninety-five against. In the city
of Brainerd, where Antoine, Louise, and their family were living at the time,
just three people cast negative votes.[19]

As the Pillsbury-financed Brainerd and Northern Minnesota Railroad
began transporting hundreds of thousands of feet of logs a day—even running
night trains for a while—a Minneapolis lumberman was already transform-
ing the woods around Brainerd. Jeremiah J. "Jerry" Howe arrived in the area
in 1876 after setting up a chain of wholesale and retail lumberyards in other
parts of Minnesota and North Dakota.[20] At the time, he was the "walking
boss" for the well-known Minneapolis company Farnham and Lovejoy, a
competitor of the Pillsburys.

Sumner W. Farnham and J. A. Lovejoy were another in the long line of
lumber merchants from Maine who saw dollar signs attached to each white
pine that towered above Minnesota's fruited plain. Howe must have seen
them too because he would branch out on his own, at least enough to put
his name above the door, graduating from "walking boss" to *the* boss. Howe
took over a mill on a small body of water on the south side of Brainerd called
Boom Lake, where the Northern Pacific had laid down track from its Brainerd
yards. Howe maintained an office in town but employed up to 225 men at the
mill. They included Antoine, his son Joseph, two other sons, and the father of
Joseph's future bride, Mary Forcier.[21] Brainerd was a place for dreamers all
right, but at its heart it was still a small town.

Howe's Boom Lake plant was state of the art, with electricity powering
rotary, shingle, and lathe saws. The plant also included a drying kiln and a

machine shop. Along with the land around the plant, Howe and his partners also owned roughly a billion feet of pine stumpage along the river.

At its peak around 1887, Howe's mill manufactured up to twenty million feet of logs a year and filled one hundred railcars a month. There were smaller operations and a bigger one, the Brainerd Lumber Company, each fueling an industry that had one serious impediment: it depended wholly on how many trees were still standing. Photographs from the period capture the complete devastation of the once-magnificent forest, with the stumps of felled trees jutting out from the ground like the noses in a prairie dog colony. Complementing this grim facade were the expressions on the faces of those in the photographs, a scowl that was apparently mandatory back in the day every time someone said, "Cheese."

Logging, particularly in the lumber camps, was a hard life. In a book of essays about pioneer life in the Brainerd area, local historian Carl Zapffe chronicled the wanderings of some of the "jacks" hired on chiefly for their brawn. One crew employed by Connor, Gaines and Company of Minneapolis took a train to Brainerd and then hiked the thirty or so miles along wagon trails through the Whitefish chain of lakes north of Brainerd to the logging camps. Companies like Connor signed up the men under a stipulation that they would receive half of their pay—as little as $15 a month—at the camp and the remainder when they returned to Minneapolis. This arrangement was most beneficial to the company but also ensured that the nearest tavern owner wouldn't tear a hole in the pocket of every lumberjack in the camp. Zapffe includes a letter from one of these woodsmen after weeks of involuntary sobriety.

> I am Suffering. I have Not had a Drink of good Whiskey for some three weeks. . . . If you have any More of that old Whiskey that you used to have in the old cellar such as you gave me once—by God send me some if you want to do a good thing and prolong a Mans Life one two or 3 Bottles would help like Hell and be Very Much appreciated.[22]

Brainerd had a wild reputation, but the log camps were a breed apart. Towns that no longer exist rose out of the swampland simply because of a nearby stand of trees. One of these logging towns, Lothrup, was in Cass County near Walker, Minnesota. The village had 1,000 people, an old-timer told a Walker newspaper in 1916—"nine hundred of whom were drunk and the other 100 fighting trying to get up to the bar." No one used the term addiction then, but it was a disease that would infect the DeChaine family in both painful and troublesome ways.

As the trees kept coming down, no one gave a thought to—or much cared about—the finite nature of what they were harvesting, believing instead the words of James Madison Goodhue, who wrote: "Centuries will hardly exhaust the pineries above us." Even depressions—and the worst in the country's history to that time came in 1893—couldn't shake the false sense of prosperity. An 1894 article in the St. Paul *Pioneer Press* stated: "The resources of Minnesota are inexhaustible and the financial Depression cannot disturb the local confidence of her capitalists in the future."

Turns out the capitalists knew better. The Pillsburys began selling their vast timber holdings in 1895, even as the *Brainerd Tribune* declared, "There is enough pine here to keep the (new) company cutting for fifteen to twenty years." Frederick Weyerhaeuser, perhaps the biggest lumberman of all and a neighbor of the railroad baron James J. Hill on Summit Avenue in St. Paul, kept his Minnesota operations going longer than the others but did so with an eye to the West. The Weyerhaeuser Timber Company bought heavily along the Pacific Northwest and even got an assist from Hill. When the St. Paul entrepreneur finished his Great Northern rail line to the Pacific, he cut the rates for the lumber producers there, of which none was bigger than Weyerhaeuser.[23]

Howe, too, began pulling up stakes. By 1895 he was selling off horses, harnesses, and logging outfits. The mill burned in 1896, and Howe and his partners didn't lift a finger to rebuild it. The NP even pulled up the tracks on the spur to Boom Lake.

Howe hung around for a while under a new company name and continued cutting logs for transport on the Mississippi, but this was clearly the mop-up phase. As the supply of pine dwindled, the industry captains abandoned the area for other virgin forests further north. In 1906, Howe left Brainerd for good.[24] By then the DeChaines were a fixture in the area and most hung around, grabbing jobs where they could—often at the railroad—or planting seeds in an industry that would prove to be far more durable and long lasting. Antoine bought farms for several of his sons, allowing them to fulfill the dream of all immigrants: to own land. Louise lived in the farmhouse Antoine built long after he passed and then moved in with their son Edward, where she hosted her famous birthday parties—community events celebrating the longevity of Brainerd's oldest resident. As she steadfastly approached the century mark, the occasions became fodder for stories in the *Brainerd Dispatch*, which annually raved about Louise's stubborn refusal to submit to the relentless pace of old age.

On her ninety-eighth birthday she "could not be aroused to see that reaching ninety-eight years was anything out of the ordinary," a reporter wrote. "She cooks and sews and works out in the garden, and during the busy season she may even be found out with the men in the field."

By her 101st birthday Louise was still rising each morning at 5:00 a.m. And although her eyesight was impaired (she refused to wear glasses), she "can still thread a needle and occasionally picks up her sewing basket," the newspaper said. "Only last year she knitted a pair of socks for her son."

But on her 102nd birthday there was no mention of knitting socks or working with the men in the field. Time was winning the race. Still, Louise was said to be "most remarkable as to good health." She died the following year, having lived through the Civil War, World War I, and part of World War II. At her death, she had six living children, thirty-eight grandchildren, and twenty great-grandchildren. According to her obituary, she stayed devoted to her faith right up until the end: "She often said her inability to attend Mass was one of the hardest things to bear in her declining years."[25]

The DeChaines came to America with little more than the clothes on their backs and their hopes and dreams in their hearts. It was a time—almost impossible to imagine now—when America extended a welcome mat to immigrants, when it took to heart the Emma Lazarus poem etched into the base of the great monument on its shore: *Give me your tired, your poor, your huddled masses yearning to breathe free.*

It's a wonderful sentiment—and a fulfilling one for countless numbers of immigrants who yearned to breathe free and ended up thriving in the comforting arms of a generous nation. But for others the promise of America was painfully out of reach. Joseph DeChaine—Antoine and Louise's oldest son—married Mary Forcier and carved out a life the way so many other Canadians did: with quiet purpose and boundless resolve. Then tragedy struck, not once, but over and over again, testing the endurance of the heart and the strength of the soul.

It was their enduring love that stitched the family together. And it was the curse of one family member in particular that nearly broke it apart.

Like her ancestors, Rose DeChaine yearned to breathe free in a world of terrifying danger and uncertainty. But just as wind and fire can destroy God's creations, man can inflict ghastly harm upon himself, sometimes without seeing from where it is coming.

NOTES

1. Evelyn Yvonne Theriault, "The Battle of Riviere-Ouelle," https://acanadianfamily. wordpress.com/2009/02/22/riviere-ouelle-les-habitants/.

2. For genealogy of the DeChaine family, source was October 8, 1985, letter to Janette Martin from American-Canadian Genealogical Society. Letter was accessed at the Crow Wing County Historical Society in Brainerd, Minnesota. For recruitment of French-Canadians of Bernard's age, see Francis Parkman, *Montcalm and Wolfe: The French & Indian War* (Cambridge, MA: Da Capo Press, 1984), 403. A number of books and articles have quoted Jefferson on predicted easy conquest of Canada at the

outset of the War of 1812. For one source, see Donald Hickey, "The Global Context of the War of 1812" article series, National Park Service, www.nps.gov/articles/series.htm?id=BDDAB89F-FCE5-5B42-606EFFF0F343F8FE.

3. "Mrs. L. DeChaine Dies at Advanced Age of 103 Years," *Brainerd Dispatch*, April 16, 1943.

4. Genealogy records. See www.ancestors.familysearch.org for Pierre Miville dit Deschenes.

5. Alfred Duclos Celles, *Louis-Joseph Papineau*, Bibliolife, LLC, 167.

6. See www.mprnews.org/story/2008/03/04/why-does-this-man-live-in-minnesota.

7. Donald MacKay, *The Lumberjacks* (Toronto: Natural Heritage/Natural History, 1998), 220.

8. Works Progress Administration interview with Mary DeChaine, June 1938. Accessed at Crow Wing County Historical Society.

9. Carl Zapffe, *Brainerd* (Minneapolis, MN: Colwell Press, 1946), 10.

10. Zapffe, *Brainerd*, 197.

11. "The Northern Pacific Riot, Twelve of the Ringleaders Awaiting Trial at Fort Ripley," *Duluth Minnesotian*, January 14, 1871.

12. William Watts Folwell, *A History of Minnesota*, vol. 3 (St. Paul: Minnesota Historical Society, 1969), 79.

13. "Indians Brought Blueberries as Brainerd Feared Massacre," BrainerdHistory.com, http://sections.brainerddispatch.com/history/stories/nat_1002030082.shtml.

14. Richard White, *Railroaded: The Transcontinentals and the Making of Modern America* (New York: W. W. Norton, 2011), 83.

15. "Important Railroad News," *Brainerd Tribune*, May 5, 1877.

16. Michael Balderston, "Fargo: 10 Behind-the-Scenes Facts about the Coen Brothers Movie," *Cinema Blend*, February 7, 2021.

17. Agnes M. Larson, *The White Pine Industry in Minnesota* (Minneapolis: Regents of the University of Minnesota Press, 1939), 38.

18. William E. Lass, *Minnesota: A History*, 2nd ed. (New York: Norton, 1998), 181.

19. For background on bond issue, see Zapffe, *Brainerd*, 63.

20. Ibid., 39.

21. WPA interview with Mary DeChaine, June 1938.

22. Carl Zapffe, *Indian Days in Minnesota's Lake Region* (Brainerd, MN: Historic Heartland Association, 1990).

23. Michael P. Malone, *James J. Hill: Empire Builder of the Northwest* (Norman, OK: University of Oklahoma Press, 1996), 243.

24. Zapffe, *Brainerd*, 77.

25. "Reaches Her 104th Year, Mrs. Louise DeChaine, Oldest Woman in County," *Brainerd Tribune*, April 12, 1943.

2

Mary

Rose DeChaine was nothing like her mother, whose wide body could scarcely contain the size of her heart. Mary Forcier was born on Christmas Day, kissed by angels and guided to do good in the world or at least to provide safe mooring for anyone with the slightest connection to family.

Whatever Rose was, she wasn't that. She took care of nobody, least of all herself, and she certainly didn't take care of her children. She was almost born on Christmas but fell a day short, perhaps a metaphor for her life. She had a beaklike nose and a homely countenance that would have been fine if not for the menacing scowl. She was a hard woman whose addiction hovered over her like a dark cloud that angrily hides the sun. If she wasn't an alcoholic as a young woman, she would soon become one, and under "cause of death" on her death certificate are the words "chronic alcoholism," as if that is a full description of who she was.

No, Rose and Mary were nothing alike. But Mary was probably most responsible for her daughter having a semblance of a normal life.

Mary Forcier DeChaine was born in Vermont but was a child of Canada in every way, including her stubborn refusal to accept life on someone else's terms. Her father was a logger who left Quebec to follow the pine, eventually settling in the Minnesota railroad town whose job prospects were as bountiful as the river that runs through it, a force of nature so great they named a state after it. Most of her siblings traced the path of the Northern Pacific to the West Coast, but Mary stayed alongside the Mississippi in Brainerd, assuming the drudgery of homemaking not as if it were a job but a noble calling.[1]

Children had always been the center of her life, perhaps because she was surrounded by them. She resembled her mother-in-law Louise in spirit and demeanor, but they were identical in one other critical sense: their fertility. Babies came so regularly in the DeChaine household you could nearly set your watch to them.

Mary was a woman of few words. As a young girl she wasn't taught the three Rs but instead learned the three Cs: cooking, cleaning, and canning. She liked to tell people that she attended only one day of schooling, not because she was proud of it, but as a simple statement of fact. She almost never brought up her childhood, but it defined her in both subtle and not-so-subtle ways. During that childhood she was always moving, leaving friends behind and starting over in a strange place. That wasn't anything she wanted for her own children. Some people see moving as adventure, as opportunity. To Mary it only meant loss.

She wore long, baggy dresses that revealed nothing of her body—not because she was modest, but because she was practical. She liked nice things, but she didn't allow them to bring her any great pleasure. She wasn't perfect: she had a sweet tooth that could put a dentist into a second home, and you wouldn't exactly call her tolerant, particularly when it came to other religions. She once told her granddaughter that she could worship in any house of the Lord that she wished, as long as it had a Saint in front of its name. For Mary, going to a non-Catholic church was the same as not going to church at all.

She was wary of strangers, which in her eyes was pretty much anybody who wasn't a DeChaine, related to a DeChaine, or friends with a DeChaine. It wasn't that she thought her family could do no wrong—she kept a stick on the top of the refrigerator and made the small ones fetch it when they misbehaved—but she held steady to the belief that the righteous among us prevail against the evil hand of adversity. As she would painfully discover, however, adversity can take many forms, and no amount of discipline, tough love, or even faith in the Almighty can truly keep it from knocking at your door.

She met her husband Joseph, fittingly, in church. They had their differences, but Mary never regretted the night she showed up at the church social and Joseph, too shy to ask her to dance, asked her if she wanted a glass of punch. He was so handsome that she would have said yes if he had asked her to go to the moon. It didn't matter that Joseph was slightly older than Mary or that his job was less than secure or even that Mary's given name wasn't Mary at all but the one she put on her marriage certificate: Melvina. To anybody and everybody, they were Mary and Joseph, and if that wasn't biblical karma, then nothing was.

In the early years, the pregnancies followed a predictable pattern, almost like the winter's first frost (which, in Minnesota, often came in fall) and the interminable rains that signaled the dawn of spring. Ida came first, followed by Lottie, Mabel, Elmer, Dora, Rose, and the twins—Clara and Clarence. There was another boy, Henry, but he didn't live a day.[2] It was the first sign that adversity wasn't just knocking at Mary's door. It was kicking it in.

When Henry emerged into the world, his still body cold to the touch, Mary prayed for guidance from above. Prayer was as important to her as the air she breathed. Maybe more important. She didn't just pray during troubled times, though. She assumed the Lord would frown on that. No, she prayed from the time she got up in the morning until well into the night, when she departed into her dreams. She prayed when it rained and when the sun peeked from behind the clouds. Most of the time she prayed for her family and made certain to thank Him—the *H* was always capitalized in her head—for providing her with so many gifts of wonderment. Anything she achieved in life was secondary to what she considered her greatest accomplishment: her family. And as the coffin closed on Henry's tiny body, she prayed that God would heal that family, now wrapped in sorrow and broken from loss.

God never talked directly to her—that particular airwave was reserved for her husband Joseph after he passed—but her faith told her there are reasons for the sufferings inflicted upon man. Maybe the reason, she concluded, was not to take things for granted, but to learn from your experiences—however agonizing they might be—and to emerge with a strength that wouldn't otherwise be possible. Maybe the lesson was to carry on.

Rose was born on December 24, 1901. Mary had the house decked out beforehand and was convinced—knew in her heart—that this beautiful child would be born on the very anniversary of Jesus's birth, just as Mary herself had been. When that didn't happen, when the first contraction came twelve hours early, she felt blessed just the same. The baby she held in her arms was perfect and, as always, living proof of the divine. Joseph always let her name the kids—"I'm no good at all that," he would tell her—but Mary had to wait until she could hold them to decide. "I need to look 'em in the eyes," she would explain.

This naming ritual had a familiar pattern. Usually she picked a family name, rotating between their two families or choosing one side of the family for the first name and the other side for the middle name. But this time she saw her daughter's face with those piercing eyes and knew instantly. No family name would do. A beautiful baby needs a beautiful name, and few names are more beautiful than Rose.

She was a difficult child. Mary believed that all of her kids were extraordinary in their own ways, but none of the others was this much work. Elmer got in trouble a few times for skipping school, but that was usually to go fishing. And he liked to play gags on his sisters, like hiding their lunch bags so they'd be late for school or putting bunny ears behind their heads as they lined up for their Sunday school pictures.

The older girls were straight arrows. Who wouldn't be after watching the spectacle of Elmer dragging the kitchen chair over to the refrigerator, crying like a baby, climbing up to retrieve the stick for his enraged mother? It didn't take him long to figure out that the louder he wailed, the softer the blows were, but the girls didn't know that. Call it sexist, but they never got the stick treatment, though Mabel may have deserved it a time or two. She was the one who was always pushing curfew.

Rose's arrow didn't follow the same trajectory as her sisters' arrows. In fact, it was as crooked as it gets. Mary taught all of her children to respect their elders, to wait patiently when someone else was talking, and to be polite. Always polite. Rose did none of those things. When she did say "please" or "thank you," it was often with a smirk, cancelling whatever goodwill might otherwise have been there. At times she was so quiet, it was as if her brain was asleep. Then she would erupt in a burst of fury that came without warning. She once tossed Ida's half-full coffee cup against the wall when Ida refused to share her shortbread.

When it came to school, Rose was no less disorderly. Mary knew not to expect miracles with Rose, though she prayed for that very thing on a daily basis. But no miracles transpired, at least not when Rose was in school. Mabel told her mom that she spotted Rose in the school office one day. On another occasion, she was seen climbing out of a window. Mary was baking bread one morning when she got a surprise visitor: the school principal. Mary didn't like chitchat, so she interrupted the introductory, nice-weather-we're-having conversation starter and insisted the man get to the point.

He did what she asked: "We can't handle Rose anymore," he blurted out. "We have to send her home."

"Send her home? Is she sick?"

"No, ma'am. Look, I don't want to be rude, but Rose can't be in school anymore. She's too disruptive. Maybe, I don't know, if she gets some help . . . "

"Help? She's eight years old."

"I know how old she is, Mrs. DeChaine. But we've looked at the law and we're under no obligation to educate someone who is"—he paused before saying the word—"feebleminded."

Mary had never heard the word before, but she had a pretty good idea what it meant. It meant they didn't want her daughter. And, just as the man said, under the laws of Minnesota, they didn't have to take her. That would change eventually. Minnesota would one day become a model for the resources it would commit to special education. But that would come too late to help Rose. Things like that were always too late to help Rose. She became another throwaway kid denied an education because of a learning disability.[3]

"I'm deeply sorry," the man said—Mary had already forgotten his name— and he began to ramble on about needing to protect the other children. *Protect the children.* What does this man know about protecting children? What about her child?

Rose was eventually readmitted to the school, but in the absence of any special help, she reverted back to her same patterns: acting out, refusing to listen, and struggling with even the simplest of tasks. One day she stuck her fingers in her ears and pretended not to listen when her teacher spoke. Another time she turned her chair around to face the rear of the room, refusing to move. At reading time, she turned the book upside down and held it in front of her face, an act of rebellion that was impossible for the teacher to miss. And this time, when the school sent her home, Mary put up no argument.

With the clarity of time, it's clear the school should have done more to help Rose. But her timing was bad. In her youth Brainerd was a place where immigrants, some with little English and no education, brought their families—children of all ages—and dumped them on the school like pieces of mail. The teachers had their hands full just handling the students who came to them from Austria, Poland, Russia, and, of course, Canada. Throw in the kids with special needs, and that was a lot to ask, particularly with a staff that wasn't trained to deal with such problems.

Special education wasn't even a concept then and federal laws mandating education for handicapped children would not pass Congress for another sixty years. There were programs for handicapped children, but they weren't mandatory, leaving districts to decide on their own what to offer kids with behavioral problems or whether to offer them anything at all. In 1899 a law was passed that stated that the board of any school district "might" maintain one or more ungraded schools for (1) habitual truants; (2) children who are incorrigible, vicious, or immoral in conduct; or (3) who wander streets or public places during school hours.[4] The trouble was, Brainerd didn't have such a school. Suffice to say that in the absence of any special help, Rose did not thrive. By the time she left school, she could barely read and had a knack, illustrated again and again, for finding trouble.

Mary did the best she could with her mentally challenged daughter. She taught her how to work the handwringer on the washer, fold sheets, and bake bread—domestic chores that she hoped would serve her well into adulthood and maybe even put a little money into her pocket. But despite the good intentions of her mother, Rose responded by doing what she always did, alternating between complete silence and spontaneous combustion. None of her behavior was the least bit constructive. And in her teen years another habit surfaced.

Brainerd had a well-earned reputation where rural kids could party, and its downtown was a drinker's paradise, or at least a landing spot for men and women whose taste for indulgence well exceeded their adherence to restraint. Rose begged, borrowed, and stole for the fuel to feed the fire in her brain, and it eventually would cost her more than her dignity. She would forfeit her possessions, her freedom, her body, and—as the state assumed control over her every move—one of her sons.[5] We often equate mourning with death, and without question, Mary suffered greatly when she lost one baby in childbirth. But Rose was a casualty as well, a wounded child who lost her way in a family where that just didn't happen. They were a family built on hard work, discipline, and allegiance to all things biblical. "Just believe," Joseph heard many times from his mother Louise as they were growing up.

Just believe. That was the mantra for all the DeChaines, a faith with no ambiguity about an all-powerful force that watches over you twenty-four hours a day. And who's to say they were wrong? Against all odds, they had made it, arriving as nobodies in a strange land yet securing a place as accepted members in an exclusive club. Antoine and Louise had long since lived in the country, but they were seen as pillars of the community who warranted the supreme compliment of being "good people." Antoine had a temper that could frighten a bear, but he also had a soft spot for those in need. When a crush of enrollment forced the city fathers to explore a possible site for a new elementary school, Antoine offered up a piece of land he owned for free, saying a growing community needs a first-class school. That's what good people do. It's what the DeChaines had always done. They came to America chasing a dream for a better life, and they knew there would be struggles. But believers find ways to survive. Those with faith—and a never-say-die work ethic—endure.

For a generation of DeChaines, that adage always had proven to be true. Rose might have been an exception, but there was always hope that God's hand would guide her to a better place. And there were signs that she was coming around. She developed a bond with several of her siblings and, though you couldn't count on them, there were occasions when she displayed real tenderness, even love. Given her circumstances—her poor upbringing, her lack of education, the sting of ridicule and rejection from society at large (and possibly other, even more damaging experiences)—her path of resistance and rebellion was all too predictable. She deserved better. They all did, and by the early spring of 1915, the hint of warmer weather signaling its annual renewal of optimism and hope, there were signs that the family's dreams of a better tomorrow were coming to pass. Then Mary's daughter Lottie attempted to light the heat stove on a cold February morning, and just like that those dreams went up in smoke. Antoine used to say that bad luck never travels alone. But for the DeChaines, it never stopped traveling at all, showing up whenever it damn well felt like it. *Just believe.* In a religious household, those two words would be needed like never before.

Lottie wasn't the tallest or the smartest of the DeChaine girls—Ida had that down on both counts—but there was no question she was the prettiest. She was ten years older than Rose but took more of an interest in her than some of the siblings who were closer in age, although Mabel would later emerge as Rose's "bestie." Lottie worked with Rose on her reading and took her along on shopping trips, introducing her as "my sis." Even after she married and moved out of the house, Lottie did her best to include Rose whenever she made invites to birthday parties or picnics. When someone is different, as Rose most certainly was, others often act as if that person will leave a bruise if you get too close. Lottie wasn't like that, as least when there weren't boys around.

They were born in the same town, but it often seemed as if the sisters were on different planets. In high school Lottie had so many suitors that Mary had trouble keeping their names straight. Rose didn't have boyfriends, certainly not the kind that you would bring home for Mary's chicken dumplings or that the family might muse endlessly whether he was "the one." When Rose was thirteen and finally had the nerve to approach a boy that she had a crush on, she was so tongue-tied he finally said, "What are you, dumb or something?"

Both sisters made mistakes, but Lottie's seemed to be written in invisible ink. She had a child out of wedlock, but that didn't seem to matter to folks.[6] Oh, sure, there was talk, but her marriage to John Verkennes largely put an end to that. Lottie lived in a railroad town and had the good sense to marry a railroad man. Even before they were married, John was such a part of the family that when they lined up for a family portrait, it never occurred to anyone not to include him. He worked in the NP shops with Joe, and after he and Lottie began dating, he agonized about what to call his future father-in-law. "Mister DeChaine" seemed too formal, but "Joe" wasn't quite right either, though he'd called him that the entire time they had worked together. Then, at the wedding, he latched on to the perfect alternative, and it would stick from that moment on: "Dad." And why not? John was one of the family—a DeChaine for all intents and purposes, and Mary treated him as such. She used to set aside an extra portion of dinner just in case John happened to come by after work. And she never let anyone else take the last slice of pie. Oh, how John liked her pie. Lottie, knowing the true path to a man's heart, begged her mother to teach her the secret to her recipe, which—Lottie would soon find out—was essentially this: add more sugar. Lots and lots of sugar.

Lottie was virtuous, wholesome, and adored by all those around her. Rose was shunned from an early age, locked up as a young woman, and defiled by the cruelest of man's blunders. Their fates were all but scribbled onto the schedule outside Brainerd's vaunted train depot. Of course, as anyone who has ever waited for a train knows, those schedules aren't always accurate.

On the morning of February 26, 1915, Lottie was alone in her home with her fifteen-month-old daughter Irene when she poured kerosene onto the heat stove to revive a dying fire. She must have been holding Irene because the explosion killed the baby instantly. When the *Brainerd Dispatch* went to press that day, Irene was already dead and Lottie was clinging to life.[7] The explosion tore the bottom and nozzle from the kerosene can Lottie was holding, burned the curtains and tablecloth in the room, and broke all the glass in the dining room cupboard.

Lottie, too, was engulfed in flames.

Newspaper accounts say she ran to the front door, crying for help before collapsing. A neighbor heard the cries and rushed to provide first aid. By this time smoke was billowing from the home and fire crews were on their way, beating John to the trauma scene by several minutes.

When John arrived, Lottie's face was covered with gauze and Irene's body lay on a chair. In graphic language shocking in its imagery, the *Brainerd Dispatch* said her hair had been burned from her head.

On the floor, blackened by the flames, lay the kerosene can.

As a deputy coroner and undertaker stood outside, John spoke to his dying wife.

"How did it happen, Lottie?" he asked.

"I poured some oil on the fire," she whispered.

In the kitchen, Mary clasped a crucifix in her hand and mouthed a prayer that the priest would arrive before her daughter would take her last breath. Neighbors attempted to console John by taking his hands in theirs. Nothing worked.

"He did not cry out loud," the newspaper account would later say. "His grief was too deep. Silent as in a dream, he walked about the little home, not fully able to realize what had happened."[8]

Lottie Verkennes died at 5:30 that afternoon. The next day's newspaper said she had been so badly burned her death came as a relief. When they finally brought Lottie out of the house, a white sheet draped over her blackened body, Mary dropped to the ground, her legs no longer able to sustain her weight. Her only communication was through her tears, which streamed down her face in a torrent of sheer agony. Two people died that day; the actual toll is beyond measure.

Mary got to her feet with the help of Joseph, who whispered something into her ear, words meant to be shared only between husband and wife. They had been through a lot together, but this—this—was new territory. This was as dark as it gets, a shotgun through the heart. Joseph held his wife that night, held her like he had never done before, and prayed to God that with the morning, a beam of light would shine through the darkness.

The following Monday, both mother and child were buried in a single coffin in Brainerd's Evergreen Cemetery. "In her hours of suffering the woman thought nothing of herself," the newspaper said of Lottie. "It was only about her baby."

Her baby. Irene hadn't lived long enough to exploit the fullness of her personality, but she was showing signs of matching her mother's passion for life. At fifteen months she was cute, cuddly, and a tear on wheels. Irene was at that stage where she got into anything and everything, testing Lottie's patience and her solemn pledge to refrain from not only cursing in front of the baby but using the Lord's name for something other than prayer.

Just the day before, Irene swatted an entire bottle of milk onto the floor, watching in glued fascination as it exploded into a million pieces, the liquid shooting out like a rocket in space. It was only when Lottie let out a deafening wail—*Ireeeene, nooooooo!*—that her child recognized the gravity of the situation and began to cry, quietly at first and then rising in intensity until her screams echoed through the quiet neighborhood as if through a bullhorn.

Lottie had been so happy when Irene took her first step, but now that she was ripping through the house like a penguin in full waddle, there was nostalgia for those peaceful days when mother and daughter would fall asleep in the rocking chair by the front window, their anxieties melted away by the mellowness of a lullaby and the soft comfort of knowing all is right in the world.

There were those who would say later, in words designed to soothe, that at least Irene didn't suffer. "Thank God she died instantly" they would say, as if that ever lessens the pain. Maybe it does. Maybe all of it does, even the well-meaning bromides: "She's in a better place now" or "God had other plans for her."

In the awful days that followed, Mary stayed mostly in her room, wearing black when she did come out. Ida took over the cooking chores, and Mabel did the laundry. They all went to Mass—even Rose, although she did so reluctantly. Mary had always soaked in the message from the pulpit almost as if God himself was blessing her family. *Just believe.* But Rose never felt that same power. Not then. Not ever.

Eventually, Mary emerged from her cocoon. She even returned to making the green bean casserole that Joseph liked so much—everyone in the family just called it "hotdish"—and she put aside a portion for John, just as she used to do when Lottie invited him to come over after work. His hands were often so covered in grease that Lottie would make him scrub them until they bled before allowing him to sit down at the table. And then she would send him back to clean up the sink.

"Just because you work around filth all day doesn't mean we have to be reminded of it every time you come over," she would scold him. At Christmas he used to dress up as Santa, with Lottie as his helper, leaving behind cookies and milk for the young ones. Now that Lottie was gone, those memories were all they had, and when silence overtook the dinner table, everyone knew not to say a word out of fear that communication in some form was being interrupted.

By fall, a routine had settled in. Joe finally had steady work at the railroad, the twins were doing what eleven-year-olds do, and Ida and Mabel stepped in whenever they sensed Mary's mood darkening. Rose was still Rose, but Elmer, long the practical joker, was developing a seriousness of purpose. He eventually would fight for his country, the first in his family to do so. His ancestors had fought for their country's independence, but as Elmer would demonstrate, they weren't the only ones whose patriotism ran deep.

Of all her sisters, Rose was closest to Mabel. Ida, the oldest, was out of the house and raising a family when Rose was still twirling around in dresses pretending to be a ballerina. Rose got a kick out of Ida's daughter Flora, though, and would make funny faces at her just to make her laugh.

Ida distinguished herself in the DeChaine family not through good looks, though she could turn heads with her smile, but through sheer brain power. She was the first DeChaine to graduate from high school and she did so with almost perfect grades. Her performance was so stellar one of her teachers suggested she do something that was unimaginable to her: attend college. A girl in college? My, how some people could dream. Still, she knew it wasn't impossible. Her favorite author, Emily Dickinson, went to college, though it was out East where such things were more natural. No, it wasn't beyond the realm, but it was beyond *her* realm. Where would she go? How would they get the money? Who would help Mama with the chores? In the end she settled on a more conventional route: marry young, get pregnant, and settle in for a life of quiet grace. Emily Dickinson once wrote how dreary it was to be somebody.[9] Well, Ida was somebody, and she didn't find it dreary at all.

The morning of Lottie's death, Ida had planned to stop by and drop off some toys. Flora was only a few months older than Irene and the moms exchanged playthings every couple of months so the girls would have something new and different, save for Flora's sock puppet that Grandma Louise—Flora called her "Maw-maw"—made from Antoine's old socks and the buttons she kept in her sewing kit. That doll was almost a part of her, an inseparable friend who took on different names for a time until Flora found one that fit: Molly.

Ida had another reason for stopping by that morning, and she couldn't wait to give Lottie the news: she was pregnant. But Flora had a slight fever—she had a tendency to kick the covers off in the middle of the night—and Ida decided to keep her home until the afternoon at least. In the aftermath of the explosion, as well-wishers came by to offer their sympathies, Ida was too embarrassed to share her innermost thoughts: "I could have been there."

In the ensuing months, it was Ida who kept things as normal as they could be. She wore the responsibility of oldest child like a scarf in winter. She even moved in with Mary and Joseph for a time, sleeping on the living room couch, while her husband, Albert, played the role of house dad at home. Even after Mary seemed better, Ida checked in on her once a day, picking up groceries when necessary and cooking dinner when Mary wasn't up to the task. Ida was in her eighth or ninth month of pregnancy—she wasn't entirely sure—and was careful not to do much bending or lifting, no matter how many candy bar wrappers Rose left on the floor. She got some help from Mabel and Dora, the precocious seventeen-year-old, as well as another family member who began popping in more and more: John Verkennes. No one gave it a second thought when John and Dora sat side by side at the dinner table, though Ida swore she saw their hands lock one night well before Joseph said "Let's pray."

On a cold afternoon in November, Ida was walking upstairs to Flora's room when she felt her water break. She tried to stay calm, but part of her knew that the sticky substance that covered her underwear and pants wasn't water. Should she be bleeding down there? And with each step, a pain shot through her body as if she'd touched a live wire. Even when she sat down, she hurt. God, did she hurt. Her husband, her father, and her brother Elmer—options one, two, and three in the family's pre-birth plan for getting her to the hospital—were all at work, and Ida at first couldn't think of any other contingencies. Flora started crying, which jumbled her mind further. Ida was the oldest child. The responsible one. Why couldn't she focus? What was wrong with her?

In full panic, she reached the phone and called Mabel, who got hold of her husband Warren at the Northern Pacific shops where he worked with Joseph, John, and two of John's brothers. Warren got there first and knew instantly that the baby was gone. And as he lifted Ida's almost limp body into his car, he had another thought: Ida might be gone too.

When he reached the hospital, nurses, orderlies, and God knows who else seemed to come from everywhere. Someone must have called the hospital to let them know that they were coming—Warren never bothered to ask who—and as Ida was wheeled away, he never got a chance to say "good luck" or "hang in there" or, as he was left to ponder later, "good-bye."

The waiting room soon resembled Mary's house on Thanksgiving, with generations of DeChaine family members lined up like bowling pins in a space no bigger than a dining room. Joseph's siblings, his mom, and each of his children were there, clasping hands as if they were locked together with a vice grip. Albert, Ida's husband, wept openly, making little effort to conceal the hole in his heart. Flora couldn't possibly understand what was taking place, but she knew there was sadness and that it had overtaken the room. Even the tree visible through the front window was bereft of life, its bare branches a fitting accompaniment to the mood inside.

Mary didn't talk or even cry. Instead, she stared at that tree so long that even when she turned away the image was imprinted into her brain. Eventually the doctors would come out, she knew that, but she also knew what they would say. *She always knew.* In another time of year, the birds would be chirping, the snapdragons would erupt into bursts of red, gold, and hot pink, and the leaves would multiply into a luxurious canopy of color. But this was November in Minnesota, and the bleakness of the sky was matched by the dearth of life on the ground. Mary was so mesmerized by the tree she didn't even notice when a man walked into the room. It was her priest.

Ida died eight months after her sister Lottie.[10] Though their deaths were very different, the aftermath had a sameness no family should be forced to endure. Mary wore black for a full year afterward and went to the cemetery every day, clutching her crucifix as if it were an appendage. Whatever her prayers were, she kept them to herself, a one-on-one with an entity whose actions she couldn't begin to understand. She loved all her children—no one would ever question that—but Ida was the closest to being her coequal. Even as a young girl, Ida had a mother's instinct for knowing whether a child needed a hug or a gentle shove. Ida could melt an ice cap with a disapproving gaze or bring on sunshine with a smile and a laugh. Mary mourned everything about her daughter, but the thing she missed above all else was that laugh. Oh God, did she miss that laugh.

Mary would go through this same experience many times in her life-time. The year before Lottie's and Ida's deaths, her father-in-law, Antoine DeChaine, died of natural causes, if there is such a thing. He had been sick for some time, however, and in many ways his passing was a blessing, an affirmation of God's plan. Mary felt somewhat similarly when Joseph died in 1920. He'd had throat cancer and was in such pain at the end Mary actually prayed he wouldn't live another day. Death is hard at any age but is more acceptable, even welcome, when the circle of life has reached its full rota-tion. At the wake following her husband's death, there was so much laughter and gaiety from all the "Joseph stories" that Elmer sidled up to his sisters and whispered, "Shhhhhhh, you'll wake up Dad."

Mary never doubted her faith, even after two of her daughters died in the same year. If anything, she became more devout. Still, she had questions. What kind of plan takes two mothers and their babies? When she was a girl, her father used to say, "What doesn't kill you makes you stronger." But Mary didn't feel stronger and there were days, fewer as time passed, when she wished it had indeed killed her.

Years later, long after Joseph passed, Mary would bury another one of her children. After her son Elmer returned from the war, he battled some of the same demons that resided within Rose. But he never lost his sense of humor or the camaraderie he shared with each of his siblings. Like many of the DeChaines, his life did not stand out, though the photograph Mary kept by her bedside spoke volumes about the strength within him. It was a picture of Elmer in his military uniform, a look of resoluteness on his face that belied the risk he faced as an American soldier on the brink of uncertainty.

Elmer survived the war. It was something else—bad luck, bad timing—that killed him. On October 19, 1939, he was walking across Highway 210 on the western edge of Brainerd with a gasoline can in his hand when he was struck and killed by an oncoming car.[11] His body was carried forward some distance by the car's grille, and his face was literally torn apart. The mortician tried using plaster to make it presentable for the funeral, but he was unsuccessful, so a veil was used to hide the damage. At the funeral, two of Mary's daughters, Clara and Mabel, held their mother's hands so she wouldn't reach out and touch the body of her fallen son, whose death would haunt her the rest of her life.

"I don't think she ever got over the shock," Rose's daughter Millie wrote me several years ago. "She cried a lot after that."

It's often said that no parent should ever have to bury a child, but Mary had to do it on four occasions, including two in the same year. It never got easier. In fact, it got harder. After all, the human heart can endure only so much.

After the deaths of her two daughters, Mary continued to open her home—and her heart—taking in boarders as if they were stray cats. There was much she didn't understand, would never acquire the wisdom to fathom, but she knew that God was with her and that no matter how dark the night, there was always morning, and in it a little light would shine through.

Fifteen months after Lottie died, her sister Dora married John Verkennes. It had come as no surprise to members of the DeChaine family, who saw how important John had become in Dora's life and vice-versa. They also saw the bulge in her belly.

Both had undergone incredible loss. John's parents had come from Germany and Holland and landed in Brainerd for the same reason most other people did: the railroad. It was woven deep into the fabric of the Verkennes family, and in the case of John's father, his soul. On August 18, 1914, August Verkennes was walking across the tracks in the NP yards in Brainerd when witnesses said he became confused and fell onto the tracks in front of an oncoming switch engine.[12]

Death, the *Brainerd Dispatch* said the next morning, was "instantaneous."

John and Dora's wedding was held in the parsonage of the Methodist church. If that bothered Mary, she didn't show it, just as she held her tongue when Lottie and John were married four years earlier. She was a Catholic first—and maybe second and third as well—but John was a Christian and she could at least take some solace in that. Besides, this was a happy occasion, and right now she needed happy. She wore a powder blue dress and accented it with the nicest necklace she owned. Actually, it was the only necklace she owned. Frills weren't something she did, except when Father O'Brien came to call. When a messenger of the Lord shows up at your home, she always told her children, you need to put out your best linens.

As the organist turned up the volume on "The Wedding March," filling the church with echoes of sound, Mary's tears were of genuine joy. She needed happiness—they all did—and when cake was served at the reception that followed, Mary treated herself to a second helping.

Three months later, on December 9, 1916, John and Dora Verkennes had the first of their four children. It had been less than two years since Lottie tried to revive a smoldering fire on a frigid February morning in Brainerd. John never forgot the frantic cries from his coworkers as he uncoupled an engine that had a leak in a steam line: "John, John, your house is burning up." He had ran the eight blocks home, arriving just as Lottie whispered her last words: "I poured some oil on the fire." The explosion had turned John's life upside down, and in the face of such grief, he turned to someone who knew what he was going through, knew what it felt like to lose someone you loved from the very bottom of your heart. For John and Dora, the pain surely lasted a lifetime—John lost his wife Lottie and his young daughter Irene; Dora lost the big sister who used to braid her hair and a niece who was just learning how to pronounce her name. Yes, for John and Dora, the pain would last a lifetime. But on this day, the hurt and sorrow gave way to something else. They had a baby that day and they named her Irene.[13]

NOTES

1. Mary's work ethic is captured in the interview done with her as part of the Works Progress Administration project in June 1938. The interview was accessed at the Crow Wing County Historical Society.

2. Numerous records attest to this. See Minnesota, U.S., Territorial and State Censuses, 1849–1905.

3. See 1910 U.S. Census for Brainerd, which shows Rose was not in school at the age of eight, though each of her siblings were. In the Faribault School for the Feeble-Minded, she was given IQ tests three times. Her scores placed her intelligence as roughly that of a nine- or ten-year-old.

4. *Laws of Minnesota Relating to the Public School System* (St. Paul, MN: Review Publishing, 1906).

5. Archived records from the former St. James Catholic Orphanage.

6. Marriage records, Minnesota Department of Health.

7. "Shocking Fatality, Mother and Child Fatally Burned from Explosion of Kerosene Oil," *Brainerd Dispatch*, March 5, 1915.

8. Ibid.

9. From "I'm Nobody! Who Are You?" by Emily Dickinson.

10. "Death's Doings," *Brainerd Tribune*, December 15, 1915. Ida's baby's death was confirmed through the website www.findagrave.com/memorial/124476816/infant-lease.

11. "Struck by Car, Killed," *Brainerd Dispatch*, October 23, 1939.

12. "August Verkennes Killed in Yard," *Brainerd Dispatch*, August 21, 1914.

13. Minnesota birth records, searchable from the Minnesota Historical Society website. Instead of DeChaine for the mother's name in the record, it is spelled "Deshau."

3

Rose

Rose was thirteen when her two sisters died. It's not hard to imagine the impact this had on her or to speculate about whether it played a supporting role in the events to follow. This was more than the loss of two sisters. It was a crossbow to the heart. Lottie had a daughter—Rose's niece—and Ida was pregnant with a child when she died. The family would never be the same. No family would. The others openly wept, their shared tears a balm to the soul. *The others*. As for Rose, she tucked her feelings away in a lockbox with no key. She always tried to disappear into the wallpaper anyway, a wounded animal hiding in a box in the corner. But when that wounded animal emerges, it acts like a tiger that had a meal swiped from under its nose. Mary had to continually tell her daughter to watch her language around the little ones.

For a time after the deaths—"the lost year," as Joseph referred to it—Rose's life seemed ordinary. She did her chores and played card games at the kitchen table with her sisters and, on occasion, John Verkennes. Elmer often played as well. They were part of a club no one wants to join, bound through unspeakable grief and eternal sorrow. They didn't talk about it much—none of them did—but it was there nonetheless, an overpowering sadness that was never far from the surface. When Elmer answered the call to serve his country, they all felt a little paranoid. After all, if the DeChaines couldn't survive in Brainerd, where the erection of a water tower was front-page news, what chance did Elmer have in occupied France?

With her brother off to war, Rose disappeared again, although it wasn't to a figurative box in the corner. She just left, a young woman exploring the possibilities of a life beyond the narrow prism of her pent-up circumstance. Only Rose wasn't a young woman—certainly not intellectually—and she soon became a fixture on the streets downtown, where she would bum cigarettes and whatever alcohol she could get her hands on. She sold her body, too, not at first, but eventually, and word got around about the family's lone black sheep.[1] The DeChaine name had always been respected without a scent of scandal. Rose changed all that, and as her daughter sunk further into a black

29

hole of peril and doom, Mary felt the embrace of a sympathetic citizenry that saw her as the victim.

It's natural for people to embrace the guardians in these situations, to see them as innocents. And, as far as anybody knows, they were. But it's far less common to come to the defense of the people acting out, to see *them* as victims. And make no mistake: Rose was a victim, perhaps in ways that no one could possibly know. Yet the well of sympathy for her was as dry as a bone. First came the cross looks and shaken heads. Eventually more punitive measures would be deployed. She was different, an anomaly. And different isn't how one succeeds in small-town USA. Maybe now. Certainly not then.

Mabel was the first to hear about the marriage, though not directly from Rose. If it wasn't the talk of the town, it was certainly the talk of the beauty shop: Rose met a farmhand from Michigan, ran off with him, and was now living sixty miles away in the town of St. Cloud. "What's his name?" "Is he—you know—like her?" "Does Mary know?" Mabel heard it all as she had her hair done, and she was so upset she canceled the errands she had planned for the rest of the day.

No, Mary did not know what her daughter had done, and when Mabel told her, Mary asked the second most important question that came to mind: "Was she married in the church?"

Mabel knew the answer and also knew what to say: "Of course, Mama."

His name was Leo Jerred, and if he wasn't the kind of man who you brought home to meet your family—he was seven years older than Rose—he was the kind of man who was perfect for her, at least at that particular moment. It's not clear whose idea it was to get out of Brainerd, but Rose wouldn't have needed much convincing. Black sheep tend to stand out even when they try to blend in with the flock.

Society is supposed to have a safety net for the Roses of the world, a landing spot for the square pegs who don't fit. But once again, her timing was off. Brainerd has always been revered for its entrepreneurial brazenness, a pretty girl with brains. But in her day, it was largely bereft of an infrastructure that could deal with the mentally ill and certainly not for the train wreck that was Rose. Trains are supposed to stay on the track, no matter how hastily and shoddily those tracks are assembled.

Rose was sixteen when she ran off with her husband, a man with little education and few job prospects beyond the menial work for which he was qualified.[2] In St. Cloud he got a job washing dishes in a dive by the highway, one of those places where a giant sign outside advertises food in capital letters. Rose wasn't pregnant when she got married—that was Mary's first question to her—but Mary knew that was just a matter of time. The DeChaines were a fertile bunch. Mary had been disappointed when Lottie and Dora got pregnant before marriage—both at the hands of John Verkennes—but John was a known entity and his commitment to the family was never questioned. Leo? He wasn't even from Brainerd. He was a drifter in the family's eyes and, worse, a con man. Joseph told him that right to his face one night and then he ordered Rose to come home.

"I ain't never goin' back there," Rose had screamed, which led to words Joseph later wished he had kept to himself.

"That's good," he said, "'cause you ain't welcome no more."

That wasn't true, of course—not for him and definitely not for his wife. Mary would never turn away a family member, even one who poured whiskey into her tea. Mary wanted desperately for Rose to find happiness. But at the same time, she knew how fragile the human heart can be. Rose was just sixteen. What would happen if she got hurt? As word arrived that Rose was indeed pregnant just months into the marriage, there was another fear: that Rose wasn't the only one who would get hurt.

The divorce occurred a little more than five months after Ernie was born.[3] It wasn't a surprise. There had been plenty of angry confrontations both before and after the baby: drunken brawls that reverberated throughout the paper-thin walls of their one-room apartment. And on at least one occasion, the cops showed up. The officers wouldn't say who called to complain, but Rose knew. They hadn't been in the place a week, just a single room with a bed that folded into the wall, when the lady with the perpetual curlers in her hair next door warned them about putting their empty bottles by her door. After Leo left, Rose packed what little she owned in a bedsheet and carried Ernie to the train station, stopping first at the neighbor's door to leave what she considered to be an appropriate good-bye gift: a pile of garbage that included the diapers she never bothered to clean.

Rose arrived back at Mary's house at the worst possible time. Joe was sick. It started as a sore throat, but before long his whole body felt like he'd been in the ring with Jack Dempsey. There were days when he couldn't get out of bed, and that just wasn't Joe. Normally he couldn't sit still for a minute. If there weren't dishes to wash, he'd dirty one just so he'd have something to do. Then the cancer struck, and he was unable to do much of anything. Rose was afraid to bring Ernie into the room to see his grandpa out of fear that this was part of another influenza outbreak.

Mary knew Joe's time was up when he told her his back hurt. "I thought it was your throat," she said.

"It's everywhere," he responded.

Joseph DeChaine died on August 7, 1920.[4] The daffodils Mary had planted by the side of the house were well past their bloom, but now they really began to droop. Mary barely had strength enough to fill a kettle for coffee or tea, much less water the flowers. Mabel even offered to hold the post-funeral gathering at her house, but Mary insisted on hosting. This was Joseph's home, and her faith told her that he would be there in spirit, drinking a beer and telling the same stories he'd told a million times before.

In the days after Joe's death the well-wishers went on with their lives while the DeChaines grappled with the reality of life on poverty's edge. They had never been destitute—Joe had seen to that—but they weren't exactly living high, not by a long shot. Asked once how he managed to support such a large and extended family, Joe remarked, "We ain't livin' in the poorhouse, but I can see it from here."

Now with Joe gone, that poorhouse came into clear focus. Mary went to work cleaning other people's houses, while the rest of the family did what they could to keep her house from falling apart. Even Rose contributed, though everyone knew when she was the one at the stove. It's hard to mess up an egg, but somehow Rose could find a way. To say she became a responsible housemate would be a stretch, but she pitched in from time to time. At least until boredom kicked in.

Like the rest of the country, Brainerd shuttered its bars during Prohibition, when liquor sales were banned throughout the United States. But that didn't mean you couldn't find a drink. In fact, there were probably more places to drink in Brainerd *during* Prohibition than before. Speakeasies popped up all over the city. They were essentially of three varieties. The more high-class establishments operated upstairs or in the back rooms of legitimate businesses and essentially barred anyone who didn't wear a bow tie at the dinner table. The second level was less exclusive, but the customers—all men, of course—were privileged wannabes, the folks who shine their shoes before going out for the evening and who keep them on to avoid revealing the holes in their socks.

The third and largest group was the subject of most of the police raids orchestrated to appease the temperance crowd. These were pop-ups that operated mostly out of private homes and served customers of varying backgrounds, including women bold enough to sidle up to the bar and thirsty enough to endure the clumsy overtures from men freed of inhibition and blinded by drink. These places moved around, but you didn't have trouble finding one if you had a nose for such things. And when it came to quenching her thirst, few had a nose quite like Rose.

Mary couldn't help but feel remorseful toward her reckless daughter and maybe some guilt. After all, she wasn't much older than Rose when she married Joseph, and there was a long history of marrying young in her family. Her parents thought she was too young, too, but they never forbade her from seeing Joe or tried to coax her into leaving him. How was Rose any different?

But Rose was different. Everybody knew that. It didn't mean she couldn't feel love, though. Who were they to deny her that one emotion so vital to a satisfying life? Leo hadn't been right for her. There was no mistaking that.

What had he said to Joe that night: "We done everything legal"? As if that was the only thing that mattered. No, Leo showed his true colors when he abandoned his family. How do you leave a child behind?

Still, Rose hadn't been herself since she returned home. She was so quiet. Mary began to miss even those times when Rose would say something inappropriate at the dinner table, inserting a cuss word that would bring the entire conversation to a halt. Mary believed that everyone begins life with a set of building blocks, and you add or subtract blocks depending on your level of fortune or misfortune. She knew Rose had lost some of those blocks in recent years. What she didn't know was how many she had left.

Whether or not Rose wanted to please her mother—she feigned indifference when it came to matters of the heart—she was incapable or chose not to show it. No one knew what she was thinking or who she was thinking about, though they were pretty sure it wasn't about her own son. When she would disappear, Ernie was left to occupy himself with the wooden spoon he liked to bang on the bottom of the pan he fetched from under the kitchen sink.

Fortunately, there were always plenty of bodies on hand to help with the feedings or dabbing alcohol on skinned knees. In addition to Rose and Ernie, Mary's small home served as living quarters to Elmer; the twins, Clarence (Bud) and Clara; Clara's husband Lloyd; Ida's daughter Flora; and someone else who hung around quite a bit: John Lorbecki, who would later become Mary's second husband. Mary waited to marry him, she told people, until she got Joe's blessing. Later, she would say it was the one time she shouldn't have listened to him.

Mary was busying herself by the stove and Mabel and Dora were folding laundry on the kitchen table one afternoon when Rose showed up at the front door. Mary couldn't figure out why she knocked first—Rose, after all, was living there off and on—but then she saw that her daughter wasn't alone. She had a man with her, and not just any man, she would come to find out. Ingram Conradson, as Rose whispered into Mabel's ear, was "the one."

Ingram was nothing like the boys Rose had associated with previously. For one thing, he was polite. When they sat down at the table for Mary's signature dumplings, Ingram even pulled the chair out for her, a gesture that didn't go unnoticed by the others. Or by Mary, who couldn't decide if he was a good actor or a really terrible one. Any lingering doubts were erased a few minutes later when Clara began to clear the plates and Ingram said, "Mrs. DeChaine, I can't possibly get up from this table without another helping of the best dumplings I've ever tasted." That was followed by the best pie he'd ever tasted and the best coffee he'd ever tasted, prompting Elmer to whisper, "Doesn't this guy ever eat?"

They were married already—the ring on Rose's finger gave that one away—but she seemed so happy that Mary put aside her skepticism about Mr.

I-can't-possibly-get-up-from-this-table-without-another-helping-of-the-best-dumplings-I've-ever-tasted.[5] What a crock. OK, there was a part of her that liked it, but she knew when someone was trying to play her, and this guy was an amateur. Still, she desperately wanted to like him—and not just because she noticed the baby bump when Rose walked in. She wanted to like him because she knew that would be best for Rose. And Ingram, by all appearances, was an upgrade from Leo. Mary wasn't sure if it was her imagination, but Rose, who was about to turn twenty, seemed more mature around her new husband. In the kitchen she even helped her mother with the dishes, washing away the grime from each dirty plate.

Mildred, or Millie as everyone calls her to this day, was born that November.[6] The name was not part of any family lore, but Ingram was insistent about it, and besides, it was a very popular name then, almost like Olivia is now. Rose had named Ernie after her brother Elmer, whose first name was actually Ernest, and she wanted some part of her daughter's name to be drawn from the same family tree. The first name was already decided, so she focused on the middle name, agonized over it, in fact. Rose wasn't one to show affection, either in public or private, but occasionally a warm heart emerged from beneath all her defenses. Mary had done a lot for her daughter, sticking by her when that wasn't the easiest thing to do. So, when the nurse with the clipboard asked her for her baby's middle name, she didn't hesitate.

"Melvina," she said. "Just like my mommy."

Rose didn't exactly quit drinking during the pregnancy—that wasn't a thing then—but she did promise herself that she'd be a better mother. And, for a while, she was. Millie was a small baby but smart as a whip with curly hair that resembled her father's. She didn't inherit his penchant for BS, but even as a girl she could spot it a mile away. As for Rose, Millie didn't pick up many of her physical features, the hard edges and punishing eyes, but she did inherit an attribute that was part of her mother's DNA. Maybe a major part.

The DeChaine women were resilient in the face of adversity, surviving body blows that would cripple most others. No matter how many times Rose was knocked down, she always got up—bloodied perhaps but determined to stand on her own two feet long enough to raise a middle finger to the world. Her daughter was blessed with that same bulldog tendency, resolute in spirit and steadfast in her refusal to let any obstacles get in her way.

As a young girl Millie would need every ounce of that inner strength. Ingram may have been "the one," but as a father, he left much to be desired. It wasn't long after that dinner party at Mary's that he did turn his back on Mary's dumplings, not to mention the rest of the family.[7] He said there was no work for him in Brainerd, and after living for a short time with his parents, he moved his family—Rose, Ernie, and Millie—to Bemidji, some one hundred miles away. It was no Garden of Eden, at least as far as Rose was concerned.

She had no friends, rarely left the house, and was dead broke—in about as many ways as the word implies. Sure, Ingram had a job at the railroad, but it meant long hours that left Rose alone in a place where she didn't know a single soul. Isolated, lonely, and stuck in a bubble with her two young children, Rose felt something she had never felt before: homesickness. Raising one child on her own was hard enough, but two was impossible. She started drinking more and Ingram began coming home less. Pretty soon, he wasn't coming home at all.

When her brother Bud came to get her, he couldn't help but notice what a pigsty Rose was living in: the back end of a narrow bungalow with just a couch and a crib in its one living space. The entire trip back to Brainerd, Rose didn't say a word, staring out the window at the tall stands of trees that would appear briefly and then disappear from view, leaving the nothingness of a landscape bereft of life.

That fall Mary was given a two-day notice of an inspection to check on the welfare of Rose's two children. Brainerd was in one of its downturns—the railroad shopmen went on strike on July 1, 1922, idling half the town's workforce, it seemed—and Mary was struggling. Everyone was. John Verkennes and his brothers joined the strikers and paid dearly for their union activity. One by one, their names were added to the famed Northern Pacific "blacklist" of workers disqualified from future employment. The list wasn't some perceived vendetta against the strikers; the company wrote down each and every one of their names and vowed never to hire them again. They didn't try to hide the list, either. It exists today, property of the Minnesota Historical Society and kept on file at the Minnesota History Center in downtown St. Paul.

On the list are machinists, electricians, blacksmiths, boilermakers, laborers, pipefitters, crane operators, apprentices, and something called a "call boy." The names of the offenders were included under a heading that was in all caps and, for added emphasis, underlined: "List of Men, Formerly Employed at Brainerd Shops, Not to Be Re-Employed."[8]

Not exactly subtle. This from a company that hired protection for strikebreakers—read: goons—and gave them free rein to crack heads. One force was said to be proficient in "machine guns, riot guns and rifles."[9] In a workhouse in Minneapolis, those nearing the end of their jail sentences were offered early release if they cared to go to work as scabs. In the first week alone, numerous shootings resulted in deaths.

Brainerd, too, had a brush with gunfire.[10] About a month into the strike, Mayor Frank E. Little—himself a shopman—was walking toward the downtown area away from the Northern Pacific shops when six shots rang out. No one got hit, but the incident occurred just days after two guards fired shots in the direction of a group of men that they said were throwing stones at them. The two were later tried for violating a city ordinance, and in court a supervisor for the railroad said the company did not equip the guards with firearms or direct that they carry them. Whether that was true or not, the presence of weapons couldn't be denied.

"It is regretted that such an attitude is taken by the guards," the *Brainerd Dispatch* opined, openly showing its bias toward the workers, "as it seems entirely unnecessary and only leads to hard feelings on the part of the striking shopmen."[11]

The shopmen did what they could to turn the tables, and when they couldn't do so at the bargaining table, they tried other means. Union "wrecking crews" tore after scabs, foremen, and men in uniform. Drive-by shootings occurred with increasing frequency, along with kidnappings, beatings, and assorted other humiliations. Floggings were common in some cities. In Utah, threatening letters with undertaker labels were sent to the houses of replacement workers. In Nebraska, the houses of scabs were painted yellow. Shops nearly everywhere were sabotaged.[12]

Concerned about the violence and the impact the strike was having on interstate commerce—OK, mostly the impact on commerce—Republican President Warren Harding gave the go-ahead to seek a national injunction. The court action, the most sweeping in U.S. history, not only inhibited picketing but limited even the types of conversations union leaders could have with their members.[13] The injunction deflated the balloon for a national mobilization, and strikers on line after line began trudging back to work following rushed contract settlements that gave them nothing or, if they were lucky, next to nothing.

In Brainerd, the strike continued into 1923, though numerous strikers had returned to work by the previous November. An agreement struck that month put an exclamation point on the failed endeavor when the NP farmed out more work to the Minneapolis shops, including the repair of a majority of the locomotives that had been serviced locally.[14] The contract meant fewer workers would be needed in Brainerd, where the Northern Pacific had already taken steps to weed out the "undesirables" who dared to challenge the company's authority.

Blackballed from the only jobs they had ever known, John Verkennes and his brothers—Matt and August, along with their families—left Brainerd for another melting pot: Flint, Michigan.[15] Flint may be a symbol of abandonment now, but at the time its booming auto plants symbolized something else: hope. John and Dora raised their family in Flint and spent the rest of their days there. Dora would see her family from time to time, but in a practical sense the move deprived Mary of another daughter and Rose of another sister. Flint was just two states away from Minnesota, but for Rose—and Mary too—it was as if another loved one had vanished from the face of the earth.

For virtually the entire forty-eight hours prior to the child welfare inspection, Mary went into full battle mode. She made sure there were clean sheets on the beds—what did she think, the woman was going to take a nap?—and that every inch of the floor was mopped, the furniture dusted, and the toys picked up and neatly put on a shelf. You would have thought the kids had their own personal maid. Mary picked flowers from her garden, which she put in a vase on the kitchen table, and she baked a chocolate cake that was still cooling on the stove when the doorbell rang.

The social worker in the black coat looked friendly enough, but Mary knew not to let her guard down. There was no telling what lurked beneath that tight smile, the kind you flash ever so briefly when you don't want someone to know what you're really thinking. Mary was always wary of strangers anyway, and despite this woman's pleasant demeanor, there was no doubt in Mary's mind: she was a stranger. After a prolonged silence, the woman, sensing Mary's discomfort, said, "Mrs. DeChaine, I'm only here to help you."

I'm only here to help you. Mary no more believed that than she believed the genuineness of the woman's smile. But politeness wasn't just something she told her children. It was part of who she was. So, stranger or no stranger, Mary put out the welcome mat. During the next three hours, they talked as if they'd known each other for years, old friends catching up over cake and coffee. The woman even volunteered to make a fresh pot.

"Don't be silly," Mary said. "Guests don't make their own coffee. Not in my house."

"Well, at least let me get the cream," the woman said, opening the refrigerator and glancing from side to side even after locating the half-full bottle.

Mary had trouble relaxing, particularly when the woman asked to meet privately with the children. Mary told the social worker that she had work to do in the bedroom, though that wasn't entirely true, and although she could hear faint voices from the kitchen, she was able to resist the impulse to put her ear to the door. After what seemed like an hour but was probably five minutes at best, Mary heard the woman say, "Mrs. DeChaine." When Mary had emerged from her hiding spot, the woman already had grabbed her coat and was taking her cup to the sink. "These are wonderful children," the woman said, adding that nothing she saw suggested removing them from the home. A wave of relief washed over Mary. The woman mentioned that Millie's legs were badly bowed and told Mary to contact a doctor if the condition grew worse. Also, she said, Ernie's teeth weren't in the best shape. She asked if he brushed regularly.

"We don't always have baking soda on hand," Mary said.

Without commenting on how little there was in the refrigerator, the woman gave Mary a phone number to call if she ever needed help buying food.

Then, as Mary opened the door, she was asked the question that had hovered between them the whole time: "Where's their mother?"

Mary didn't like to lie—she took her commandments as seriously as she took her marriage vows—so she came up with an answer she thought could possibly be true.

"She's working," she said.

Mary had heard all the stories about what her daughter was doing for money, and at first she dismissed them as "just talk." But deep down, she knew. *She always knew.* Father O'Brien once preached that "adulteresses" were sorcerers and devil worshippers who forfeited their rights to inherit the kingdom of God. Mary agreed with most of what Father O'Brien had to say, but that one seemed unduly harsh. While Mary disapproved of her daughter's activities, she refused to believe she was touched by the devil or, good heavens, a sorcerer. She didn't know exactly what an adulteress was, but she knew Rose wasn't *that*. Forfeit the kingdom of God? Good Lord. Mary knew there was room for her daughter in heaven whether Father O'Brien realized it or not.

One of the women for whom Mary cleaned homes suggested that Mary use something called "tough love" on Rose: make it hard on her as a means for changing the behavior. Mary rejected that advice right off. She didn't like to give her children more than they could handle. Ida could do complex math equations that Mary could scarcely begin to understand. Elmer could take apart an automobile transmission and then put it back together without missing a single part. Rose? It wasn't clear what she could handle. She appeared lost in space almost from the minute she was born. While Lottie brought a sparkle to everyone around her, Rose had the opposite effect. In an otherwise clear sky, she was the one dark cloud. No, the way Mary saw it, "tough love" translated to "no love."

Mary had tried so hard with Rose. Sure, her other kids had their struggles. When Lottie got dumped by a boy, you'd have thought the world came to an end. Clara could be mouthy at times. And Clarence—now there was a bucket full of piss and vinegar. But all of them put together didn't measure up to Rose when it came to giving their mother heartburn. Yet, once in a while, a different Rose would surface, what Mary liked to call "the real Rose." Mary had back trouble throughout her life, and when the pain became too bad, she had to sleep upright in a chair. When morning came, there was always a pillow behind her head and a blanket pulled up to her chin. Mary had always assumed it was Clara or maybe Dora doing what they could to ease her suffering. But one night she woke just as Rose was tucking the blanket under her feet so they wouldn't get cold during the drafty night. Mary rested easy that evening, knowing "the real Rose" was close at hand.

Not long after the social worker's visit, Mary opened the door to two police officers standing on the steps. *Why did they send two?* Rose, they told her, was going away.[16] She is immoral, they said—said it like it was a barefaced fact—and the state had a place for people like her.

People like her. They made it sound like she was a leper.

"What did she do?" Mary asked.

"Ma'am, we're just here to tell you where she is," one of the officers said, the pudgy one with the shirt that was at least a size too small. The other one was younger and too skinny for Mary's taste. Doesn't his mother cook?

"We can't get into all of that," the fat one said, then under his breath but loud enough for Mary to hear: "She got what she deserves, you ask me."

"I ain't asking you," Mary said and then slammed the door in his face. Mary was nothing if not polite, but you could push her too far. Joseph found that out when she found him sleeping in the bushes one morning after being out all night. Mary told him if he tried that again, he could sleep there permanently. He never tried it again.

The two police officers had told Mary that Rose was headed to the state hospital—a school, they called it—in Faribault, which she assumed was in Minnesota but could have been in Alaska, for all she knew. Mary had never heard of it. She didn't regret slamming the door in the man's face. Sure, he had a job to do, but that didn't give him the right to be rude. *Got what she deserves.* What about Rose's children? Did they get what they deserved?

As the officers drove away, Mary realized she didn't ask an important question. They told her where Rose was going. What they didn't say—and she was now kicking herself for failing to ask—was when she was coming back.

NOTES

1. Intake records for the Faribault School for the Feeble-Minded. Two people testified that Rose was immoral, alleging she was a prostitute. The records were accessed at the Minnesota Historical Society.

2. Leo's job as a restaurant keeper is confirmed in the birth record for their son Ernie from the State of Minnesota Division of Vital Statistics, December 22, 1919.

3. Birth certificate for Ernie from Stearns County, Minnesota Division of Vital Statistics.

4. "Death's Doings," *Brainerd Dispatch*, August 13, 1920.

5. Rose's marriage to Ingram Conradson is recorded in her marriage certificate from Beltrami County, Minnesota. The date was May 21, 1921.

6. Birth record, Minnesota Department of Health, November 19, 1921.

7. Ingram's abandonment of the family is recorded in various records, including the adoption petition from Rose's third husband, Orvel McClain, that was approved by a judge on March 21, 1942.

8. Northern Pacific Railway records, accessed at the Minnesota Historical Society.

9. Colin J. Davis, *Power at Odds: The 1922 National Railroad Shopmen's Strike* (Urbana: University of Illinois Press, 1997), 64–82.

10. "Six Shots Greet Mayor's Walk," *Brainerd Dispatch*, August 18, 1922.

11. Ibid.

12. Davis, *Power at Odds*, 73.

13. Ibid., 131.

14. Carl Zapffe, *Brainerd* (Minneapolis, MN: Colwell Press, 1946), 129–30.

15. See 1930 U.S. Census for Flint, Michigan. Record was accessed through Ancestry.com, www.ancestry.com.

16. Intake records, Faribault School for the Feeble-Minded, Minnesota Historical Society.

4

"Feebleminded"

Before pulling up outside the front door of the State School for the Feeble-Minded and Epileptics in Faribault, Minnesota, the green-and-white bus that picked up Rose from the train station in St. Paul made seventeen stops: from Prior Lake to Farmington to Northfield to Cannon City. Onboard were men and women adjudged to be slender of mind and empty of soul. In the slang of the institution, they were all "cracked."[1]

Rose landed on that bus because two people testified that she was a "common prostitute." And that's all it took to commit her. On her paperwork, next to a box that says "reason for commitment" are the words: "Is immoral."[2]

Is immoral. On the basis of that subjective judgment, Rose spent the next five-and-a-half years in and out of that institution, where the occupants were essentially branded with a letter—*F* in Rose's case, for feebleminded—and given all the compassion of a modern-day Hester Prynne.

The Faribault state hospital, long since closed, was an imposing structure—three stories throughout with a four-story tower in front.[3] Boys and men were on one side and girls and women on the other. All of the "patients," regardless of age, were referred to as children. It was a collection point for those deemed unfit for society, and although we now know better, it was believed at the time to be a forward-thinking and compassionate method for treating the mentally deficient and physically handicapped.

It was also a convenient ruse for getting them out of the way.

Institutionalization was passed off as humane public policy, done to keep the mentally ill (a wide category that could mean anything from mental retardation to even depression) from harming themselves. Certainly there were those who needed such protection, but the bulk of the population—which kept growing with each loosening of the commitment laws—posed little danger to themselves or anyone else. Many were just poor.[4]

Warehoused in institutions built in far-off-the-beaten-path rural areas, their real sin was not being like everyone else. And in 1920s America, not being like everyone else was among a list of forbidden directives, right up there with "thou shall not steal" and even "thou shall not kill."

Local child welfare boards and their accomplices, county court judges, were governed by the state's commitment laws, which called for certain criteria to be met. But in reality, committing those seen as different—or slow of mind—required little provocation. These local jurisdictions were the eyes and ears of an all-powerful statewide body with an ominous but apt name: the Board of Control. It was this board that assumed responsibility for protecting children from their defective parents, or as the feebleminded are referred to in some Board of Control reports, their "subnormal" parents. It was that board that held sway over Rose for much of her twenties, dictated her movements, and subjected her to the evil hand of eugenics, one of the most hideous social experiments in the history of America.

Committing those with intellectual disabilities meant getting them off the street—and out of the community—so judges often took a hard line with minimum risk of being second-guessed. Judges, in fact, were all but insulated from criticism. As a *Minnesota Law Review* article points out, there was "no post-commitment judicial review of any kind—even of a decision to institutionalize a ward."[5]

As for the wards themselves, they had little sophistication about the legal system—they were "subnormal," remember—and no defense against the most powerful weapon of all: the IQ test. In 1905, the French psychologist Alfred Binet developed the first practical intelligence measurement—the Binet-Simon test—as a means for calculating an individual's cognitive ability. Eugenicists saw it as something else: a chance to apply true science to their theories of inherited intelligence. Using Binet-Simon test results as affirmation, eugenicists soon were making alarmist—and often inaccurate—claims about the number of immigrants and prison inmates who tested below normal.

Intelligence testing was far from universal in Minnesota during the 1920s, largely because of the cost, but it was used religiously at both the local and state levels to determine whether a person should be committed to an institution. Later, the same tests were used to justify decisions on sterilization.

The person who authorized Rose's tests—she was tested three times while in the Faribault institution—was Frederick Kuhlmann, the research director at the Board of Control and the state's leading advocate of intelligence testing.[6] Kuhlmann was an influential voice in the mental health community and a firm believer that mental tests were all that was needed to certify someone as feebleminded. Rose's records from Faribault state: "Tested by Miss Charlotte Lowe of Kuhlman's [*sic*] office."

Critics argue that IQ tests have an inherent cultural bias and don't accurately account for a person's environment or level of educational attainment.

For example, how could anyone expect Rose, who had little formal education, to test at the same level as someone who finished high school or junior high? Taking those factors into account, her test results—she never tested above sixty-eight, the mental acuity level of a ten-year-old—are not atypical.

In the hierarchy of intelligence as measured by the Binet-Simon test and its variations, a sixty-eight is well within the range of what was considered feebleminded. In a January 1920 address before the Minnesota State Association of Probate Judges, Kuhlmann said a score lower than seventy "means that such adults will not be able permanently to make an independent, honest living without supervision and guardianship, under any and all circumstances they are likely to meet in their lives. The chances of their doing so are practically nil, and the risk of leaving them unprovided for is too great."[7]

Kuhlmann went on to say that "one-half of professional prostitutes are feebleminded" and "probably about the same figure holds for the occasional sex offenders and the mothers of illegitimate children." Rose was alleged to be a prostitute and the mother of two children whom society considered illegitimate. You do the math on her chances of scoring normally on the tests.

Rose also had another hurdle to climb, and it was one that would forever stand in her way: her timing. Research on the perils of aberrant behavior was coming out of the shadows just as Rose's so-called moral failings were gaining local attention. And as Faribault grew into one of the largest institutions of its kind in the country, it was on the cutting edge of the eugenics movement, which by then was achieving national relevance. More bad timing, you might say. To the people who now held her fate in their hands, her handicap was more concerning than any physical disability, and far, far more dangerous. Moral degeneracy had to be stopped, or at least slowed, to preserve a way of life that was increasingly under siege.

Women were a particular target. Because of their ovaries—those nasty things—women deemed to be of low morals and intelligence were seen as potentially corrupting to future generations. (The concept that it takes two to tango didn't seem to register with the all-male legislatures and judiciaries of the day.) There was disagreement about the methods needed to stop women like Rose from reproducing; there was virtually no argument about the need to stop them.

In Minnesota, bills authorizing the use of forced sterilization were introduced in both the 1911 and 1913 legislatures. Neither passed, but there was momentum for taking more aggressive measures to address the growing threat of degeneracy. In 1917, Minnesota adopted the so-called Children's Code, which was lauded by many for its much-needed reforms aimed at protecting children.[8] For example, among the thirty-five laws encompassed in the code was one curtailing the practice of "baby farms"—the name given poorly run maternity hospitals that provided shoddy care and extracted huge fees for placing infants. To remedy the outrageous abuses that were occurring, the Children's Code established a licensing system for maternity hospitals, infant homes, and child-care and child-placing agencies, with state-administered standards for quality care. One writer called the package of reforms "perhaps the greatest achievement in the history of Minnesota's social legislation."

Yet for all its good, the Children's Code also led the way to a Big Brother–esque commitment of people like Rose. Under the law, county probate judges were given immense powers, including committing neglected, dependent, and delinquent children—and any person alleged to be feeble-minded, an inebriate, or insane—to state guardianship *without* the approval of a parent or guardian.

That opened the floodgates and soon institutions like Faribault were packed with inmates—or, if you prefer, patients—who got hauled before a local judge for any number of reasons, including financial hardship.[9] As in so many public policy decisions, addressing one problem inevitably led to another, and just as "tough on crime" laws today result in expensive solutions like building more prisons, the compulsory commitment law left too many people in too few facilities. More would have to be built unless—and this was the ingenious part—the population could be reduced through a quick medical procedure. There was just one problem: it wasn't yet legal.

When Rose first arrived at the Faribault institution in 1924, eugenics was no longer a fringe movement. Immigration was becoming more of a concern, and eugenic fire-breathers fueled those anxieties with maniacal warnings of widespread mayhem. The general thought process was this: along with all the homegrown and foreign-born idiots, the country would soon be subsumed by their morally degraded offspring. A psychologist, Henry H. Goddard, capped the hysteria in 1912 with his book *The Kallikak Family: A Study in the Heredity of Feeblemindedness.*[10]

Kallikak was a fictional name Goddard gave to a family line that extended back to the Revolutionary War and supposedly tainted by an illicit affair its patriarch had with a feebleminded girl. Using doctored photographs, Goddard sought to illustrate the string of defective descendants sown through that immoral coupling. Advocating for mass sterilization, Goddard wrote that the unfortunate Kallikaks who followed in the line were "feebleminded, and no amount of education or good environment can change a feebleminded individual into a normal one, any more than it can change a red-haired stock into a black-haired stock."

No amount of education or good environment. So much for weighing the merits of nature versus nurture.

Not to be outdone, Minnesota had its own Kallikak-like propaganda with which to scare the masses. In 1919, a researcher named Maud Merrill completed the work of her former boss, A. C. Rogers, the longtime director of the

Faribault institution. Rogers was in charge at Faribault for more than thirty years, guiding its gradual transition from a teaching institution into a custodial environment in which the "children" were segregated, indefinitely if necessary. For the women, this meant getting them past their childbearing years.

Although Rogers did not endorse mandatory sterilization as a means for culling the population of degenerates—making him something of a moderate on that point—he became a firm believer in eugenics as a backbone of public policy. The research he initiated, which was completed after his death, helped to lead the state into this regrettable era of social engineering.

Merrill pulled together Rogers's fieldwork into a collection of stories—some clearly fabricated—about a line of supposedly degenerate offspring that settled along the Root River valley in southern Minnesota. The book, *Dwellers in the Vale of Siddem*, advertised itself as "a true story of the social aspect of feeble-mindedness," but it was mostly an alarmist screed of bogus science that would be laughed out of any research institution today. Consider this passage:

> It is not the idiot or, to any great extent, the low-grade imbecile, who is dangerous to society. In his own deplorable condition and its customarily accompanying stigmata, he is sufficiently anti-social to protect both himself and society from the results of that condition. But from the high-grade feeble-minded, the morons, are recruited the ne'er-do-wells, who lacking the initiative and stick-to-itiveness of energy and ambition, drift from failure to failure, spending a winter in the poor house, moving from shack to hovel and succeeding only in the reproduction of ill-nurtured, ill-kept gutter brats to carry on the family traditions of dirt, disease and degeneracy. Such communities as the Vale of Siddem bear eloquent testimony to the futility of trying to cope with such social inefficiency from the standpoint of the criminologist of holding the individual responsible for his misdeeds when he is fundamentally irresponsible, or from the point of view of the philanthropist improving his condition and helping him to help himself when he is fundamentally incapable of self-help. A laissez-faire policy simply allows the social sore to spread.[11]

A laissez-faire policy simply allows the social sore to spread. My goodness.

The face of the eugenics movement in Minnesota for a long time was a man named Charles Fremont Dight. He was a bit of a kook—Dight was said to have lived in a treehouse for a time—but he developed a huge following as a tireless advocate of what researchers call negative eugenics: invasive intervention that rejects the notion of supporting families through more positive measures, such as job training or family counseling. A good house, he once said, "cannot be built with rotten lumber."[12]

Seizing on that sentiment—or fearing the political repercussions if he rejected it—Minnesota's Republican governor, Theodore Christianson, signed a eugenics sterilization bill into law on April 8, 1925. Although a turning point, it wasn't the muscular sea change favored by Dight and his like-minded peers. For example, the law specified that no sterilization could take place *without* consent, a ridiculous requirement in Dight's eyes. Even a "blank idiot," he complained, couldn't be sterilized under the new law.

The bill had critics on the other side as well. The Catholic Church opposed eugenic sterilization in principle, seeing it as a violation of moral law.[13] But the church wasn't the reason Minnesota adopted the more restrictive language, at least not directly. More persuasive was the assumption that the U.S. Supreme Court would never sanction a law permitting involuntary sterilization. And on that, the policymakers in Minnesota couldn't have been more wrong.

Indiana opened the door to eugenic sterilization as a state-sanctioned policy in 1907.[14] Although there were illegal sterilizations performed long before then, Indiana's law placed that state in a sort of rarified air. According to author Edwin Black, Indiana was the first jurisdiction *in the world* to legislate forced sterilizations on mentally impaired patients.

California soon followed, along with a host of other states, but an uneasiness was creeping in. Courts began siding with those who claimed that the bills were unconstitutional, and it was becoming obvious to all that a test case was needed that could pass a vigorous court review. In Virginia—and a young mother named Carrie Buck—sterilization advocates had their poster child.[15] And what a poster child she would prove to be. In *Buck v. Bell*, the court established that states can mess with the reproductive organs of any woman they deem unworthy of the privilege of motherhood, provided a few minor safeguards are put in place. In other words: game on.

The story of Carrie Buck is worth examining here, not just because of the similarities between Carrie and Rose, but as an example of the type of thinking that was sweeping the country just as Rose became an institutionalized ward of the state of Minnesota. The theory that bad stock ultimately breeds more bad stock was backed by no real science but caught fire in a nation that saw its destiny being undermined by the morally unfit. Many of the country's top thinkers believed strongly that if something wasn't done, not only would these people become a burden on society, they would lead to its eventual ruin. George Washington Carver wasn't talking about eugenics but might have been when he wrote, "Fear of something is at the root of hate for others." Hate was a driving factor in the country's tilt toward eugenics: hatred toward the poor, hatred toward black and brown people, and—most of all—hatred toward women.

Carrie Buck was the daughter of Emma Buck, who was declared to be feebleminded because of a record of prostitution. That was enough to send her to the Virginia State Colony for Epileptics and Feebleminded for the rest of her life. When her daughter Carrie got pregnant at the age of seventeen—the result of a rape in all likelihood—her case went before the same judge as her mother's. Talk about a stacked deck. After hearing testimony about the soon-to-be teen mother's "outbreaks of temper" and hallucinations—alleged by her foster parents—the judge committed her to the same institution.

A pregnant teen with temper tantrums. Hmmm.

Like Rose, Carrie's timing wasn't great. Her baby, Vivian, was born a little more than two months after Carrie was committed and just days after Virginia passed its model eugenics sterilization law. Eugenicists could scarcely contain their enthusiasm. After all, Vivian held the key to proving the very premise behind eugenics, that defective genes are as hereditary as height and hair color. It's one thing to demonstrate two generations of defectives. Eugenicists could cite many such examples. But with three, they had the Holy Grail.

Vivian was seven months old when a social worker first examined her mental fitness. Asked in a subsequent hearing to assess the child, the social worker responded, "It is difficult to judge probabilities of a child as young as that, but it seems to me [she is] not quite a normal baby."[16]

"You don't regard her child as a normal baby?" she was asked.

Somewhat reluctantly, the social worker responded: "There is a look about it that is not quite normal, but just what it is I can't tell."

There is a look about it that is not quite normal. With those words, Vivian Buck became the third generation in her family to be declared feebleminded. Harry H. Laughlin, the superintendent of the Eugenics Record Office in Cold Spring Harbor, New York, and a prominent educator at the time, summed up the views of eugenicists in a deposition that was included as part of the court case: "These people," he wrote, referring to the Buck family, "belong to the shiftless, ignorant and worthless class of anti-social whites of the South."

"Shiftless and ignorant" pretty much summed up the attitude in America toward anyone, particularly women, who had the misfortune of possessing a mental handicap. In clipped language as if it came directly from a medical diagnosis, Laughlin then said Carrie Buck "has record during life of immorality, prostitution and untruthfulness; has never been self-sustaining; has one illegitimate child, now about six months old and supposed to be mental defective."

Laughlin's testimony about Carrie's mother Emma was similar, but he added that she should not be allowed to marry, having been divorced from her husband "on account of infidelity."

It mattered little, of course, that the infidelity, even if true, was hardly confined to those among the lower social and economic strata. Or whether Emma was the offender. (After all, aren't men guilty of infidelity as well? Studies, in fact, show that men are far more likely to cheat than their female counterparts.) But alas, facts weren't really important or even the least bit relevant.

For example, on Rose's paperwork from Faribault, there is a reference to the origin of her alleged feeblemindedness. "Inherited," someone wrote. And they knew this, how?

The deck was stacked so heavily against women like Rose and Carrie Buck (both of whom were committed in the same year) that it was like sending toddlers to do battle against gladiators. Fear carried the day. In the court case involving the Buck family, both the trial and appellate courts upheld the Virginia law and, in a vote of eight to one—all nine justices were men, of course—the U.S. Supreme Court followed suit on May 2, 1927. Compulsory sterilization was now the law of the land, and in his majority opinion, Oliver Wendell Holmes showed just how accepted the very concept of feeblemindedness had become in the American mainstream: "Carrie Buck is a feebleminded white woman who was committed to the State Colony," he wrote. "She is the daughter of a feebleminded mother in the same institution, and the mother of an illegitimate feebleminded child."[17]

At the time of the ruling, Vivian Buck was all of three years old. She was snatched from her mother in a theft as outrageous as the kidnapping of the Lindbergh baby. Yet it wasn't seen as wrong. At an age when kids are just beginning to explore the vastness of their potential, Vivian's destiny was stamped in concrete by one of the nation's foremost legal scholars. In words that would become immortalized in the sad chapter of eugenics in America, the eighty-six-year-old Holmes concluded:

> It is better for the world, if instead of waiting to execute degenerate offspring for crime, or to let them starve for their imbecility, society can prevent those who are manifestly unfit from continuing their kind. The principle that sustains compulsory vaccination is broad enough to cover cutting the Fallopian tubes. . . . Three generations of imbeciles are enough.

The Holy Grail came home.

The truth about the Buck family would eventually emerge, and for eugenicists who yearned for a return to glory, it was a gut punch: all of the Bucks— every last one of them—were normal.

In 1983, the paleontologist Stephen Jay Gould revisited the landmark Supreme Court case for an article in *Natural History* magazine.[18] Citing the work of author/scholar Paul Lombardo and others, Gould noted that Carrie Buck had lived a long and productive life *after* she was released from the institution.

"As scholars and reporters visited Carrie Buck . . . what a few experts had known all along became abundantly clear to everyone," he wrote. "Carrie Buck was a woman of obviously normal intelligence."

Writing a year after Carrie's death, Gould noted that during her lifetime Carrie was an avid reader with a fondness for crossword puzzles. *Crossword puzzles*. Better lock her up.

There is ample evidence that Vivian—the supposed third generation of "imbecile" referred to in Holmes's opinion—was mislabeled as well. Her report cards from the elementary school she attended in Charlottesville, Virginia, show that, at least in the first and second grade, she was as normal as can be. There are no records beyond that because she died of an infection at the age of eight.

Had Holmes and the court received the case a few years later, they would have had to reconcile their own rank prejudice with some of the As and Bs Vivian received on her report cards and the fact that she was named to the school's honor roll in April 1931.

As a court-declared feebleminded person, Carrie wasn't even told that her daughter had died. It was July 3, 1932, the day before all of America celebrated its independence.

When Rose entered Faribault, the Supreme Court had yet to make its landmark ruling in *Buck v. Bell*, but Minnesota was so desperate to begin sterilizing the wombs of its mentally deficient moms that it put its program into practice *before* the high court settled the question of whether sterilization for eugenic purposes was constitutional. Although men too were targets for sterilization—often through the prison system, which was concerned about excessive masturbation—the overwhelming majority of eugenic sterilizations in Minnesota, as elsewhere, were done on women.

Rose was a prime candidate. Her entire identity was wrapped up in the one-word label assigned to her as a permanent reminder of her repulsiveness: she was feebleminded. In Minnesota, that meant she met the following criteria: "Any person, minor or adult, other than an insane person, who is so mentally defective as to be incapable of managing himself and his affairs as to require supervision, control or care for his own and the public welfare."

"Incapable of managing himself and his affairs" would seem to fit about half the twenty-something population. But unfortunately for Rose, it also fit her to a T. Not only did she carry the twin labels of "feebleminded" and "morally corrupt"—judges tended to conflate the two—she was unmarried, young enough to bear children, and demonstrably fertile, as evidenced by her son and daughter. The reality, of course, is it wouldn't have made any difference if she had one child or none. At twenty-four, she was *able* to have children, and as Minnesota's eugenic sterilization law hit the ground running in January 1926, the idea of giving someone like her control over her own body was crazy talk. Consider this statement from William Hodson, the Minnesota Children's Bureau director: "Children of defective parents are almost sure to carry the defective inheritance. The state cannot permit its feeble-minded girls and women to corrupt the human stream."[19]

It would be easy to condemn Rose for her behavior, which was less than exemplary and certainly damaging to her children. But there is no denying that her options were limited. A single mother with her education and intellect had roughly two legitimate occupational opportunities: waitressing and housekeeping. But women working at all was still frowned upon by many, particularly if children were involved. And even though attitudes toward women in the workplace were changing, women like Rose were seen as powerless to defend against their sexual impulses. In a 1922 report to the State Board of Control, Hodson wrote:

> Two occupations of a somewhat similar character stand out as dangerous . . . as to the temptations which they afford. It is probably true that the house maid, with long hours, inadequate living quarters, uninteresting drudgery and lack of opportunity for proper recreation is particularly open to destructive influences. The waitress, of course, suffers from a somewhat different situation. In serving all types and conditions of people, she becomes the object of much loose talk and many improper advances. This occupation needs more constructive attention from the intelligent forces of the community.[20]

The biennial reports to the Minnesota State Board of Control read like mad experiments on the manipulation of human behavior, which of course they were. "Defective" women, the word used to describe people like Rose, were considered either immoral or helpless to resist the sexual advances of men and deeply dangerous to society.

Hodson, who left Minnesota in 1922 to assume a similar post in New York City, was considered an enlightened voice in the country on issues of child welfare and sexual behavior, and he wrote often about the perils of the feeble-minded in society. In that 1922 report he argued for a law prohibiting the marriage of feebleminded individuals and said his office would send all the clerks of court in the state an alphabetical list of committed cases so they would know to hold up any marriage licenses, at least until "interested people" could take steps to prevent the marriage of those known to be mentally defective.

"In the long run," he wrote, "the development of a strong public opinion against the marriage of the unfit is the only remedy."[21]

By the early 1920s, Minnesota was routinely locking up women like Rose and taking steps to ensure that they were not allowed to marry. But that wasn't enough. With the sterilization law, their campaign of hatred was taken to a whole new level. Rose was first tested upon admission using Kuhlmann's variation of the Binet-Simon IQ test, which included questions like this: How many fingers are on your right hand? How many fingers are on your left hand? How many fingers are on both hands?

Based on those results, Faribault officials had little doubt that Rose was feebleminded. And in their minds, of course, they already knew her to be immoral. What they didn't know, and were loath to discover, was that she was pregnant.[22] And there was another problem as far as the institution was concerned: no one (except Rose perhaps) was sure who the father was.

Eugenicists were of like mind when it came to the offspring of two feebleminded parents: the child was almost certain to carry the defective gene. But the pairing of a feebleminded and normal person carried a ray of hope. In studies purporting to be fact-based and scholarly reviewed, children with one parent of normal intelligence (and the other one feebleminded) were found to have a one-in-four chance of adding another defective person to the gene pool. In other words, there was at least a fighting chance that the baby would be normal. Rose knew Faribault's administrators were interested in the identity of the father for reasons that were less than altruistic. No matter what the Binet-Simon test said about her, she had a keen sense of her environment. What were they going to do if she didn't answer? Kick her out? So she did the equivalent of putting her fingers in her ears, turning her desk to the rear of the classroom, and pretending to read a book upside down. Like her mother and other members of her family, Rose wasn't one to jump just because it was suggested as a worthwhile thing to do.

Rose's third and final child, Robert, was born on April 20, 1925—eight months and eight days *after* she was admitted to the institution. That means that she was either a week or two pregnant when she got there, or she became impregnated during the early days of her incarceration. Rose's daughter Millie has always believed her biological father, Ingram Conradson, was Robert's father as well. After all, Robert's name during the first years of his life was Conradson. But it is far from certain that Ingram was Robert's father. According to Millie's adoption papers—she was adopted by Orvel McClain, Rose's third husband, when she was a teenager—Ingram deserted the family in September 1922.[23] That was nearly three years before Robert was born. Rose's intake records at Faribault say that Ingram, who was still legally married to her at the time, "abandoned her." Since those notes were written the same month Robert most likely was conceived, Ingram would seem to be disqualified—or at least questionable—as a potential sperm donor.

Which raises an obvious question: If it wasn't Ingram who fathered Robert, who did? One of Rose's johns? A fellow inmate? A guard? There certainly were fine guards at Faribault—or "aides" as the state liked to call them—but personal testimonials provide a contrast to the sanguine portrayal of the staff found in government reports from the period. Rose was in Faribault at the same time as William Sackter, whose life story was later made into the TV movie *Bill* starring Mickey Rooney. It was only after the movement to deinstitutionalize those with disabilities that Sackter was set free after spending forty-four years in the same institution Rose was in. He struggled outside of the institution for a while, but soon his true character as a warm person with a tender soul was revealed. Folks also discovered he could play a mean harmonica. Bill became so beloved in the college town where he ran Wild Bill's Coffee Shop—Iowa City, Iowa—that flags in the town were flown at half-staff when he died.[24]

In an autobiography about his life (written by Thomas Walz using passages dictated by Sackter), Bill described some of the Faribault guards as sociopathic bullies. Faribault had about 2,000 inmates (or wards) in all, so Sackter's experience wasn't likely mirrored by everyone. Most of the folks who work in this industry do it out of a sense of duty and empathy, enriching the lives of people who don't always encounter such kindness. Let's hope some of the staff at Faribault was cut from that same cloth. But as Bill's book showed, it was a tough place where personal safety wasn't a given. One night, he awakened a guard because a fellow inmate—a child—was having a seizure. After Bill shook him a few times, the guard jumped up and screamed, "What the fuck do you want?"

Bill told the guard his friend would die if he didn't get help. There is no corroboration for this, just Bill's account, but he said the man responded, "Let the bastard die." When Bill persisted, he said the guard led him to a stairwell and beat him so savagely he ended up in the infirmary.

Compassion was often lacking in the Faribault that Bill describes. He had an ulcerated leg that was a souvenir from a kick he received from a drunken aide. When inmates didn't conform to the rules of the institution, they were made to lie naked on the floor or immersed in a cold tub of water. Some experiences can be corroborated: when Bill was released from the Faribault institution in 1964, not only couldn't he read or write, but no one had taught him how to tell time from the hands on a watch. That he struggled upon getting out was not only understandable, it was preordained.

There are scant records from Rose's time in the institution, but at least one surviving record suggests she wasn't particularly happy to be there.[25] On January 29, 1925, Rose tried to run away from the attendant who was taking her to the laundry. A typed, cryptic account of the incident says: "Was caught after running a short distance by the attendant."

Rose was five or six months pregnant at the time, so she couldn't have gotten far. But it was recorded in her file as if it were a significant event. Yet not recorded in those records is any mention of her pregnancy, the birth of her son, or the health of her baby. It's as if it never happened. And as far as the state was concerned, it never did.

Like his older brother and sister, Robert Conradson was brought into this world under conditions that were less than ideal. It's not even entirely clear where he was during the first year of his life. Was he in the institution with his mother? Perhaps. The Faribault "school" did house a number of the inmates' younger children. But as an anchorage for child development, it was unsuitable, and someone decided—it's not clear who—that Robert would go live with his grandmother in Brainerd.

Unfortunately, that wasn't ideal either. Even in the best of times, Mary DeChaine struggled financially, and these were far from the best of times. The shopmen's strike was over, but there was no question who had won, and it wasn't the workers on whose incomes so many households in Brainerd depended, including the DeChaines. The little money that Mary brought in working as a housekeeper was hardly enough—the credit she'd gotten from the grocery store was close to tapping out—and ever since Joe died, the house was in continual need of repair. Mary kept the kids fed and bathed, but their clothes were ragged, and at sixty years of age, the energy she needed to calm a toddler screaming into the night wasn't so easily summoned. As always, she did the best she could, relying on a higher power to push her through.

In the early spring of 1926 Mary was about to head outside to hang another load of laundry when a knock on the front door echoed through the house like a shotgun in the middle of the night. *Bang. Bang. Bang.* Then somewhat louder: *Bang. Bang. Bang. Bang.* Mary could always tell by the force of the knocking whether her visitors were friendly or not. Friends and neighbors don't pound on the door like they're trying to wake a sleeping lion.

The man and the woman standing on the landing looked uneasy as Mary said, "What do you want?" through the screen door, thinking they were bill collectors, agents from the revenue office, or traveling salesmen peddling some miracle cure for wrinkles or warts.

"Can we come in? It's a little cold out here," the man said. "I really think you want to hear what we have to tell you."

"I really don't have time," Mary said gruffly. "Go bother someone else."

Mary was about to shut the interior door when the woman said, "Mrs. DeChaine, we're from the Board of Control. It's about your daughter."

Mary swung the door open so fast it banged against a chair leg. "Is she OK?"

"Oh, she's fine," the man said. "In fact, we want to send her home."

"Home?" Mary said, somewhat surprised. "So why ain't she here? What do you mean, send her home?"

The two people looked at each other, annoyed to be pushed off their well-rehearsed script.

"Well, Mrs. DeChaine, there's something we need to take care of first," the man said. "Please, I really think you're going to want to hear this, but we can't do it out here. It involves paperwork. Signatures."

"Signatures?" Mary said. "What on earth for?" She was always distrustful of those who wanted her signature. Friends don't ask for signatures.

"Please, ma'am," the man said, definitely irritated now. His spotless brown suit looked out of place beside the peeling paint, the missing hinge on the screen door, and the broken railing on the front steps that Joe never got around to replacing.

Mary eyed them both. Signatures. Good grief. But it was cold and they said they had information about Rose. She opened the screen door. "Best you come in then."

Normally, Mary would offer visitors coffee, but this wasn't that kind of visit. After both sat down, she said, "What is this about? Where is Rose?"

"Again, she's fine," the man said.

"I asked where she is."

"She's at school," the woman offered.

Mary laughed. "You call that a school? She's locked up like a criminal. School, my foot."

"Now Mrs. DeChaine," the woman said. "I resent the inference that your daughter is not well cared for. We've given her training, taught her an occupation . . . "

"An occupation? What occupation?"

"Housekeeping," the woman said. "She's assigned to the laundry."

"The laundry?" Mary laughed again. "She don't need no training for that. She can do that at home."

"That's why we're here," the man said. "We think she would be better off in her home environment."

Mary hadn't expected visitors, so her "home environment" was less than tidy. The daybeds were covered with dirty clothes, the kitchen was a mess—Millie liked to play with her dolls on the floor and not necessarily neatly—and the baby was crying in the back bedroom, which used to be Mary's bedroom until her son Elmer converted it into a makeshift nursery. Mary slept on the couch where her two visitors were sitting now, on opposite ends separated by the pile of papers that apparently needed signatures.

"Look, Mrs. DeChaine," the man said. "We've come all the way from Faribault, well, frankly, to make your life better."

Mary glared the way she did when she knew one of her kids was lying to her. "What's the catch?" she said as she fetched Robert from the bedroom, where he had awoken from his nap. "I have to feed him and I have work to do. I ain't buying that you're trying to make my life better. You never met me before."

Mary walked to the stove, struck a match, and began heating milk for the baby. Millie was playing quietly—thank goodness for that—but Mary wasn't entirely sure where Ernie was. She hoped he was in the backyard where she last saw him. She thought about calling for him, but she wasn't sure if this would get put in some report. They did say something about signatures.

When the milk was warm to the touch, Mary poured the contents of the pan into a bottle and put Robert on the floor. His wails subsided as he began to suck, holding the bottle of milk as if it were a trumpet. Mary was tired. Anybody could see that, and as she struggled to get up from the floor, the man jumped up to help her to her feet. Mary sat down, rubbing the right side of her back in a futile effort to lessen the pain.

"We don't want to take up a lot of your time, Mrs. DeChaine," the woman said at last. "I don't know if we've introduced ourselves properly. This is Mr. Overson and I'm Miss Short, but you can call me Linda. I know we're strangers, but we care about you and we care about your daughter. This is a good thing. Trust us."

Mary knew not to trust anyone who says "trust us." But she was also looking at Robert's bottle, which was now half full. "What is it I'm supposed to trust you about?" she asked.

The man—what did she say his name was, Overson?—jumped in with a lot of words Mary didn't understand. The legislature did this, and the governor did that, and women were getting freed from the institution because of eugenic something or other. Then he said a word she did understand: sterilization. Hell, her dad used to do that with cattle.

"Wait a second. You want to sterilize my daughter? Is that even legal?"

"It is," Linda Short said. "Has been since January. And we've yet to get a complaint. Families love it. They get to reunite with their loved ones, and they no longer have the burden of raising more children. They can concentrate on the ones they have. And Mrs. DeChaine, this is completely voluntary. The legislature made sure of that. They didn't want to strip families of their right to choose."

"Right to choose? What about Rose? Does she get to choose? How do I know this is what she wants?"

"We're coming to you," the man named Overson said. "That's what the law specifies. And frankly, if you don't take advantage of this opportunity, someone else will. And Rose will stay where she is."

Mary didn't know it at the time, but the man was telling the truth. Under the law of Minnesota at that time, feebleminded individuals were stripped of their basic legal rights, meaning they couldn't vote, own property, or marry without the state's permission.[26] They also couldn't give the written consent that was required for sterilization. That was no deterrent, of course, because such consent could be granted by the patient's spouse or nearest of kin or, in rare instances, the Board of Control. But the simplest way to avoid any legal entanglement was to get permission from a parent or legal guardian. Hence, the visit to Mary's house by the two Board of Control employees.

Mary wished Bud would come home. She didn't like being double-teamed, and she didn't appreciate having to decide this without talking to Rose. The bottle was three-fourths empty now, and she knew she should give Robert a burp. But her back was hurting, and it would really flare up if she bent down to pick him up. She thought of asking Miss what's-her-name to help—she must be a mother—but there was that business with the signatures and the paperwork and that godforsaken brown suit of the man in charge. The words, "If you don't take advantage of this, someone else will," began to ping-pong back and forth inside her head. She looked at the bottle one more time and heard a slurping sound. Any second now Robert would start screaming and, back be damned, she would have to pick him up. Where was Bud? *Slurp. Slurp. Slurp.*

She closed her eyes and began to pray. *Slurp. Slurp.*

"How do I know this is the right thing to do?" she whispered to herself, or maybe to Joe, but certainly not to the brown suit and the woman who was adjusting a pin in her hair.

"Ma'am, we wouldn't be here if we didn't believe in the rightness of this," the man said. "Dozens of women have already done this. People are lining up for the chance to make their families whole again."

Robert tossed the empty bottle aside, where it rolled toward the freshly polished shoes of Miss Pin in Her Hair.

"You can make your family whole again, Mrs. DeChaine," the woman said. "You can bring Rose home."

NOTES

1. Thomas Walz, *The Unlikely Celebrity: Bill Sackter's Triumph over Disability* (Carbondale: Southern Illinois University, 1998). For Sackter's treatment inside the institution, see 13–26.

2. Faribault School records. The two individuals who testified that she was "immoral" are not named.

3. Molly Ladd-Taylor, *Fixing the Poor: Eugenic Sterilization and Child Welfare in the Twentieth Century* (Baltimore: Johns Hopkins University Press, 2017), 33–37.

4. Ibid., 38–43.

5. See Robert Levy, "Protecting the Mentally Retarded: An Empirical Survey and Evaluation of the Establishment of State Guardianship in Minnesota," *Minnesota Law Review* 49, no. 5 (April 1965): 833.

6. Faribault School records, Minnesota Historical Society.

7. State Board of Control Published Records, Minnesota Historical Society.

8. "The Minnesota Experience," Minnesota Department of Public Welfare, 1967.

9. Ladd-Taylor, *Fixing the Poor*, 56.

10. Edwin Black, *War against the Weak* (Washington, DC: Dialog Press, 2012), 76–79.

11. Maud Merrill and A. C. Rogers, *Dwellers in the Vale of Siddem: A True Story of the Social Aspect of Feeble-Mindedness* (Boston: Gorham Press, 1919), 15.

12. Ladd-Taylor, *Fixing the Poor*, 78.

13. "Catholics and Eugenics: A Little-Known History," *National Catholic Reporter*, September 9, 2013.

14. Black, *War against the Weak*, 211.

15. For the Supreme Court's decision in the Buck case, see the following Library of Congress website: https://tile.loc.gov/storage-services/service/ll/usrep/usrep274/usrep274200/usrep274200.pdf.

16. Black, *War against the Weak*, 115.

17. "Buck v. Bell majority opinion," Oliver Wendell Homes, 1927, Library of Congress.

18. Stephen J. Gould, "Carrie Buck's Daughter," *Natural History Magazine*, July 1984.

19. See "What Minnesota Has Done and Should Do for the Feebleminded," by William Hodson, *Journal of the American Institute of Criminal Law and Criminology*, August 1919, 208–17. Also see: https://mn.gov/mnddc//past/pdf/10s/18/18-WHA-WNH.pdf.

20. Eleventh Biennial Report of the State Board of Control of Minnesota. Period Ended June 30, 1922, 46.

21. Ibid.

22. Robert's birth date is recorded in the Child History Record from the St. James Catholic Orphanage. Rose was in the Faribault state hospital at the time, confirmed through records accessed at the Minnesota Historical Society.

23. Adoption record from Anoka County, Minnesota, March 21, 1942.

24. Walz, *The Unlikely Celebrity*, 16.

25. Faribault School records.

26. Molly Ladd-Taylor, "Eugenics and Social Welfare in New Deal Minnesota," in *A Century of Eugenics in America*, ed. Paul Lombardo (Bloomington: Indiana University Press, 2011), 119.

5

Orphans

Rose DeChaine was sterilized on April 23, 1926. She wasn't in the first group of Minnesotans to have that operation. That "honor" went to the six women (one still in her teens) sterilized three months earlier during the law's first week. But she was among the early guinea pigs. At the end of 1926, fifty-three women (and two men) were sterilized at Faribault, each given the same get-out-of-jail-free card: sterilization in exchange for freedom.[1]

Over the years, thousands of "cracked" individuals made that same choice or, to be more accurate, had it made for them. By 1945, at least 1,800 sterilizations had taken place inside the Faribault institution, according to data compiled by Molly Ladd-Taylor for her book *Fixing the Poor.* The high-water mark was set in 1937, when 188 surgeries were performed, a rate of one every two days.

World War II largely put an end to the practice, but as Ladd-Taylor points out, the slowdown had more to do with an absence of nurses during the war than any enlightenment about the cruelty inherent in what the state was doing. In fact, although sterilizations were rare after that, the law remained on the books for thirty years *after* the war was over. No, eugenics wasn't just a passing fancy in Minnesota; it occupied a half-century of its history.[2]

Rose was released into Mary's custody on May 20, 1926, almost one month to the day after she was sterilized and just one day after Mary married John Lorbecki.[3] That was Mary and John's honeymoon: a trip to Faribault to pick Rose up from the institution. The celebration at Mary's house that night was one to behold, a gathering of friends, neighbors, family, and anyone who happened to drop by. Joseph's brothers were there and so was Grandma Louise, still a spry ninety-two. She made a bun cake.

There are moments in everyone's life when cares and worries take a back seat, when life slows to a speed so relaxing you can take time even to smell the tea, and for Rose it came at the precise moment she opened the door to a roomful of people who loved her unconditionally. Ernie had scribbled "Welcome Home" on a banner he and his sister hung in the kitchen. Mary had the house looking spotless, or at least as spotless as it ever got, and Bud built a folding partition in the corner of the living room so that Rose could have some privacy when she changed clothes. Clara even offered up her own daybed, the most comfortable of them all. Rose soaked it in, felt the pure ecstasy of the affectionate embrace, and then asked, "Anybody got a beer?"

Unfortunately, it didn't take long for the beer to go stale. In a fairy tale, Rose would have found her prince and lived happily ever after or at least found some measure of happiness. But nothing about Rose's life comes close to a fairy tale. Given her situation, what happened next was perhaps predictable. When you live near a crater, sometimes you fall in, and Rose had encountered plenty of craters. But the hole she fell into this time was so deep that she took someone important with her: her mother.

Mary had always been able to read people. She couldn't read much of the written word—the letters always got mixed up in her head—but when it came to deciphering someone's thoughts, she was almost without peer. But she always had a soft spot for family, and occasionally that soft spot became a blind spot.

In December 1927, just a few days before Rose's twenty-sixth birthday, Mary was awakened from a nap by another urgent pounding on her front door. The same two Board of Control officials were on the steps along with two other women that Mary later learned were from the Crow Wing County Child Welfare Board. One held Robert's hand as she stood to his side and the other one had both of her hands on Millie's shoulders. Ernie was in the back. No one had his hand.

"What's this about?" Mary said as she gathered up the children.

"Ma'am, is there someplace we can talk privately?" said the male Board of Control official, in a gray suit this time. Mary had long ago lost his name and had no interest in asking. She was in her normal work clothes, a baggy black dress and flat shoes that didn't aggravate her corns too much.

Mary called for Clara, who herded the kids into the kitchen where she promised them cookies. Mary turned back to the four people standing in her living room, none of them daring to sit before being directed. Despite her short height, Mary had a way of intimidating people, demanding their immediate attention. She removed a pile of dirty laundry from the couch and offered up the chair she had just been dozing in to whoever wanted it. It had been Joseph's favorite chair, broken springs and all, and those who sat in it—Mr. Gray Suit in this case—would sink down so low you'd think they were a foot shorter.

Miss Pin in Her Hair—Mary swore her hair was lighter the last time she was here—started talking, and for the next ten minutes Mary listened without interruption as each visitor took turns offering up one sordid detail after another. There was no promise to make Mary's life better, and though she knew by now to expect the worst when it came to Rose, she wasn't prepared for this. Never this. She had called the sheriff's office when Rose didn't come home with the kids for two days, but she didn't put two and two together until Mr. Gray Suit finished his spiel. Mary sat silently for a few seconds before blurting out, "He did what?"

It's not entirely clear what John Lorbecki was doing with Rose and her three children, but this much was clear: if it was entirely innocent, these people wouldn't be here. Here are the facts: John, Rose, and her three children were picked up just outside International Falls near the Canadian border, some 200 miles from Brainerd.[4] Rose was sent back to Faribault and John was—well, Mary didn't much care where John was. The kids were safe— that was the important thing—but Mary knew they'd be without their mother again, knew it the minute Mr. Gray Suit and Miss Pin in Her Hair showed up at her door.

The questions about Rose and John flooded Mary's head with the force of a tsunami: What were they doing? Where were they going? What will happen to the kids? And then there was the question that kept circling back in an endless loop: how could she be so blind?

Sure, she and John had been having problems. He wanted things that she just wasn't willing to provide. They'd had their share of fights, but those were usually over money. But John taking off with her daughter? That never entered her thoughts. But now, she realized, these strangers knew more about what was going on in her house than she did. All of her life she had tried to do what was best for those around her, and she definitely had tried to do what was best for Rose. That had been her guiding philosophy from day one. But this was about as bad it gets. Her marriage was in shambles, the kids were without their mother, and she was tired. Oh, God, she was tired. And there was that question again: "He did what?"

By the time Clara read her mother the January 25, 1928, story in the *Brainerd Dispatch*, Mary had already filed desertion charges against John Lorbecki. Rose was old enough under normal circumstances to make responsible decisions. At twenty-six, you're an adult. But Rose wasn't an adult, not really. If you believe the Binet-Simon test results, Rose had an IQ equal to that of a ten-year-old. What kind of man hightails it off with a ten-year-old?

Mary was weary—actually bone-tired—but now the pain that was always present went straight to her heart. She wanted to punish John—OK, maybe Rose, too—but not the kids. Never the kids. What had they done to deserve this? Yet they were the ones who would suffer the most. Mary could no longer hide the family's dysfunction with flowers on the kitchen table or a chocolate cake cooling on the stove. It was out in the open for everyone to see. She may have raised the kids, but she had no legal claim on them. With their mother back in the institution and upheaval in the home of the grandmother, the

Child Welfare Board recommended an outside placement—bureaucrat talk for getting the kids out of Dodge. To the board members it was reasonable, smart. Rose was an unmarried woman—unacceptable for a mother at that time and place—and for all practical purposes, Mary was, too. Yes, to the board members, the recommendation was smart. But to the children—Ernie, Millie, and Robert—it was something else entirely. Their mother was out of their lives. Just when they needed someone who knew which stuffed animal they couldn't sleep without or wouldn't forget to put a penny under their pillow when a tooth fell out, Mary, for all practical purposes, was gone as well.

Brainerd was no outlier when it came to punishing mothers whose husbands were absent, but women like Rose had a special burden. They weren't supposed to have children at all. Consider this monthly report from the Child Welfare Board that ran in the *Brainerd Dispatch* just a few days after Mary's visit from the Board of Control:

> During the past year, there were twenty-six unmarried mothers in the county, a deplorable condition that the board cannot remedy without the wholehearted support of the parents in the county.[5]

A subsequent report put the number at sixty-eight, of which thirty-eight were said to be "feebleminded."[6] Here's a question: if it was deplorable to be a mother who was unmarried, what word best described a mother who was unmarried *and* feebleminded? With eugenics fever sweeping the land, the children were mere collateral damage in a war in which the marauders all wore suits and ties. The innocents—and there were many—could do little more than wave a white flag.

For Mary, not only were her husband and daughter out of the house, but her grandchildren were, too. One minute they were playing marbles in the front yard. The next they were standing before a judge whose desk was taller than Ernie, the only one of the three children—and a good many of the adults—who made it through the whole hearing without crying. Robert, in fact, wailed so uncontrollably, Mary was asked to come forward to calm him down.

"We don't blame you," the woman from the child welfare office whispered into her ear.

Mary thought about what that one cop had said to her when Rose was first hauled off to the institution: "She got what she deserves, you ask me." That's it, isn't it? The person who gets the most blame is often the one least responsible. Rose was essentially a kid in an adult body, yet she would pay an adult price, separated from her family and stuck in what was commonly referred to as a mental asylum. Sure, it claimed to be a school, but the schools Mary was familiar with had doors that opened both ways. Faribault wasn't a school. It was a prison. Actually, worse than a prison. At Faribault, the sentences they gave the inmates were indefinite, with no reduction for time served. Ask Bill Sackter if he ever got a sentence reduction. He spent forty-four years there.[7] His crime? His brain wasn't wired the way society thought it should be.

Rose was released after her first stint in Faribault because she got sterilized. She no longer had that particular card to play, and this time she would have to show that she could function normally outside the institution—not easy to do when half the people running the place didn't believe that was remotely possible. Remember the words of Frederick Kuhlmann: feebleminded individuals with Rose's level of intelligence "will not be able permanently to make an independent, honest living without supervision and guardianship, under any and all circumstances they are likely to meet in their lives. The chances of their doing so are practically nil."

Practically nil, as in no chance. As for Mary, she did what she always did when her life took a terrible turn: she leaned on her faith. Oh, how she missed Joe. She even missed his corny jokes, which for some reason he never grew tired of. He used to do this one card trick over and over again. "I get Mary with that one every time," he would boast. At the dinner table he and Elmer would go and on about who was better: Babe Ruth or Ty Cobb, whom Joe called Ty Corn-on-the-Cob. He had a nickname for everyone—even the Babe, who, of course, already had one. But Joe never called him by *that* nickname. It was always "the Big Lug," "the Dumb Goon," or "the Boob." As in, "The Boob couldn't shine Corn-on-the-Cob's shoes." When the Red Sox sold Ruth to the Yankees in 1919, Joe said, "He'll be working in a car wash by the end of next year. You mark my words." That was a thing with Joe. Whenever he said something outrageous, it was always followed by "you mark my words." Then he'd wink, just to make sure no one took him *too* seriously. He was always clever that way.

Clever isn't a word too many people would attach to John Lorbecki. Decent didn't come to mind anymore, either. He knew his actions would blow up the household, yet he did it anyway. What was the endgame there? To live somewhere in Canada? What were they running from? And why bring the children?

At first, Mary didn't believe it could possibly be true. She thought maybe John had given Rose and the kids a ride somewhere. But if that was the case, why didn't he tell her where he was going? And when Rose was taken into custody, did he think to let his own wife know what was happening? A phone call would have been nice. Instead, she had been humiliated in front of strangers. *Ma'am, is there some place we can talk privately?* She agreed to drop the charges against John on one condition: that he disappear from their lives forever. And that's what happened. Within a year he was at the altar with another girl, an occasion marked by a small mention in the newspaper. If Mary blamed him for her own misfortune, she didn't let it show. Like the loose-fitting dresses she wore because they were comfortable, putting John out of her mind was a gift to herself, as calming as a warm bath.

In the end, Mary did blame herself for what happened, furious that she didn't ignore the voice in her head. "I just want you to be happy," Joe had told her. Happy? What does that have to do with anything?

The *Brainerd Dispatch* story was a rewrite of an earlier article that ran in the International Falls newspaper. Mary insisted that Clara read it to her, though Clara balked at first.

"Are you sure, Mama?" Clara protested.

Mary shot her a look. "You think the whole town don't already know it?"

Mary sat down in Joseph's chair, the weight of her body bending the last of the springs keeping her from touching the floor. She listened as Clara read, her eyes closed to the world. Clara began:

"County supports children," Clara read, causing Mary to scoff.

"That the title? Who wrote this, that Overson fella?"

"It doesn't say," Clara said. "But there's more to the headline. It says, 'Returned to county from International Falls when aid is asked.'"

"Good Lord," Mary said. "I don't know where International Falls is, but it ain't nowhere around here. Can't wait to hear what comes next."

"Mama . . ."

Mary shot her a look, the kind of look that means you better do what's asked. Clara continued reading.

"Support for three children, their mother feebleminded and under care of a state institution has finally been placed in the hands of the county following their transportation to this county from Koochiching County, it was learned here today."

"Koocha-what county?"

"Koochiching, Mama. I think that's where International Falls is."

"OK, whatever. What else?"

"The children are now in the care of their grandmother," Clara read. "The International Falls paper had the following news item recently: At a meeting of the Child Welfare Board, held yesterday, John Lorbecki, who came here from Crow Wing County with Rose Conradson, a feebleminded woman and the wife of another man, and her three children, appeared before the board and in as much as the mother had been scut back to the home for the feebleminded, that he was unable to take care of the children and asked for the help of the board in making arrangements for their care, now and hereafter."

Mary couldn't sit silent any longer. "Wife of another man? Why don't they just come right out and say she's a slut? And why did they have to use John's name? Whole town knows he's married to me. The whole blasted town. Now I'm a laughingstock."

"I don't have to read the rest, Mama," Clara said.

"Doesn't matter, girl. Can't get any worse, I figure."

"It's almost over," Clara said, then started reading again, a little faster now: "The members of the board, after considering the matter, ordered the children to be transported to their rightful place of residence in Crow Wing County. It is probable that the officials of that county will place the children in a state institution."

"A state institution?" Mary said. "What state institution? Institutions are for bad kids." That's the thought Mary couldn't get out of her head. These kids didn't do anything wrong. Robert was just three, for crying out loud. And Millie, you don't get much smarter than that girl. Her legs were getting worse, but what would an institution do about that? Do they even have doctors? Sure, Ernie was wild, but he was eight. Mary remembered Elmer at that age and saw some of the same tendencies. The kids didn't do anything wrong. They almost never do.

The commitment hearing was held before Judge Louis B. Kinder, the same judge who sent Rose to Faribault nearly four years earlier. The children were dressed in their Sunday clothes, and though their shoes were worn, the kids wouldn't have looked out of place in a church pew. The judge said several times that he only wanted what was best for the children and he hoped by sending them to an orphanage they would have more stability.

Stability, Mary thought. How would sending them away give them stability?

Before the kids were escorted out of the room, Mary hugged each one as if she would never see them again. And when it came to Robert, she never would. The children, the judge said, came from a broken home. That's the word he used: *broken*. Mary didn't think her home was broken. Rundown maybe, but broken? Sometimes the human eye sees only what it wants to see—the peeling paint, the torn wallpaper, the leaky roof—and completely misses the most important attribute of any home.

Rose's three children were committed to the St. James Catholic Orphanage in Duluth, Minnesota, on March 3, 1928, roughly three months after their mother lit out for points unknown with the husband of her own mother.[8] As unseemly as Rose's flight with her mother's husband might have been, it's difficult this many years later to see what crime was committed. The children weren't being abused. There is no record of that, anyway. And although things would have been icy at home between Mary and Rose, adultery—if that's what this was—doesn't normally result in an extended stay in an institution. But once Rose was labeled with the dreaded crucible of feeblemindedness, it was a stain that could never be erased. The 1917 Children's Code gave the state such power over feebleminded children—and adults—that families had little or no say about whether their loved ones were committed to an institution or how long they would stay there.

So Rose was returned to Faribault, fulfilling the expectations that most mental health officials had for her. Meanwhile, her children were sent to the St. James Catholic Orphanage some 200 miles away. Judge Kinder, who died in 1966, apparently believed he had little choice, and given the prevailing wisdom at the time about mental retardation and its many cousins, he may have been right. There were foster homes then, but it was not yet an integral part of the child welfare system. Certainly not in Brainerd. Kids from unstable homes were sent away. That's just how it was done. No, Judge Kinder apparently believed he had little choice. But the decision would have a profound impact on each of those children, every member of the DeChaine family, and maybe hundreds of others who were touched in some way by the outcome. Sometimes, the most obvious choices aren't necessarily the best ones. Rose may have been the one to bring her family to the edge of the cliff, but she had a whole lot of help in pushing them in.

Since the late 1800s Minnesota had been working to establish a more humane system for administering to neglected children, opting for alternatives to prisonlike institutions. The first and most famous of these opened in 1885. The Minnesota State Public School for Dependent and Neglected Children in Owatonna was a national model. Wards were housed in cottages, given training in various jobs—including farming—and then placed in permanent homes as soon as possible.[9] Unlike the St. James Catholic Orphanage, which opened in 1910, the Owatonna home was secular, its flock watched over by matrons and not nuns. But the general premise in the two institutions was the same: provide a foundation of discipline and purpose and then send the newly enlightened on their way.

Although adoption wasn't the primary purpose at St. James, it was an option, and as a feebleminded ward of the state, Rose would have no standing to object. This much was made clear: they weren't her kids anymore. The state, through its Board of Control, could seek adoption without her approval or that of anyone else in the family, for that matter. In fact, the state could have put all three of her children up for adoption. Given the prevailing attitude toward women of Rose's intellectual deficiencies, it's not hard to imagine that happening. Women like her were seen as incapable of much of anything, much less raising children, and the cheapest way of preventing a reunification between the children and their "cracked" mother would be to get a normal couple to adopt them. In chess it's the pawns that get sacrificed. In 1920s America, the mentally deficient and intellectually disabled were seen as just as expendable.

Rose's daughter Millie crashed the adoption party. Upon entering the St. James, all children were examined for their overall health, and in her case it wasn't good. Both of her legs were badly bowed, most likely because of a nutritional deficiency. She was advanced for her age mentally but extremely underdeveloped physically, at three feet, six inches tall and weighing just thirty-eight pounds. Her chart from the orphanage used the words "leg deformity" to describe her condition along with the term "saber shins." Rickets is a common cause of saber shin, a marked bowing of the tibial cortex, but there is another possible factor that can't be excluded: congenital syphilis. Millie inherited none of her mother's scandalous behavior, but she couldn't escape every byproduct of Rose's unhealthy lifestyle.

On August 13, 1928, roughly five months after entering the St. James, Millie was sent home to her grandmother.[10] In simple terms, the orphanage didn't want her. It wasn't just that she couldn't work, though that was an essential aspect of life at the St. James. She was a charity case, and, for an institution struggling financially, that was a nonstarter. She wasn't at Mary's house long, however. Roughly two weeks later, a social worker came to visit, took one look at Millie's legs, and had her transported to the Gillette Hospital for Crippled Children in St. Paul, whose mission was to provide care and treatment to indigent children.

During the course of the next several months, Millie underwent a series of operations on both legs. She spent her seventh birthday in the hospital but went home the next month to the one family member who had always been there for her: Grandma. Millie knew nothing about what had happened to her mother or where she had gone. When she would ask, Mary gave her the answer that she thought would cause the least harm: "Why do you want to know about all that stuff?"[11]

Ernie could have been adopted out as well, but his age got in the way. That and an attitude toward authority that didn't leave him when he left the orphanage. Parents who adopt children prefer them to be young, cute, and, above all, huggable. Ernie, who became Ernie McClain after Rose married her third husband, was none of those things. Though he would later charm the pants off any girl who got within three feet of him, at eight he was a handful, the rebellious teen years making an early appearance. Since no family was approaching the orphanage with a request like "Give me a temperamental kid who likes to challenge authority," Ernie was tossed out of the adoption pool. Which left Robert.

At three, Robert was the perfect age: old enough to be out of diapers and too young to carry around a vat of hostility. He wasn't just cute, he was adorable, with dimpled cheeks, a ready smile, and a penchant for fits of giggles. When he ran, his legs looked like slightly askew pinwheels, but he could throw a ball if he cocked his arm far enough to the side. Looking at him, you wouldn't know he never knew his father and barely knew his mother. You wouldn't know he was born in an institution and was back in one because his mother was a mess. And you definitely wouldn't know the bond he had with his siblings, who used to take turns pushing him on the swing at the park as he screamed "higher, higher" or would run in a circle alongside the roundabout until they all collapsed together in a dizzying euphoria.

You wouldn't know that he was loved by those who would never see him again. But then again, that was never a factor. All that mattered was that there was a couple who wanted him, and the needs of his brother, his sister, and his mother—particularly his mother—were of no consequence. Being feeble-minded meant losing everything that belonged to you, including those things most sacred. Maybe especially those things most sacred. In Rose's day, the mental health system that was so carefully constructed by individuals with long titles and advanced degrees had as its guiding principle this: punishment.

Adoption is a wonderful concept that has saved the lives of countless individuals, giving them an opportunity to thrive amid chaos. But not everyone benefits, and by wiping out Robert's past, he too may have suffered. His brother and sister loved him, as did his extended family and—although we don't know this for sure—Rose may have as well but was simply unequipped to show it. Let's be honest about this: left on her own, Rose may well have carved out a trail of destruction that would extend far beyond the people closest to her. But we don't know that. And here's the thing: the people who did this to her didn't know it either.

Like his brother and sister, Robert was examined upon admission, measured for his vitals—he was thirty-six inches tall and weighed a shade under thirty-three pounds—and vaccinated. Unlike Millie's file, however, which clearly lists her father's name as Ingram Conradson, a question mark is given on the form for Robert's father. In fact, there were question marks all over his form. It's as if he had no past, and maybe that was the point. As Robert was taken away by his adoptive parents—Raymond and Santa Anderson of Eveleth, Minnesota—Ernie watched from an upstairs window, his life unraveling before his very eyes. Robert was his little brother, the cute kid who would grab his leg and hold on for dear life as Ernie dragged him about the house. Now that cute kid was gone, and like the towns stripped bare by the 1918 Cloquet–Moose Lake fires, his existence was erased from the map.[12]

For a while Ernie tried to fit in at the orphanage, though his mother could have told him how difficult that is when you are labeled—in his case, with a T for troubled. Labels don't always take into consideration mitigating factors. He was a skinny, unimposing kid whose height when he entered the St. James was listed at four feet even and his weight at fifty pounds. Of course, no scale can measure the weight of terror felt by a young boy who finds himself disconnected from family and confined in the mesh of strangers.

His daughter Carolyn says her father told the family he ran away from the orphanage, and although that isn't mentioned in the records still encased in books stored in boxes in the building's interior, there is a troubling notation on the form for Ernie. Perhaps it happened before he got there and may have been a complete accident. It might be nothing at all. But listed after the question "Deformities?" on the form, someone wrote: "Burn, left hand."[13]

It's not known if Ernie was physically abused in his youth, but he had enough of what researchers refer to as "adverse childhood experiences" to haunt him for the rest of his life. In recent years, researchers have linked adverse childhood experiences to specific outcomes in adults, including physical and mental health issues. In 2008, the Centers for Disease Control developed criteria that states could use to determine the status of their residents' mental health and what services are needed to deal with issues related to childhood trauma.[14] In Minnesota, as elsewhere, researchers found it is not unusual to have negative experiences as a child—divorce being a common one—but the more traumatic the childhood, the greater the likelihood for long-term damage.

Data was collected specifying nine so-called adverse childhood experiences, or ACEs: physical abuse, sexual abuse, emotional abuse, mental illness of a household member, problematic drinking or alcoholism by a household member, illegal street or prescription drug use by a household member, divorce or separation of a parent, domestic violence toward a parent, and incarceration of a household member. Minnesota's survey, published in 2011, reported that 55 percent of adults had been exposed to at least one of these experiences as children, with many encountering more than one. Those with five or more had the most trouble adapting to adult life.[15]

Given the dysfunction that surrounded them, the number of ACEs for the children of Rose DeChaine could easily be put at five, and possibly more for Ernie, whose youth was spent either in the presence of a neglectful, alcoholic mother or in a prisonlike orphanage. Emotional abuse. Check. Mental illness of a household member. Check. Problematic drinking or alcoholism by a household member. Check. Divorce or separation of a parent. Check. Incarceration of a household member. Check.

Did Ernie encounter physical, sexual, or domestic abuse? Impossible to know. But he had enough negative experiences to raise serious alarms. All kids encounter stress, but there is a separate category for what the researchers called toxic stress: recurrent child abuse or neglect, severe maternal depression, parental substance abuse, or family violence. These experiences act like chemical agents that attack the brain and, if untreated, get worse with time. Individuals with multiple ACEs often experience anxiety and depression as adults, along with overall health problems that many treat by self-medicating. All of this, of course, can trigger other issues that then come into play: divorce, employment problems, financial strain, criminal behavior, and, finally, violence.

Ernie made his own choices, and his actions later in life can't be condoned no matter how many childhood stressors he might have had. Rose had her childhood stressors, too—plenty of them—yet she didn't take a gun into a courtroom. In fact, there is no record of Rose ever causing physical harm to another human being. No, what Ernie did was reprehensible. But it's important to understand that it wasn't something that just surfaced that morning—it was, in fact, many years in the making. At a critical juncture in his life, Ernie lacked the "protective factors" that researchers say kids need to lessen the pull from all the bad stuff. For Ernie, those protective factors didn't come from his mom and couldn't come from his siblings. And, perhaps when he needed it most, the church—which ran the orphanage he was housed in—failed him as well.

Billie McClain, Ernie's fourth wife and his principal target when he took a gun into that Oregon courtroom in 1979, says he spoke often about his time in the orphanage.

"He was severely beaten by the nuns," she said.[16]

Breanna Schueller, a former development associate at the now-closed Woodland Hills residential treatment facility in Duluth, which offered programs in the same building that once housed the orphanage, said former St. James wards—particularly the ones who were Ernie's age when they were there—often talk about how mean the nuns were. It's not uncommon even today for Catholic children to think of nuns that way or to rail against their belief in the structure of discipline. But Ernie went to prison twelve years after leaving the orphanage, harbored negative thoughts the rest of his life about his time spent there, and ended that life in a murderous cataclysm of blood and pain. Whatever the lessons meant to be absorbed by him during his two years at the St. James obviously did not take hold.

Sister S. Luce Marie of the St. Scholastica Monastery in Duluth said the nuns during that period were overworked in general with various other ministries and demands on their time and many were in declining health. The Benedictine sisters' community was also in financial hardship. A story about the orphanage in the monastery's internal publication, *Pathways*, speaks to the budget woes during that period: "Stories of providential donations of clothing for the children and food for all abound, as do records of constant trips to parishes soliciting funds," the article states.[17]

The writer had this to say about the occupants of the orphanage, which was incorporated as an institution of the Diocese of Duluth in 1916:

> Children came and left for many reasons. They came because of the death or illness of a parent, or because of family disruptions. And as many as half of the children might leave each year. Yet for many, St. James Orphanage was the only childhood home they would remember. An educational assessment declared that classes were well conducted, although 60% of the students came from conditions both at home and at school (which) were decidedly unfavorable.

It was undoubtedly true that the kids came from "unfavorable" environments. But the really sad thing is the state and the church made matters worse for some of them.

What happened to Ernie at the St. James Catholic Orphanage is not entirely clear. He may have simply rebelled against the strong arm of nuns who had the kids' best interests at heart. But conflicting accounts of what took place there have emerged in recent years, including confirmation that priests sexually abused children going back many decades. The St. Paul law firm Anderson and Associates filed five lawsuits on a single day in 2016 naming two priests who molested boys at the St. James home between 1948 and 1969.

Mike Finnegan, who handles many of the firm's priest abuse cases, said he believes the actual abuse count far exceeds what has been documented to date, with children in orphanages serving as prime targets for pedophile priests.

The Anderson firm, led by founder Jeff Anderson, has filed more than 1,000 clergy sex abuse lawsuits—more than any other law firm in the country. In 2018, Anderson sued the Vatican, seeking files on more than 3,400 priests around the world.

Finnegan said the church is actively engaged in a cover-up even as it releases the names of priests—most of whom are now deceased—on lists of "clergy with credible claims against them concerning sexual abuse of a young person."

"All these lists are underreported by them," Finnegan said, adding that the strategy from the Vatican on down is to "keep everything secret and out of the public eye."[18]

The abuse that occurred at the St. James stayed out of the public eye for a long time. Victims began coming forward in large numbers only after press attention on dioceses in Boston and elsewhere lifted the veil on the immense scope of the priest abuse scandal. In 2013, Minnesota opened a three-year window for unlocking the statute of limitations on clergy sex abuse cases, giving victims who had buried their memories in anger, alcohol, and other destructive measures an outlet for retribution. Dioceses from coast to coast were put in the spotlight, including the small but sprawling diocese based in Duluth, which had oversight of the orphanage where Ernie was housed for two years.

In October 2019, a bankruptcy judge in Minnesota approved a $39.2 million settlement of 125 claims against the Diocese of Duluth.[19] In addition to the money, the diocese—which includes seventy-two parishes in ten counties—released documents, adopted a whistleblower policy, and agreed to redouble its efforts to police sexual misconduct and identify clergy members with a history of abuse.

No one outside the church believes the list of thirty-six names currently on the diocese's published list of abusive priests is an accurate tally. But even if incomplete, the list reveals a pattern of astonishing deception and complicity on the part of the Catholic Church, which repeatedly ignored warnings about abuse, took steps to conceal the behavior when it was discovered, and then allowed priests it knew to have problems stay in close contact with children. To get a sense of the potential number of victims, consider this: the thirty-six priests on the Duluth Diocese list collectively logged more than 1,000 active years in ministry in at least 200 parishes. And these are only the priests whose names were made public by the church. What about those who haven't been made public? What about the potential cases that occurred before the church was forced to reveal its ugly secrets?

Four of the five lawsuits filed by Anderson and Associates against the Diocese of Duluth named Father Frederick Fox.[20] He was an assistant pastor from July 1957 to January 1965 at St. John the Evangelist Church in Duluth, which is just down the hill from the orphanage. Fox was also director of the orphanage from 1965 to 1970. According to the lawsuits, he lived in the home from 1957 on, using his position as director to gain even greater access to children.

Two of his known victims were fourteen and fifteen years of age. Another was twelve or thirteen—the lawsuit isn't clear about when the abuse occurred. And one was between the ages of six and eleven—that's right, as young as six—when he was abused by numerous priests, according to the lawsuit he filed in 2016. Fox molested the boy when he was between the ages of nine and eleven, according to the lawsuit. A chilling thought: Ernie entered the orphanage at age eight and left when he was ten, the precise age when many of these cases occurred.

The plaintiff in the Fox lawsuit, identified only as John Doe, did what he was told: attend church services, engage in youth activities, and trust Father Fox and the other clergy members to provide the spiritual guidance necessary to put him on a brighter path. That the priest strayed from those duties should not have been a surprise to the diocese, according to Finnegan, because Fox had presented himself as a danger to children *prior* to his assignment to St. James.[21]

"Defendants negligently or recklessly believed that Fox was fit to work with children and/or that any previous problems he had were fixed or cured," the lawsuit states.

Fox went on to a long career in the priesthood, retiring in 1987. He was removed from ministry in 1988 and died in 1999.[22] It was only when the Diocese of Duluth released its initial list of "credibly accused" priests in 2013—more than four decades after his stint at the St. James—that the public learned that he had been sanctioned by the church because of sexual misconduct. But how extensive that misconduct was—and exactly when the church knew of it—remains a closely guarded secret.

A fifth lawsuit naming the diocese over abuse that occurred at the St. James was also a John Doe, but the victim has since come forward and courageously lent his name to a narrative that, sadly, has become all too familiar.

Eugene Saumer was nine years old when he and his three brothers were dropped off at the front door of the St. James in the late summer of 1948.[23] There was upheaval in their parents' marriage, and the family—mostly the boys' grandmother—insisted the children get a Catholic education until their mother could get back on her feet.

That particular Catholic education, however, included lessons no child should be forced to live through.

The priest who abused Saumer—Father Gregory Manning—was shielded by the church long after there was any reason to believe his behavior was something that could be managed. Manning's "unfortunate ailment," as one superior described it, was so well-known to the church that he was sent to a retreat in New Mexico that became a way station for clergy members caught committing sexual violence. Letters unearthed as part of the lawsuit Saumer filed show that Manning was reassigned to other parishes even after he was found to be unresponsive to treatment in New Mexico.[24]

Learning of these covert efforts to hide the truth infuriated Saumer, who said he pursued the lawsuit because he saw the church as protecting the man who abused him. Those who file claims against the church often do so for that very reason. Quin Buchtel was molested as a young girl in a Brainerd church at the hands of the late Reverend Charles J. Gormly. Decades later, in 2015, she filed a lawsuit against the Duluth diocese. Why make the church pay for something one of its priests did years earlier?

"Father Gormly molested me," she told reporters, "but I feel the diocese abused me."[25]

Saumer feels similarly toward the church because of what Father Manning did to him. Manning was the assistant pastor at St. John the Evangelist Church, the same parish where Father Fox was assigned a few years later. Ministering to the children in the orphanage was considered part of the church's mission, and Saumer remembers how the priests there would pull up in their "big, beautiful Buicks." As any young boy would in the presence of such authority, Saumer trusted Manning, enough at least to unburden himself in confession about his newfound interest in girls.

He realizes now that was a mistake.

"I personally believe what you tell a priest during confession, they use that," Saumer said.

Verne Wagner of Duluth, who served as the northern Minnesota director for the Survivors Network of Those Abused by Priests for more than two decades and an abuse survivor himself, said children from unstable backgrounds get special attention from priests, which puts orphanages in a line of fire because they teem with kids who meet that very description.

"These kids are looking for some kind of structure and along comes the priest," he said.[26]

Manning came along for Saumer in the middle of the night during a field trip held in a cabin deep in the woods. Each of the boys were asleep, including Saumer, who woke up when he felt Manning on top of him. He doesn't know for sure if the priest ejaculated, but he remembers being "all wet." Manning, he said, then left his bed and acted as if nothing had happened.

Did Saumer tell anybody at the time what Manning had done to him?

"I didn't say nothing to nobody," he said, which is consistent with the experiences of many, many others who are abused as children. Some stay quiet about it for decades, burying the experience deep into their subconscious or pushing it aside out of fear, shame, or a belief that no one will believe them. Saumer's lawsuit talks about the culture that existed in the church and how it created pressure not to report what was done to them.

When Saumer finally did open up about what happened, it wasn't to a priest or a nun or anyone else in authority, but to his brothers. It was then that he found out that his oldest brother, Jerome, had also been molested by Father Manning. Another brother, Bob, was molested, too, but Saumer doesn't know if it was by Manning. At the St. James, numerous clergy members had close contact with children.

Saumer, now in his eighties, recalls the time he spent in the St. James almost as if it occurred last week. Not all the experiences were bad. He liked the food and said each kid was given new shoes—"I never had shoes like that"—as well as clothes that were laundered regularly. He still remembers the number on the tag sewn into the inside of his pants, shirts, and underwear: S4B. He thinks the S was for "small boys."

Saumer's two older brothers—Jerome and Bob—were housed on a separate floor from where Eugene and his younger brother John lived. The St. James had four floors with separate dormitories for the girls and boys and a special wing for babies. The classrooms were on the first floor, along with the dining room and lobby. The nuns lived on the second floor.

The nuns were a commanding presence in the St. James, and some of them clearly loved children. But one in particular—Saumer remembers her as Sister Constantine—lost her cool whenever a certain boy, a notorious bed-wetter, soiled the sheets. She would grab the boy by the pants to see if he was wet and then lift him up and haul him down the hall as the other kids listened to his screams. In one terrifying episode, Saumer had to pull the same nun off his brother Bob after she began beating him with a broomstick, causing deep welts on his arm. She was the dormitory supervisor and chief disciplinarian, and it didn't take much to incite her to anger. All it took on this day was a wind gust that blew through the door of the fire escape, knocking a plant over and spilling dirt onto the floor. Bob wasn't misbehaving. He had opened the door to shake out a rug, per one of his chores.

Wagner, who was molested as a boy by a Catholic priest in a parish outside of Duluth, said he has heard many stories about abuse of all kinds occurring in Catholic orphanages, including physical abuse.

"These priests and nuns felt that to get people to obey, they had to beat them," he said. The comment lends credence to the stories of the beatings Ernie said he took at the hands of nuns during his time in the orphanage.[27]

After leaving St. John the Evangelist Church in 1950, Manning was assigned to two Minnesota parishes. Complaints surfaced, and in 1957 the bishop of Duluth, Thomas Anthony Welch, wrote to the church-affiliated Via Coeli treatment center in Jemez Springs, New Mexico, to see if Manning could be helped with his "unfortunate ailment."

Via Coeli was a retreat house founded by Father Gerald Fitzgerald, an exalted figure within the church who had started the facility as a treatment center for clergy members with drug or alcohol problems. Later, it became a dumping ground for priests accused of sexually abusing children. It was closed in the 1990s as court dockets began to fill with lawsuits from victims who began telling their stories and exposing the depth of the church's efforts to hide the truth.

Welch's letter to Fitzgerald is as good an example of that as any you will find.

Writing more than seven years after Manning abused both Saumer and his brother, the seventy-two-year-old Welch wrote:

> A priest of our diocese, Gregory Manning, 39 years of age, is afflicted with an unfortunate ailment although physically well as far as we know. Up to the recent disclosure of his ailment, nothing was known about it. As a matter of fact, he has been very successful in the fulfillment of his pastoral duties.[28]

Nothing was known about it? Manning in 1950 was transferred from the St. James in the diocese's largest city to a parish in the small Iron Range town of Biwabik. That could hardly be viewed as a promotion. And at the St. James, Saumer's father—in full view of others—drew blood from Manning's nose when he confronted him about what he had been doing to his sons.[29] Nothing was known about it? Not likely.

Welch, who was nearing the end of a more than thirty-year reign as the diocese's bishop, had to have heard stories about Manning's behavior because in his letter to Fitzgerald he expressed deep skepticism about whether Manning could be helped. In fact, Welch told the priest he was referring Manning to the treatment center "not with any thought that you should work a miracle."

Fitzgerald's response was unambiguous.

> We are fully convinced from our wide experience that this type of aberration is
> not curable. They [pedophile priests] are dangerous . . . and whenever we have
> gone against conviction and approved their activation, we have had uniformly
> cause to regret. The dog returns to his vomit.[30]

The dog returns to his vomit. If only the church had heeded that particular
piece of wisdom—with Manning and with so many others.

With the church's blessing, Manning left Via Coeli and went to live with his
parents in California. But records show he returned to active ministry in that
state, beginning in 1963 and continuing until his death in 1969. It is beyond
outrageous, but after Manning climbed into the bed of a ten-year-old boy in
1949, the church held him in its warm embrace for another twenty years.

It's not fair to assume that because two priests molested children in a home
full of orphans, others would do the same or to assume that all the nuns were
mean and nasty. But it does make you wonder: if it happened in the 1940s—
if someone like Father Gregory Manning was allowed to chaperone young
boys to a cabin in the woods—is there any reason to believe the 1920s were
somehow better?

Saumer doesn't think so. He said he's talked to too many victims with
experiences much like his own: preyed upon by powerful individuals and
thrust into situations in which they had little or no control. He was just a boy,
powerless to defend himself in a den of wolves.

I didn't say nothing to nobody. That makes sense. After all, in a den of
wolves, there is no one to tell.

Predictably, the shame and humiliation Saumer felt as an abused child
morphed into anger as he got older. When he was a teenager, he was out with
friends one night when a priest walked into the restaurant that was the kids'
hangout. The boys all jumped up and surrounded the man in the robe as if
he were a rock star. All except for Saumer, who remained seated. It wasn't
that he blamed that particular priest for what Father Manning had done to
him. Rather, he saw the priest as an extension of something evil, and that
burning rage stayed with him. When the Duluth settlement was announced,
a reporter for the Minneapolis *Star Tribune* asked Saumer what impact the
abuse had on him.

"I had trouble sleeping sometimes," he said. "I drowned it in a bottle of
whiskey lots of times."

His wife Bonnie confirmed that and said she knows of many other priest
abuse victims who took that very same route. "Most people overmedicate
with alcohol or drugs," she said.[31]

That wasn't Ernie's thing. He didn't smoke or drink. But his time at the St. James was no picnic, and his daughter Carolyn says he attempted to run away from the orphanage, hoping to disappear amid the jack pines that surround the place and provide the illusion of grace. Which begs a question: what was he running from? He was young and young kids do impulsive things, but the desire to escape was not unheard of. When Saumer and his brothers finished the school year in the spring of 1950, they went to live with their mother and uncle at a farm outside the town of Brimson, about forty miles north of Duluth. One day a group of kids from the orphanage showed up at the farmhouse, hoping Mrs. Saumer would take them in. She couldn't, she told them, explaining that she could get into a lot of trouble housing runaways.

What was Ernie running from? Whatever it was, apparently he wasn't alone in his desire to escape.

In Minnesota, orphanages have provided a salvation for children since the 1850s, carving out a safe space from illness, neglect, drug abuse, homelessness, violence, and a host of other dangerous situations. For some kids, at least, the St. James was desperately needed to silence those devils. Not long after Ernie left, two brothers and their sister arrived at the St. James, becoming long-term residents who would have a decidedly different story to tell about their treatment there. Richard Partika, who later became Father Richard Partika, wrote often about how blessed he was to live in the orphanage. His mother was terminally ill and his father was, as he has described it, a victim of the Depression.

In a 2011 article in the *Duluth News Tribune*, Partika wrote:

> St. James Orphans Home was a very nice place to live. We had very good nuns and priests running it. It was as normal as you could possibly make it. Sure, kids were lonesome for their families and wanted their families restored. But it just couldn't be.[32]

Partika, who died in 2020, said daily chores kept both the boys and girls busy, including sweeping and scrubbing the stairs, halls, and dormitories. For Partika, those memories are mostly positive, though the place operated as a work camp of sorts. Boys would weed the garden beds and hoe the raspberry patches in the summer while the girls washed dishes and worked in the laundry.

Three priests lived in the orphanage when Partika was there and ministered to roughly seventy to eighty children. Some of the kids were adopted out, but most were there as boarders, temporary in some cases, longer in others. As for Partika, he was there for ten years, leaving after finishing eighth grade. His mother had died by then and his father had remarried. On the advice of a priest who offered to pay his tuition, Richard enrolled in ninth grade at

Cathedral Junior High School, a private Catholic school. Before long, he heard the call: he wanted to be a priest.

In 1986, Robert Fulghum published a series of essays in a book that became a best seller: *All I Really Need to Know I Learned in Kindergarten.*[33] In it, he argues that the basic rules engrained in children at that age—sharing, thoughtfulness, cleanliness, and a healthy balance between work and play— are touchstones that can help guide us to a healthy life.

To Partika, those touchstones were all present in the St. James he knew, a place where sweat and toil went hand in hand with the word of God.

> The haying and threshing seasons were my favorite. The days were the longest and warmest. In those days we had no tractors, balers or such. We pitched the hay with forks onto horse-drawn wagons and brought it to the barn. When the orphanage fields were cleared, we went to Calvary Cemetery and cleaned the open spaces there and brought the hay home. In some years, when more was needed, we went out to the Lepak farms in Gnesen Township and brought in hay from there. I loved getting to drive the horse-drawn wagons, and I made sure I was first to volunteer.[34]

The St. James that Father Partika remembered included baseball in the summer, sledding and skating in the winter, and a chapel on the third floor where the children celebrated Mass on school days and Sundays. It was at the St. James where he took his first Communion and where the seeds for his life's work in the priesthood were nurtured. But Ernie wasn't so smitten. For some, organized religion provides a gravitational tug that is impossible to resist. For Ernie, it had the opposite effect. He didn't like to be called to do something—by God or anyone else. Father Partika had his siblings and a spiritual wonderment to guide him through his experience at the St. James. Whatever Ernie had—and it wasn't that—he would carry with him the rest of his days. Whether he was beaten, scolded, or merely counseled by the nuns, this much is clear: he wasn't inspired by them. When the newspapers tried to make sense of his actions in a Portland courtroom on February 13, 1979, they all mentioned that Ernie was "raised by nuns" in an orphanage.[35]

Of course, that wasn't true. Ernie McClain wasn't raised by anybody.

NOTES

1. Rose's records from Faribault. For data on institution's sterilization practices, see Molly Ladd-Taylor, *Fixing the Poor: Eugenic Sterilization and Child Welfare in the Twentieth Century* (Baltimore: Johns Hopkins University Press, 2017), 57–83.

2. Ibid., 173–76.

3. Faribault School records. Mary's March 19, 1926, marriage to John Lorbecki was accessed through the Minnesota Official Marriage System (MOMS), www.moms.mn.gov.

4. "County Supports Children, Returned to County from International Falls When Aid Is Asked," *Brainerd Dispatch*, January 25, 1928.

5. Ibid.

6. Ibid.

7. Thomas Walz, *The Unlikely Celebrity: Bill Sackter's Triumph over Disability* (Carbondale: Southern Illinois University, 1998), 11.

8. Faribault School admission records on file at the Minnesota Historical Society.

9. See www.orphanagemuseum.com.

10. St. James Catholic Orphanage records.

11. Author interview with Millie Sivanich.

12. Robert's adoption is confirmed in records housed in the basement of the former St. James Catholic Orphanage.

13. Ibid.

14. The Adverse Childhood Experiences (ACE) study was a collaboration between the U.S. Centers for Disease Control and Kaiser Permanente. See www.thepermanentejournal.org/issues/2020/spring/7363.html.

15. From "Adverse Childhood Experiences in Minnesota: Findings & Recommendations Based on the 2011 Minnesota Behavioral Risk Factor Surveillance System," Minnesota Department of Health. See https://health.state.mn.us.

16. Author interview with Billie McClain, Ernie's fourth wife.

17. *Pathways* 29, no. 3 (Lent 2018). *Pathways* is a publication of the Benedictine Sisters in Duluth, Minnesota.

18. Author interview with Mike Finnegan.

19. "Bankruptcy Judge OKs Settlement between Duluth Diocese, Abuse Survivors," *Catholic News Service*, October 23, 2019.

20. *State of Minnesota v. St. James Children's Home, Inc., et al.*, District Court, Sixth Judicial District of Minnesota, April 12, 2016.

21. Author interview with Finnegan.

22. See www.bishop-accountability.org/accused/fox-frederick-1952/.

23. Author interview with Eugene Saumer.

24. Saumer lawsuit, U.S. District Court. *Doe 350 vs. St. James Children's Home, et al.*, District Court, Sixth Judicial District of Minnesota, April 12, 2016.

25. "Woman Sues Duluth Diocese, Claims Priest Sexually Abused Her as a Child," *Duluth News-Tribune*, May 18, 2015.

26. Author interview with Verne Wagner.

27. Ibid.

28. *Doe 350 vs. St. James Children's Home*, District Court, Sixth Judicial District of Minnesota, April 12, 2016.

29. Author interview with Saumer.

30. See: www.andersonadvocates.com/Documents/priest_files/Fr.%20(Thomas)%20Gregory%20Manning%20documents.pdf.

31. Author interview with Bonnie Saumer.

32. "Meet the Man Behind the Many Letters," *Duluth News-Tribune*, May 29, 2011.

33. From Robert Fulghum, *All I Really Need to Know I Learned in Kindergarten* (New York: Ivy Books, 1989).

34. From "Meet the Man Behind the Many Letters."

35. "Gunman Described as 'Brilliant,'" *Daily Astorian*, February 14, 1979.

6

Transition

While her son Ernie struggled with the rigidity of the St. James Catholic Orphanage, her daughter Millie endured surgery and learned how to walk again, and her son Robert was lifted from one world and dropped headlong into another, Rose was locked away as if none of that was her concern. It's not even clear if she was told what was happening to her children. What is clear is this: they didn't have to tell her.

To be mentally deficient in America in Rose's day—to be a woman of her age and intellect—meant more than being the subject of ridicule and scorn; it meant enduring man's vilest tendencies. We now have precise definitions for various types of mental impairments, though labels have gone in and out of favor as once scientific terms become playground slurs. President Barack Obama in 2010 signed Rosa's Law, which removed mental retardation in federal statutes, replacing the words with "intellectual disability."[1] Thus, the term "mental retardation" went the way of "idiot," "moron," "imbecile," and other once-accepted classifications of mental deficiencies. In Rose's day, "feebleminded" was a catchall term that referred to a wide variety of backward behavior, differentiating between "high-grade" feebleminded people and those who were "low-grade." In Minnesota, judges could automatically commit the people that they considered low-grade without consulting so much as a medical professional. The higher-grade folks—and judges had sole discretion to decide who these were—required a sign-off, which was easily obtained. The definitions didn't really matter when sterilization came into vogue, because feebleminded women of all types were seen as menacing threats.

It took a long time, but the state of Minnesota in 2010 apologized for its legacy of treatment toward "all persons with mental illness and developmental and other disabilities who have been wrongfully committed to state institutions."[2]

The proclamation, signed by Republican Governor Tim Pawlenty, acknowledged a multitude of injustices, including subjecting women inmates to

involuntary sterilizations, punitive shock treatments, and even frontal lobotomies. The resolution states:

> Many of these Minnesotans have died and been buried in unmarked graves or
> graves that bore only a number. These fellow Minnesotans were portrayed by
> some as subhuman organisms, as deviant individuals to be feared by society, and
> as eternal children unaccountable for their behavior and incapable of speaking
> for themselves or shaping their own lives, which greatly diminished their fellow
> citizens' ability and willingness to accept them for their own unique qualities.

The resolution goes on to say that the state regrets its history of institution-
alizing the mentally ill. That's nice. After all, Minnesota has nothing to be
proud of in that regard. But the apology, however well-meaning, would come
long after Rose went to her grave and long past the time when women like
her were treated like "subhuman organisms."

In other words, it came long after it would have any practical meaning to
Rose or her family.

When Rose was returned to Faribault after getting picked up with her
three children and her mom's husband, her timing, for once, worked in her
favor. Although the state still segregated those with mental deficiencies, a
slight softening in treatment methods was underway. Those deemed insane
or feebleminded were still housed in giant institutions where abuse was com-
monplace, but a door had opened to more humane practices that were less
costly. The compulsory commitment law had flooded the state's institutions
with thousands of "subnormal" wards and the pressure was on to find more
affordable alternatives.

"It will never be possible to herd all defectives into institutions," the Board
of Control wrote in one report.[3]

Enter the "clubhouse" concept, essentially a halfway house for feebleminded women. On July 2, 1928—six days before Robert's adoption became
final and a month before Millie was hospitalized in St. Paul—Rose entered
the Club House for Girls at Harmon Place in Minneapolis.[4] There, she was
housed with twenty like-minded women who had all been sterilized and
whose mental handicap was judged to be "high-grade." For Rose, it was a
light at the end of a very long tunnel.

Rose's second stint at Faribault coincided with Mildred Thomson's appoint-
ment as director of the Board of Control's "Bureau for the Feebleminded and
Epileptic." Thomson's lengthy title spoke to the emphasis the state placed on
managing the folks whom no one wanted to see walking down the sidewalk
or—God forbid—the aisle of a grocery store. She was a staunch believer
in eugenics, but unlike many in her field, she also championed community placement. In other words, Thomson had an expansive view about the

potential of some feebleminded individuals for existing outside an institution-alized setting. It doesn't sound radical now but it certainly was then.

Thomson became a huge advocate of the clubhouse concept after visiting the Rome State School in New York where the superintendent, Dr. Charles Bernstein, pioneered the concept of "colonies" for feebleminded girls.[5] The women worked in private homes and their earnings "beyond a certain allow-ance" were used by the institution toward meeting the cost of their housing.

Thomson took what she learned from the Rome example and doubled down. In her 1963 book on Minnesota's history of dealing with mental retardation, Thomson said the concept used by the Harmon Club was more progressive than other so-called colonies, such as the one in New York. She wrote:

> If a girl at Harmon Club was earning enough, she paid her board—not includ-ing the expense of supervision—and any other money she earned was her own for clothing, other personal expenses and, usually, a savings account. Return to the institution was always possible, but supervision was by persons outside the institution staff.[6]

Paying for your board and managing your money was a huge leap from life inside the institution. But there were restrictions, and the women transferred to the clubhouses were closely monitored. Consider this passage from a 1926 Board of Control report about the track record of the Harmon Club during its first two years:

> During the two-year period, 38 girls were enrolled there. Four were placed out for domestic work within a few days after entrance; one was discharged by court order within a few days; two were returned to the institution because both had evaded the rules and managed to be in the company of men when they were supposed to be at work, though neither had committed an immoral act; one was returned because of homosexual acts; one was returned after a short period because of her own desire to go back; five others were placed out of the Club House as maids in homes after having been there for periods varying from three to 13 months; one received from a hospital for the insane, was returned after a diagnosis of tuberculosis; one was entered in the House of the Good Shepherd because it was felt she might be helped to suppress periods of rebelliousness; two entered a sanitorium for tuberculosis.[7]

That's quite a list: getting sent back to the institution after getting caught "in the company of men," engaging in a homosexual act, or exhibiting "rebelliousness" that needed to be suppressed. It was all from the handbook of known behaviors of feebleminded individuals. (And many "normal" people as well.) The House of the Good Shepherd, where two of the expelled parolees were sent, was a convent that operated in St. Paul from 1883 to 1969. There's a courtyard there now along with a sign commemorating its long history as a refuge for those who need a "place in the sun."

God knows Rose needed a place in the sun, but it's not likely she was ever considered for the convent. Church may have been a big part of her mother's life, but it was never Rose's sanctuary.

Most of the women at the Harmon Club worked in laundries or as maids, where they earned about $5 a week—roughly $80 today.[8] And because there was more freedom there than inside the institution, the women were chosen based on certain criteria, including whether they had been sterilized and their mental abilities had been deemed "high-grade." Rose passed the test on both counts, which raises another question: if she was able to function normally—if she was considered "high-grade" by the institution—why was she institutionalized in the first place? Yet it was these so-called higher-grade feebleminded women who gave the state the most discomfort. Consider this passage from Charles Hall, the Children's Bureau director at the time of Rose's confinement:

> In spite of disappointments, the clubhouse as a means of parole seems successful, especially for the girls who have not adequate homes. The big problem still exists as to whether eventually these girls and others of the higher-grade feeble-minded may become sufficiently stable and independent to be discharged from guardianship.[9]

"Sufficiently stable" was the stated goal of the reformers within the mental health industry in Minnesota: program these feebleminded women to be functional in public life—after stripping them of the ability to reproduce, of course. But it wasn't entirely accepted that these women could ever be made whole, or even useful in a modest sense, and plenty of officials treated with scorn the very philosophy of recovery as it applied to the mentally ill or deficient.

One of them was Guy C. Hanna, who was the Faribault superintendent much of the time during Rose's tenure. Hanna saw little merit in the alternatives to segregating the mentally ill, once writing, "The commitment of the feebleminded is for life."[10]

Hanna would eventually accept parole as an economic necessity, but at the same time he worked to block the release of women he saw as "oversexed." Not all Faribault administrators hated the people who passed through their doors, but Hanna clearly did, summing up his general philosophy with this sentiment: "No amount of training could make a moron normal."

He didn't stop there. Feebleminded women weren't just a burden in his eyes. They were among society's greatest threats. He said as much when he wrote:

> It does not follow that a high-grade feebleminded woman who is a passable or even good cook and housekeeper is capable of properly rearing a family, nor does the offspring escape the taint of heredity. Countless thousands of high-grade feebleminded females, both married and unmarried, who appear fairly efficient at their tasks, are bringing their kind into the world and constitute the greatest menace to the social structure.[11]

Fortunately for Rose, Hanna left the job while she was under consideration for placement in the clubhouse program. However, debate continued regarding the wisdom of community placement and the belief that the mentally ill could live normal lives outside an institutional setting. The prospect of any of them enriching society? Well, that was considered well outside of the realm of what was possible.

In the end, the clubhouses—there would eventually be three until they became Depression-era casualties—had mixed success. Nearly one of every two women sent there was returned to the institution.[12] For that, the state may be as much to blame as the women who, after all, were given their first taste of freedom in a long time—years in most cases—and then expected to become model citizens. And the freedom they had while being housed at the clubhouse was fleeting to say the least. When a return to the institution is determined by such vague and minor infractions such as being seen as "rebellious" or found "in the company of men," the roughly 50 percent failure rate was wholly predictable.

On March 30, 1929, after failing her stint at the clubhouse, Rose was admitted to the Faribault institution for a third time. The Guy C. Hannas of the world could take heart. Their policy of hate scored another win.

After leaving the St. James Catholic Orphanage, Rose's daughter Millie underwent osteotomies on both of her tibias and was hospitalized for 117 days.[13] Permission for the surgery was not granted by any member of the family, but by Rebecca Cassell, the executive director of the Child Welfare Board—more evidence of the little sway the DeChaine family had over the welfare of their children. On Millie's chart from the hospital, her condition was described in the politest way possible by her doctor, W. H. Cole: "Bowing of both tibia, slight enlargement of the end of the radius. Question of whether it is due to rickets or congenital anomaly."

Rickets has always been what the family has subscribed to, but the words "common prostitute"—the description provided in Rose's commitment papers—echo. The commitment laws were insanely unfair and Rose was institutionalized on the testimony of two individuals who described her as immoral. What steps were taken to determine whether they were telling the truth? But Carolyn says her mother once told her that Rose was a prostitute, and Joyce McClain—Ernie's second wife—could only have gotten that information from one person: Ernie. Behavior has consequences, though it is not always immediately visible to the naked eye. It could have been rickets that caused Millie's leg deformity. But we'll never know.

Millie was discharged from Gillette Hospital on December 8, 1928. The word "impaired" was written on the chart in response to a question about the results of her operations. It is an almost comically understated answer, yet it would prove to be an exaggerated prognosis. Nine decades later, she still bears the physical scars from her surgeries but walks without so much as a limp.

After leaving the hospital Millie returned to the house at 319 South Second Street in Brainerd where Mary, the five-foot-tall bowling ball, stood as a towering presence. She was the epitome of the prairie matriarch: bighearted, methodical when it came to running the household, and fiercely dedicated to family. None of the DeChaines ever considered anything they did to be out of the ordinary, but the Works Progress Administration (WPA) in the 1930s profiled several members of the family for a retrospective on pioneer life.

To Mary, that was a hoot. "Missy, I'm old," she told her interviewer in June 1938, "but I ain't no pioneer."

In Brainerd, interviews with immigrants about their life stories were among the make-work jobs the WPA came up with as America struggled to climb out of the Great Depression. The effort didn't leave behind a building or a park, but the transcripts provide an invaluable resource about early immigrant life in America, using unimpeachable sources: the people who actually lived through it. Immigrants weren't always easy interview subjects, however. Some, like Louise Marineau, Joseph's mother, didn't speak English, forcing her interviewer to describe the color of a barn or the pattern on a dress rather than to glean insights about the experience of coming to America from a far-away place without knowing the language, the history, or the culture. Mary liked to tell people she attended only a single day of schooling, but that's probably not why her answers were so cryptic. She wasn't one to waste time on anything that wasn't family related. For her, keeping the household running was more important than documenting her life's work. In the interview the WPA did with her, Mary said her parents "had eleven or twelve children, some of them born after I left home and I've never seen them. Many of them are dead."[14]

It is understandable that this woman would describe death in such matter-of-fact terms. For her, tragedy was endemic in God's plan, its mysteries shrouded in a spiritual force beyond man's comprehension.

Her home was a rooming house for her extended family, who were welcomed no matter how much she struggled to put food on the table. It was a small, dilapidated structure that probably would be condemned today for violating city codes. When I told Millie a few years ago that the house no longer exists, she wasn't surprised.

"It wasn't very nice back then," she said.[15]

She remembers how daybeds were spread throughout the small house and how "Grandma" did laundry for her many occupants daily, using the backyard clothesline as a dryer. Sometimes small things stand out in our lives. It was in that home that Mary's son Bud taught Millie how to play cards—a lifelong passion—and she remembers a bet he made with her one day. Mary baked a dozen loaves of bread twice a week, and Bud bet Millie that she couldn't eat an entire loaf. She carefully sliced the bread, covered each slice with lard and sugar and downed the whole thing. After that Bud had a nickname for her: "Pig."

In the months after the surgeries, Mary got Millie to discard the crutches she felt she was relying on too much. Mary took a dim view of doctors, putting them in the same bin as lawyers, politicians, and bill collectors. To her mind, it was the doctors with their all their drugs and medical theories who turned people into namby-pamby couch sitters. Mary didn't like couch sitters. So when the doctor told Millie to stay off her feet and not walk for six weeks, looking directly at Mary when he said it, Mary gave him a look that caused him to amend the statement slightly. "Unless she can do so without pain," he added.

Pain. These doctors act like no one should suffer. Which just proves they're not God. God understands what these doctors don't: that pain is part of the life experience, maybe even an essential part. To reject it, to mask it with drugs and the like, is tantamount to denying the will of God, ignoring His wisdom. And to Mary's way of thinking, that is never a good idea.

"Grandma, I can't find my crutches," Millie said one day near the end of the six-week period.

"Have you looked in the kitchen?" Mary said, knowing full well that's just where she put them.

Mary may have had only a single day of schooling, but she knew an essential part of recovery is overcoming fear. Part of it, too, is knowing that someone is always there for you. Growing up, Millie wasn't used to hugs—that wasn't part of Rose's repertoire—but after she made her way across the living room and into the kitchen, stopping just once to brace herself on the back of a chair, Mary held her granddaughter close to her bosomy frame, the softness of her touch a soothing balm for the pain in Millie's heart and the ache in her soul.

"I did it, Grandma," Millie screamed as if she'd just climbed Mount Everest.

"Of course you did, dear," Mary said. "Of course you did."

While in the clubhouse on Harmon Place in Minneapolis, Rose violated one of its bedrock rules: Don't fraternize with members of the opposite sex or—as homosexuality became a concern—the same sex. It was among the more unnecessarily punitive measures aimed at controlling the feebleminded charges under the state's purview. Sex, and even friendship, was treated as a crime against humanity. And when someone slipped, which happened often, they were returned to the institution and stripped of their privileges. This threat of punishment worked for many of the inmates. But it didn't work for Rose, whose so-called feeblemindedness was high-grade in the hierarchy of intelligence measurements and thus considered dangerous to one and all. Recall this passage in the book *Dwellers in the Vale of Siddem*:

> It is not the idiot or, to any great extent, the low-grade imbecile, who is danger-ous to society . . . he is sufficiently anti-social to protect both himself and soci-ety from the results of that condition. But from the high-grade feeble-minded, the morons, are recruited the ne'er-do-wells, who lacking the initiative and stick-to-itiveness of energy and ambition, drift from failure to failure, spending a winter in the poor house, moving from shack to hovel and succeeding only in the reproduction of ill-nurtured, ill-kept gutter brats to carry on the family tradi-tions of dirt, disease and degeneracy.

Well, well. Someone who has a bad reputation and is perceived to be lacking in ambition can't possibly be given a chance at redemption. And by all means, keep her away from men. Nothing good could come of that.

As it turned out, something good did come of Rose's relationship with Orvel McClain. In fact, he may be the primary reason she was released from the Faribault institution for the third and final time.

Orvel grew up on a farm in Iowa but was selling and repairing typewriters in Minneapolis when he met Rose. Just how their paths crossed is difficult to say. Orvel was a lifelong teetotaler whereas Rose—let's just say—wasn't. But in May 1929, barely a month into her third stint at the Faribault institution, someone wrote on her chart, "Oriville McLain [*sic*], friend, not to see Rose unless he has permission from M. Thomson."[16]

The notation, which refers to Mildred Thomson, the Board of Control bureau director, is more evidence of how controlling the state was about what its institutionalized wards could do and who they could see. But it also reveals a more open attitude toward allowing feebleminded wards to marry. (Providing they had been sterilized, of course.) If the administrators at Faribault didn't want Orvel around, he would have been banned from the premises. Instead, he was allowed in under certain circumstances, namely permission from the Board of Control's director. Faribault was a prison, but massive overcrowding brought about a change in philosophy, at least for some people. As Rose approached her twenty-eighth birthday, some of the administrators at Faribault even thought it might be OK if she were allowed to be in the company of a man. Small potatoes perhaps, but potatoes nonetheless.

Listed on her chart along with the notation about Orvel is the name of his mother, Myrtle McIntyre, along with a date: November 3, 1929. In all likelihood, that was the date Myrtle met with the Board of Control to discuss Rose and Orvel's marriage plans. Those under state guardianship—even well into adulthood—had to meet certain criteria before they could marry. Sterilization was obviously one requirement. Good behavior was another. A third was having a spouse who, after thorough vetting, was deemed to be a proper match.[17] Orvel was employed, didn't drink, and must have said the right things during his interviews. There was one small matter that had to be dealt with, however. On paper, at least, Rose was still married.

On November 14, 1929, the court finalized Rose's divorce from Ingram Conradson. It hadn't been much of a marriage. They hadn't seen each other in years. And although it did produce a daughter—Millie—you will find no mention of her in Ingram's obituary. We often speak of biological fathers as if they are the "real" fathers. But Ingram wasn't a real father in any sense of the word. Fortunately for Millie, a real father would emerge, and no one would ever attach the word "abandon" by his name.

On Christmas Eve, Rose's twenty-eighth birthday, she was discharged from the Faribault School for the Feeble-Minded for the third time.[18] But she still wasn't free. Instead, she was placed in another clubhouse: the Lynnhurst Girls Club at 471 Lynnhurst Avenue in St. Paul, where she worked as a housekeeper.[19] It had been nearly six years since she first set foot in the Faribault institution. Much had changed, both inside the institution and out, where the country was spiraling into a deep depression, but there was one constant that couldn't be altered no matter how many steps were taken to erase that fact. Rose had brought three children into this world, and although one had been taken from her, he didn't disappear—except from the only family he had known—until the day that Ray and Santa Anderson drove away from the orphanage.

Later in this book, you find out what happened to Robert, information Rose and Ernie were deprived of during their lifetimes. His adoption was decided by people who believed they had the boy's best interest at heart. Maybe they were right. Maybe a life with Rose as his "real" mother would have been unbearable. But there were times during their lives when Millie and Ernie could have used a brother, the kind of bond only siblings have. And Robert—the boy with the moppy hair who towered over his big sister and made her laugh—might have benefitted from that bond as well.

Rose's release from the Lynnhurst clubhouse—her last confinement in one of the state's mental institutions—occurred just before her marriage to Orvel McClain on May 14, 1930.[20] Rose was free at long last, and a picture of her on her wedding day captured something frequently missing from her photographs: a smile. She was now free to live wherever she wanted, and she and Orvel settled into an apartment in Minneapolis, the normal life her mother had long wished for her daughter finally within reach. No, she didn't exactly live like a monk after that, but she never again was returned to the institution that considered her incapable of living independently. Apparently, "practically nil"—the words Frederick Kuhlmann used to describe a feebleminded woman's chances of surviving on her own—didn't apply to Rose. Whether she was released because of costs, good behavior, progress in mastering daily work skills, or a womb that was now barren didn't matter. She was free—free of the long arm of the state and the injustice of a system that saw her as less than human. As Robert Frost once said, "the best way out is through."[21] Well, Rose had experienced hell and somehow made her way through.

Ernie's hell may have just been beginning, though nobody could possibly have known that then. On June 2, 1930, two weeks after Rose married Orvel McClain, Ernie was released from the St. James Catholic Orphanage and transported by a representative of the Child Welfare League to Mary DeChaine's home in Brainerd.[22] There he was reunited with his sister for the first time in nearly two years. It was awkward at first—most reunions are—but soon they were playing Catch Me If You Can in the backyard and violating Mary's orders not to run in the street. Rose wanted Ernie with her, so within days he went to live with his mother and her new husband in Minneapolis. There Rose was reunited with a boy who understood as she did that freedom is precious. It was a marvelous homecoming that gave all of them a taste of normalcy. They were a family—two parents and a child in a home no one could say was broken. But Rose was Rose, and she had her secrets, which she managed to keep from Orvel. After Ernie came to live with them, one of those hidden truths from her past came to be revealed.

She had a daughter.[23]

NOTES

1. "Obama Praises Maryland Girl Who Inspired New Law," *Baltimore Sun*, October 8, 2010.

2. Minnesota Legislature Office of the Revisor of Statutes, SF 1135, introduced 86th Legislature, 2009–2010.

3. Report to Minnesota State Board of Control, June 30, 1928.

4. Faribault School records, Minnesota Historical Society.

5. Molly Ladd-Taylor, *Fixing the Poor: Eugenic Sterilization and Child Welfare in the Twentieth Century* (Baltimore: Johns Hopkins University Press, 2017), 71.

6. Mildred Thomson, *Prologue: A Minnesota Story of Mental Retardation Showing Changing Attitudes and Philosophies prior to September 1, 1959* (Minneapolis, MN: Gilbert Publishing Company, 1963), 50.

7. Board of Control report, June 30, 1928, Minnesota Historical Society.

8. See Ladd-Taylor, *Fixing the Poor*, 130–37.

9. Board of Control report, June 30, 1928.

10. For background on Hanna, see Ladd-Taylor, *Fixing the Poor*, 73–76.

11. Board of Control report.

12. Ladd-Taylor, *Fixing the Poor*, 70–72.

13. Gillette Hospital records, Minnesota Historical Society.

14. Works Progress Administration interview with Mary DeChaine (Lease), June 1938. Interview is on file at the Crow Wing County Historical Society.

15. Author interview with Millie Sivanich.

16. Faribault School records, Minnesota Historical Society.

17. See Ladd-Taylor, *Fixing the Poor*, 130–36.

18. Faribault School records.

19. 1930 U.S. Census available on numerous sites. I accessed the records through Ancestry.com.

20. Marriage records, Minnesota Department of Health.

21. From "A Servant to Servants," Robert Frost.

22. St. James Catholic Orphanage records.

23. The information that Rose kept the existence of her daughter a secret from her husband came from my interview with Millie Sivanich. Millie went to live with her mother a short time later.

7

Ernie

Millie has always insisted it was Orvel's doing that forced her mother to take her in. His almost mythical stature as the parent who could do no wrong may well be overblown. But whatever faults he had, he became a father to two kids who never had one. At least not a responsible one. Millie used that word "Dad" so much to describe Orvel that few people even knew his given name.

Orvel was a tinkerer, particularly with automobiles, and that may have rubbed off on Ernie, who loved to work on cars and had a knack for putting things together. Ernie built Millie's first bicycle from parts he found in a junkyard. He used to borrow books on woodworking from the library, and he and his sister once built a wooden car that was big enough to sit inside. There is a comic side to the story: although it was big enough to sit in, it was too big to get out the front door of their home so Ernie had to cut it in half.[1]

In Minneapolis, the family moved numerous times as Orvel struggled to pay the bills during some of the leanest times in American history. At one apartment in southeast Minneapolis, Orvel worked as the janitor and Rose as the building's housekeeper. People did what they could to get by. By 1933, when Ernie was a teenager, unemployment was 25 percent while incomes throughout the country were, like the car Ernie and Millie built, cut in half. In his autobiography, *The Education of a Public Man*, Hubert H. Humphrey described the bleakness of the Depression-era landscape as his father drove him from South Dakota to the Twin Cities to finish his schooling and begin his mercurial political career in Minnesota.

> Grasshoppers had devastated the area in 1935 and 1936, chewing up the crops, gnawing into fence posts, and 1937 had been another dry year. I wondered if those fields would ever be green again. It took us more than ten hours to get to Minneapolis, and as we bounced along the highway through little towns that had been a part of me—Cavour, Iroquois, De Smet, Lake Preston, Arlington, Brookings—watched the gaunt faces of men standing, staring in front of buildings laminated with dust. Life seemed so static. Only the wind seemed to move.[2]

Only the wind seemed to move. That bleak description would seem to capture much of Ernie's life until that point.

The family would have more than one connection to Humphrey. One of the apartments the McClains lived in was near the campus of the University of Minnesota and the drugstore where young Hubert worked as a pharmacist while attending school. Years later, Ernie would tell his family that the future U.S. senator and vice president worked as a "soda jerk" in his neighborhood, implying that the two had met. When Humphrey was campaigning for president during one of his runs in the 1960s and visited the state of Washington, Ernie's then-wife Joyce asked him if he wanted to go see his pal from the old neighborhood.

No way.

"I didn't like him then," Ernie said, "and I don't like him now."[3] Later, the son of Humphrey's right-hand man—referred to as his "bagman" in some books—would coach Millie's son John's baseball team.

Not all of Ernie's childhood was scarred. He may have faced the wrath of mean-spirited nuns in the orphanage, but in Rose's home, he could do no wrong. Orvel convinced Rose to open their home to Millie, but opening her heart was another matter. Some of the favoritism seems trivial now, typical sibling jealousies like the time Rose took Ernie's side when he trampled Millie's flowerbed. Or how he was always given the second bedroom whenever they moved while Millie was confined to the couch in the dining room.

"It's not fair," Millie complained to her mother.

"You don't like it, lump it," Rose responded. "Ernie's the oldest. When you're the oldest you can get your own bedroom. We ain't rich like some folks where everyone gets their own room."

Small memories reveal a lot. And so do missing ones. Millie can't remember a single occasion when her mother hugged or praised her. And she wasn't the only one to notice the resentment. Rose's sister Mabel frequently reminded Rose that she had a daughter too.[4]

Millie was the short kid with the bowlegged walk whereas Ernie had a brilliant mind, movie-star looks, and a mischievous streak that girls found irresistible. He was the focal point of his mother's attention, as well as everybody else's. But in a true tragedy, the hero always meets with disaster. And once Ernie crossed that Rubicon and descended into the darkness, there was no turning back.

His childhood was far from normal, but there are many instances of people rising from a tough environment and achieving success, even greatness. But that's not what happened here. When Ernie dropped out of high school during his sophomore year, it led to nothing good. He kicked around in various jobs, but they never lasted long: a few months at a filling station, another couple of months spray-painting cars, a short stint hauling scrap iron. Somewhere along the way he found a more lucrative pursuit: boosting cars.

In December 1940, Ernie was arrested on suspicion of auto theft and received a suspended sentence.[5] The judge who let him off easy didn't know the half of it. Ernie and a couple friends had been committing burglaries and car thefts for months. Later, he would tell his family he was a modern-day Robin Hood, taking only from the rich. But Roy W. Olson, whose Standard Oil station was burglarized by Ernie that month, probably didn't see himself as Ernie did, as a man of wealth.

Ernie's luck ran out a short time after the first judge gave him that slap on the wrist. At approximately 2:00 a.m. on December 22, 1940, Ernie broke into Olson's station at 5400 Chicago Avenue in Minneapolis while an accomplice, Donald Murray, waited outside in a car they had borrowed from a friend. The plan was to load the loot onto a truck that was parked at the station and drop the merchandise off the next day at a garage owned by a proprietor who had apparently agreed to sell it for them. Everything worked according to plan until one of the gang spilled the beans. At least some of the haul—tires, batteries, radios, and other auto accessories—was recovered, and Ernie had little choice but to plead guilty to a charge of third-degree burglary and admit there was more than altruism involved with his crime spree. All told, he owned up to nine burglaries and four car thefts. When a police officer asked the reason for the criminal acts, he responded that he "wanted money." Robin Hood apparently wasn't above pocketing a few of the coins for himself.

The stolen merchandise from the gas station was valued at a mere $226, but Ernie would spend nearly four years in prison because of it. Well, that and his behavior in prison. True to his nature, he wasn't a model prisoner. He broke prison rules, refused to work on numerous occasions, damaged prison property, and—in a letter that really enraged the warden—disrespected his jailers.[6] At the St. Cloud Reformatory, where he spent the bulk of his incarceration, a prison psychologist expressed concern about Ernie almost from the minute he walked into the institution. On March 25, 1941, just a month after Ernie got there, the psychologist wrote:

> A peculiar looking and acting fellow. Is withdrawn, introverted and reticent. Looks down at floor and replies only to direct questions. Offers no explanation of his crimes except that he was out of work and no expression whatsoever of future intentions.

Surely the prison doctor had encountered sullen inmates before, so Ernie's demeanor must have been demonstrably uncommunicative. Prison was difficult for him, just as the orphanage had been years before, and a few months after his initial evaluation Rose, in a typewritten letter to the warden's office that is very clearly stated and seems to defy her prognosis as "feebleminded," wrote, "I was wondering if it would be possible to give him a chance in the machine shop or auto mechanic shop, as he always wanted to learn that trade and never had the chance."

The letter worked. A month later, Ernie was transferred to a vocational automobile mechanic class, and he must have absorbed some of what he learned there because he became immersed in cars the rest of his life. But his prison record shows it was a bad fit in other ways. He first appeared before the parole board on January 23, 1942, less than a year after entering the prison. Just a week earlier he had been written up for stealing food, and his case was continued for one year. If he stayed clean, he might have served two years instead of four, but that was a little bit like asking a dog to ignore his fleas. Trouble soon followed.

In April 1942, Ernie was banned from having visitors after he was placed in what the prison referred to as "third grade," which meant no privileges for thirty days. His various infractions included refusing to work (this happened on two occasions), purposely ruining a stone he was working on in his job as a stonecutter, and overall violations of prison rules. He made at least three trips to solitary and was written up ten times, including twice when his privileges were suspended.[7]

His most serious infraction (in the eyes of the prison administrators) occurred in October 1942 when he was ordered into isolation for three months. The penalty resulted from a letter Ernie wrote requesting a job change. The letter, which was considered disrespectful, accused his handlers of having it in for him. This is what it said:

> I was getting along swell in the carpenter shop until Patterson and Muldune started spreading propaganda around that I was a troublemaker. If it wasn't for these two, I'd probably be holding down the late [unintelligible word] boy in E house, but they had to queer the works by sticking their nose in someone else's business.

"Sticking their nose in someone else's business" may well meet the job description for corrections officers, but in Ernie's eyes it was a violation of the code. Later in the letter he accuses one of the guards of lying to him when he asked for a transfer to another cell. He concluded:

> I haven't kissed any screw's ass since I've been in here and I don't intend to start now. If nothing else, you can have me transferred to Stillwater, where the screws at least treat you like a man.

The screws. Maybe they treated him decently and maybe they didn't, but to Ernie's way of thinking, every single one of them was worthy of contempt. *I haven't kissed any screw's ass since I've been in here and I don't intend to start now.* It was a vow he would never break.

The most revealing part of Ernie's prison file is how often Rose visited him—like clockwork once a month except for the times when Ernie lost his visiting privileges. Millie visited on a few occasions, too, and Orvel at least once, but usually it was just Rose. Ernie also wrote his mother often, at least as often as he was allowed, and must have smoked in prison or used cigarettes for barter because Ernie—a lifetime nonsmoker—had several cartons of cigarettes delivered on multiple occasions. His IQ was listed as eighty-two, which was higher than his scores at the orphanage but below the typical adult average of one hundred. Since many people would later describe him as having an engineer's mind, one has to wonder about the legitimacy of the tests or his engagement while taking them. On the form used by the prison system, a single word described Ernie's interest in education: "indifferent." His vices were all tame—he admitted to gambling a little—but another one-word answer spoke volumes about his life at that time. On a line on the form for character associates, someone wrote "bad."

Ernie was in prison from February 24, 1941, until October 11, 1944—years when he almost certainly would have been sent off to war had he not been incarcerated. Instead, he grappled with his own demons in a place where his sentence was lengthened with each violation of the rules. It was a pattern that persisted when Ernie was finally discharged. For Ernie, rules were meant to be broken—again and again and again.

He hooked up with his first wife—Elizabeth "Betty" Taylor Allen—after his release from prison.[8] Betty possessed the two traits Ernie required of all his women, even long after his hair thinned: she was young and she was pretty. She lived a few blocks from the McClains in Columbia Heights and was a friend of Millie's, though she was a few years older than Ernie's sister. In fact, Betty was the only one of Ernie's four wives who was older than him. Carolyn once said to her mom Joyce that the older Ernie gets, the younger his women get. By the time Ernie married his fourth wife, Billie, she was even younger than his daughter Carolyn.

Millie didn't want Ernie and Betty to get married, ostensibly because of Betty's seizures.[9] She was an epileptic. Maybe the real reason was more veiled. Betty wanted to move out West, which meant Millie would be separated from Ernie yet again. Sure, the siblings had their differences—a younger sister bruised over the praise heaped on a favorite son—but Millie had already had one brother stripped from her life. When Ernie left, those feelings of abandonment resurfaced. The siblings would see each other from time to time, but when Ernie left for Oregon, he pretty much extended a middle finger to Minnesota, attempting to leave his past behind. We now know that wasn't possible.

At the wedding, Millie was Betty's maid of honor. The ceremony was held in a Lutheran church, which Ernie may have seen as more palatable than a Catholic mass. Certainly, it wasn't Rose's choice. When Millie, who became a Lutheran, told her mother that she was going to go to church one day, Rose threw up her hands and said, "Do what you want."

The seeds of mental illness in Ernie were probably visible for everyone to see even then. Those who knew him well describe Ernie as extremely bright but with a mean streak that could surface at odd times. When Carolyn was pregnant with her first child, Ernie, who lived just a few blocks away, would bike over to her house and they'd get hamburgers. "He was happy-go-lucky," Carolyn says, "but boy could he turn on a dime. One time I was at a restaurant with him and he just exploded in the restaurant and started screaming."

She never found out what set him off.[10]

Another time she did know. Jean Buckman, Ernie's third wife, bought him a suit that Ernie, for inexplicable reasons, left in the closet at the house of his second wife, Joyce. She understandably wanted to get rid of it and asked Carolyn to tell her father to fetch his suit. When Carolyn approached Ernie with Joyce's request, he turned and smacked her above the eye. She still has a scar from the blow.

Ernie wasn't big—maybe five feet eight or so—but there wasn't an ounce of fat on him. It's not clear if any one incident ended his marriage to Betty, who died in 2000, but Carolyn says it is no mystery: "My dad couldn't keep his fly closed," she said.

Ernie met Joyce Frances Becken in Silverton, Oregon, sometime around 1950. Carolyn isn't sure how they met, but it was most likely in a restaurant. Ernie was a big coffee drinker—and a big talker—and he liked to hold court in restaurants and coffee shops, including the Pig 'n Pancake restaurant in Astoria, where his son Michael would one day join his father in a headline-ripping act of madness. Ernie's presence attracted people of all ages, particularly young women. When they met, Joyce was nineteen and not more than a year out of high school and Ernie was twenty-nine. They married a year later.

Ernie's marriage to Joyce was the longest lasting of his four marriages and resulted in three children: Carolyn, Michael, and Nancy. Ernie got a job at the hospital in Astoria, where he raised his family and spent much of the rest of his life. They bought a forty-acre farm, which Joyce received in their subsequent divorce. When she died in 2009, she left it to her daughter Carolyn, the only child still alive by then. Massive tragedy—and mental illness—wracked the McClains, but Carolyn somehow emerged with a sweet soul intact, a testimony to perseverance and survival. We never know our influences, but it's possible she got that from Rose, whose perseverance and survival may have been her most endearing quality.

Carolyn doesn't recall Ernie being around much when she was young and says he wasn't particularly close to any of the children. She has one endur-ing—and terrifying—memory, which involved Rose.[11]

Orvel's steadying influence and teetotaling ways were probably the pri-mary reason the state agreed to release her from the institution. They were in sync on many things but parted ways on one of their biggest disagreements: her drinking. In William Saastamoinen, Rose found a partner whose habits were more in line with her needs. They were both big drinkers and didn't, as a general rule, wait until the sun went down before starting the pouring.

In the early 1960s, Rose and Bill moved to Astoria so Rose could be nearer to her son. Bill also thought he could get work there. But to hear Millie tell it, Joyce wasn't enamored with the idea and ran them off.

She had her reasons. One day, Joyce dropped off Carolyn and Nancy at their grandmother's house while she tended to errands. Nancy was probably three or four at the time and Carolyn nine or ten. They went into the bath-room to take a bath and Carolyn instinctively decided to lock the door. That's when Bill and Rose, both stumbling drunk, decided to have some fun at the girls' expense. As Bill knocked on the door, Carolyn heard Rose say, "Go get 'em daddy, go get 'em daddy." Bill kept knocking and Rose kept laughing. "Let me in. I want to wash your backs," Bill said to more laughter from both adults. Carolyn kept the door locked. Eventually Bill stopped or Joyce arrived to pick up the girls. Rose and Bill left Astoria and returned to Minnesota a short time later.

In August 1960, Ernie took his family to Minnesota to visit his sister and her family. Carolyn remembers Millie buying her a cowgirl outfit and hunting for agates on the shore of a lake. For Millie, lakes have always given her a sense of solace. She may have endured neglect and rejection as a young girl, but as she peruses the shore for hidden gems in the sand, those troubles are as distant as the far-off boats seen bobbing up and down in the water, their protruding fishing lines appearing as black specks against the setting sun.

A few years after the visit to his sister, Ernie returned to the Midwest, only this time he wasn't looking for agates. On his agenda was something far more important: reuniting with a father he barely knew.

None of Rose's three children knew their biological fathers. Ernie's and Millie's fathers were gone by the time they turned one and Robert's remains a complete mystery.[12] Lots of children grow up without a father, but most of the time they know who that father is. In Millie's case, she didn't even know her father's name. She thought it was England, maybe because she misheard "Ingram" when she was a little girl.

Ernie's estrangement from his father was just as pronounced and maybe more damaging. For two long years he was in an orphanage whose history, we now know, included harboring sexual predators. During that time, he at least knew where his mother was. From his father he inherited little more than a last name.

Leo Jerred could have chosen to occupy a larger part of his son's life, taken him on fishing trips, or just been there for critical moments. Instead, he chose a different path. Rose was hardly the ideal mother (or wife), but it's possible she did the best she knew how. Leo did nothing, and when Ernie could have benefitted from a father who loved him, Leo was missing in action. Unfortunately, Ernie would later mimic those same tendencies.

Leo left Minnesota sometime in the 1930s and bounced around a bit before returning to his native Michigan. Ernie's prison file lists his father's occupation as a machinist and his last known address as Elgin, Illinois. But when Ernie went to visit his dad in the early 1960s, Leo was back in Michigan, near Flint, where John Verkennes and his brothers found work in the auto plants.

It's not clear when Ernie last saw his father—he at least knew where he lived when he went to prison—but it's safe to say they didn't go to ballgames together. It could have gone badly. Such get-togethers can result in awkward silences and even bursts of emotional anger. But this homecoming had all the explosiveness of a Hallmark movie. Millie has a photo her brother sent her. In it, Leo is holding a cat in his backyard next to Ernie, whose hands are clasped together in an otherwise relaxed pose. Nancy, three at the time, is directly behind him and Michael plays near the car. It's as normal a visual as you can have of a family picnic in the warm summer sun. Innocence never looked so good—and a photograph has never been more misleading.

A few years after Ernie's trip to Michigan, Michael went to live with Millie and her family.[13] Ernie and Joyce may already have divorced by this time, and Michael was proving to be a handful. Ernie asked Millie if his son could live with them for the summer and enroll in school in the fall. Michael eventually would land in prison and make headlines afterward, but there was no indication of that in his brief tenure in Minnesota. He may have upset the dynamic in the household of two adults, four boys, and their beloved dog, Sam, but he wasn't disruptive.

Still, there were signs. Millie and her husband Ellsworth, or Al, weren't big drinkers but kept a supply of booze on hand for parties. Michael, to the astonishment of his ten-year-old cousin, not only discovered where the alcohol was, but he knew to substitute water for the vodka he drank. Later, he wouldn't be so adept at covering his tracks.

When fall came, Millie told Joyce that Mike would have to return to Oregon, explaining, "I have four boys. I don't need a fifth."

Ernie and Joyce's marriage ended in 1964, but truthfully, it was over before then. That's usually how it happens, no one incident blowing things up. And Ernie lit plenty of matches. One of his dalliances resulted in a blow to the head from the woman's husband. When it came to women, Ernie had an unquenchable thirst.

In the mid-1960s that wandering eye of his stopped to rest on a young woman at Bumble Bee Seafoods in Astoria. Jean Ann Buckman had gone to school to learn how to fillet fish and was the first woman to drive a forklift at Bumble Bee. She was in her early twenties when she and Ernie met—Ernie was probably forty-four—but the attraction must have been mutual because Jean became Ernie's third wife and the mother of his fourth child, this time a son. The name—DuShane Ernest McClain—seemed to echo from Ernie's past, as DuShane is similar to Rose's surname of DeChaine. DuShane had heard of the DeChaine name, a slight variation of his own, but wasn't aware of its significance until I told him a few years ago.[14] Unfortunately, the past would repeat itself in terms of the relationship between Ernie and Jean—known as "Jeannie" to the family. She divorced him in December 1969.

Jean died in 2010 after a long and successful marriage to Herb Dockter, a nice man who delivered gas for a fuel distributor. Later he drove a log truck. Herb knew both Michael and Ernie—Astoria, like Brainerd, is a small town where the business of others is often shared—and he has insights about both of them. Many people have compared Michael and Ernie, but Herb says they were nothing alike. Ernie used to hold court in the Pig 'n Pancake, talking the ear off anyone who would listen. Michael, on the other hand, would sit by himself and "not say anything." He was a loner and, as many others would come to learn, a time bomb waiting to erupt.

Ernie, too, had a fuse capable of causing harm. Herb described him as a "little man" with a constant chip on his shoulder as well as a vindictive streak. After Ernie's divorce from Jean, Herb says Ernie forged her signature on the title of a new horse trailer that she was supposed to get in the settlement and then sold it without her knowledge.

"He could be very bitter," Herb said.

But unlike his son Michael, who to hear people tell it had no good qualities, Ernie had genuine admirers, even among those he crossed.

Herb called Ernie a first-rate handyman whose skills were virtually unmatched. He was a poor money manager, though, and wasn't always compensated adequately for his services.

"He could do anything he wanted to do," Herb said. "People took advantage of him."[15]

Those close to Ernie, including Millie, often say he had an engineer's mind. He told his family he designed the first double-decker bus, and that story would get told over and over again. Whether it was true or not, he was sought after as a carpenter, even if he did have trouble hanging on to steady work. His great-grandfather, Antoine, was once described as a "journeyman" in census documents, and that description was an apt label for Ernie as well. He never stayed long in any one endeavor. The last job he had was tearing down an old cannery in Astoria. He also constructed a building for Van Huesen Beverages, a company owned by the mayor. At one time, he owned an entire city block in Astoria. He could be generous with his money, though that generosity didn't necessarily extend to his ex-wives or to his children, for that matter. After his divorce from Joyce, Ernie enjoyed a lavish lifestyle, driving a Cadillac, living in a beautiful house, and buying expensive presents for his girlfriends. During that same time, Joyce and their kids were in a house with no running water and no electricity, according to Carolyn.

"We had a woodstove, so we had heat," she says.[16]

Ernie eventually lost it all, including the city block. That life story would be dispiriting if that's all there was to it. Unfortunately, it would take a more destructive turn. Ernie McClain's final breath came not in the noble pursuit of any internal reward, but at a hearing in which he was fighting about paying child support to Billie, his fourth wife and the mother of their son, Ernie's fifth child, Ernest McClain Jr.

He could be very bitter. The world was about to find out just how bitter Ernie McClain could be.

Billie McClain was seventeen and already had a child when she laid eyes on Ernie for the first time. It was in a restaurant and, as usual, Ernie was the center of attention.

"Everyone in town knew him," she says. "A lot of kids hung around him."

Billie was a kid, too, but she was attracted to Ernie in much the same way women always were. He was handsome and seemed to have the world tucked into his sleeve.

"He was a nice guy," says the woman who almost had her life ended by him. "He had a heart as big as life."

Billie witnessed Ernie's dark side, too. She was holding their son, Ernest, one day when Ernie tried to rip the boy out of her arms.

"He was a pretty violent guy," Billie says. "The people close to him knew that."

Billie said she can't recall many high moments from the marriage. "I was kind of like going on, doing my own thing, raising the kids," she said. "He wasn't into that."[17]

That seemed to be a pattern with Ernie, the detached father whose self-interest was manifest. A theory emerged after the shooting, probably put forth by Joyce, that Ernie had a brain tumor. Recent research has associated brain damage with a number of violent episodes. The most famous of these is probably the 1966 clocktower shooting at the University of Texas. An autopsy on the brain of the shooter, Charles Whitman, revealed a tumor the size of a walnut that extended into his amygdala, a part of the medial temporal lobe that controls behavior and emotion. Hallucinations have been known to occur during seizures in that part of the brain, as well as voices barking out instructions of murderous intent.[18]

Did Ernie hear voices the day he brought a gun into a Portland courtroom? If so, they came early. He drove to Portland from Astoria with his son Michael in the car and something else: a .357 Magnum revolver. The killing wasn't spur of the moment. It was orchestrated and planned. It was also preceded by another factor that researchers say can trigger mass violence: a crisis of major proportions, either real or imagined. And in Ernie's case, the crisis that occurred in the late summer of 1978 was as real as real can get.

Nancy McClain, Ernie's third child from his second marriage, was the girl next door in a small town—drop-dead gorgeous but with tomboy tendencies. You wouldn't hesitate to ask her to the prom or to play poker with the guys. She was *that* girl. Neil Stein, a cousin of Carolyn's then-husband Chris Tucker, needed a fishing partner because his girlfriend had left for California to tend to some family business. Although Nancy had never been on a tuna boat before, this seemed to be an easy way to make some quick cash. And she needed the money.

Oregon tuna fishing is big business with a fishery that is almost unrivaled in the world. In the late 1970s it mostly consisted of big charter operators and small independents like Stein, hoping to cash in during a season that runs roughly from July to October. On August 23, 1978, Stein and Nancy, who was nineteen, set out on a boat called the *Roundup*. Fog and rain were rolling in, but that wasn't unusual for the Oregon coast. And the wind was manageable, topping out at maybe ten miles per hour. The haul can be great in those conditions, and that might have been the case on this day. Of course, we'll never know. Because after the two set out that morning, they were never seen again. According to the U.S. Coast Guard, the *Roundup* was likely caught in a storm about thirty miles off the coast of Coos Bay. The only wreckage that turned up was part of a life jacket and the boat ring.

"My mom just about went crazy afterward," said Carolyn. "It was horrible."

Months later, speculation would center around whether Ernie's courtroom violence was the byproduct of his depression over the death of his youngest daughter. That's certainly possible, although Nancy's death wasn't his only setback. Billie had left him and moved to Portland to attend school some one hundred miles away. Ernie's son Michael was showing signs of extremely bizarre behavior. And after a life in which he earned much and was free with his money, Ernie was dead broke. Instead of owning a farm or a city block, he was living in a house with nothing on the walls and just a few pieces of furniture. Call it the emptiness of divorce. Add in Nancy's death, and Ernie's life was empty, too.

Around this time, Carolyn visited her father. She hadn't done that in quite a while and doesn't remember why she did it that night. But they had a great time. Ernie had just seen the movie *Every Which Way but Loose*, starring Clint Eastwood as a mild-mannered sort who becomes a great prizefighter and roams the countryside with a pet orangutan in pursuit of a love interest. Ernie laughed as he related scenes from the movie, which was a departure from the shoot-'em-up westerns that had been Eastwood's calling card to that point. He was being cast against type and maybe that's what appealed to Ernie the most. Carolyn remembers something else from that evening. In a serious moment, Ernie said he felt bad about Michael.

"He's such a mess," he told his daughter. It was the last time she would see her father.

That December Ernie was ordered to pay $200 a month in support for Billie and $275 for their son, Ernest Jr., who was two years old at the time. For Ernie, who was doing remodeling work for a wine and beer distributorship, the order must have rankled. Whether he agreed with it or not, he didn't pay it and another hearing was scheduled in Portland for Tuesday, February 13, 1979—nearly four years to the day since their wedding. Billie thinks Ernie was under the false impression that the hearing related to custody of their son.

"That wasn't even what it was about," she said. "It was a contempt hearing."

The night before, Ernie called a friend, Lyman Cornish, who owned an antique shop near where Ernie was doing his remodeling work, and asked if he would testify on his behalf. Cornish said he couldn't but that his wife, Marilyn, would.[19] However, at 6:30 the next morning—the time Ernie said he would pick up Marilyn Cornish—he didn't show. There was just one person in the car with him that morning accompanying him to the courtroom: his son Michael. Whether Michael knew what Ernie was thinking and was fully on board would be a matter of speculation in the family for years to come. Billie is convinced that Ernie hatched the plan along with his son, who she says adored his father. Before the shooting, she said, Ernie transferred his car into Mike's name, perhaps realizing he would no longer need it. The firearm he brought into the courtroom also belonged to Mike originally.

"He stuffed a .357 Magnum into his pants with Mike in the car and [Michael] didn't know?" she asks incredulously. "He knew. It was planned."

Carolyn isn't so sure, believing instead that Michael was there simply to provide moral support for their father. Carolyn, however, doesn't question Billie's account of what happened in the shooting's immediate aftermath. Billie says Michael leaned over the fallen body of his father after the shooting and whispered, son to father, brother-in-arms to fallen comrade: "We'll get 'em." Billie, who was rushed to the hospital and underwent surgery for powder burns on her face from the shooting, has no doubt who Michael was referring to with the words "We'll get 'em."

Just before the start of the hearing, Ernie—sitting on a bench behind Billie in the courtroom—leaned forward and said, "You just need to come home with me and I'll forget the whole thing." While doing research for this book, I asked Billie what she thinks would have happened had she done what Ernie asked.

"I wouldn't be here," she said.

When the case came before Circuit Judge Mercedes Deiz, Ernie and Billie took their seats at the short table in front of the benches. One of the ironies from that day is that Judge Deiz reduced the amount Ernie was to pay in support during the hearing. Most likely, though, Ernie wasn't paying attention. In addition to the fully loaded .357 Magnum he was carrying, he had twelve bullets clanging around in his coat pocket should he need to reload.

When the hearing ended, Judge Deiz prepared to leave the courtroom. Standing left to right in the courtroom well were Billie, her attorney Candise Jones, Ernie, and Ernie's attorney, Ronald Miller. After the first shots rang out, it was Miller who reached Ernie, who had just turned and fired at Jones from three feet away. As she fell, Ernie aimed the gun at Billie, grazing her shirt but missing her body entirely. Miller then grabbed Ernie and wrestled him for the gun, which fired again, this time into the ceiling. Miller then backed away in one of those moments frozen in time that can't be replicated even in the mind's eye. Ernie McClain then leaned over in that courtroom in Portland, pointed the gun at his own head, and fired one last time.

NOTES

1. Author interview with Millie Sivanich.
2. Hubert H. Humphrey, *Education of a Public Man: My Life and Politics* (Minneapolis: University of Minnesota Press, 1991), 37.
3. Author interview with Carolyn Phillips. The reference to the baseball team is from my own reflections.
4. Author interview with Millie Sivanich.
5. Ernie's prison record, Minnesota Historical Society.
6. Ibid.
7. Ibid.
8. Ernie's marriage to Elizabeth "Betty" Taylor Allen occurred on September 12, 1945. The record can be obtained through the Minnesota Official Marriage System. A story about the wedding also appeared in the *Minneapolis Tribune*.
9. Author interview with Millie Sivanich.
10. Author interview with Carolyn Phillips.

11. Ibid.

12. St. James Catholic Orphanage records.

13. Author recollections.

14. Author interview with DuShane McClain.

15. Author interview with Herb Dockter.

16. Author interview with Carolyn Phillips.

17. Author interview with Billie McClain.

18. From "How Responsible Are Killers with Brain Damage," *Scientific American*, January 30, 2018.

19. Ernie's shooting in a Portland, Oregon, courtroom on February 13, 1979, was widely covered. Most of the details I included were taken from interviews with Ernie's family members and news stories from the *Daily Astorian*, the *Oregonian*, and the Associated Press.

8

Michael

The shooting in Portland had echoes that extend far beyond the court-room. Selfish acts tend to work that way. The biggest tragedy was the death of Candise Jones, Billie's attorney, who at age twenty-six was just beginning to show the promise of her upbringing. Not only was her father a lawyer, but the Brooklyn-born Jones's three brothers had each launched legal careers as well.

An hour after the shooting, Judge Deiz emerged from her chambers fight-ing back tears.

"Candy! I just can't stop thinking about Candy," she told a reporter from the *Oregonian* newspaper. "I never got to tell her how much I liked her. This isn't an afterthought. I liked her very much. She was a special lady. That child had such a good future."[1]

Coworkers told reporters how proud Candise was about passing the bar barely a year earlier. One said she once told him she was relieved to be in Portland rather than in her native New York where "you lived in fear all the time." In Ernie's blind rage, Candise Jones was collateral damage, a means to an end however twisted. But from all accounts, she was a beautiful soul whose death cast a wide shadow. Her husband, Randall, said he and his wife had recently taken ballroom dancing classes at a local community college. The shooting took place a day before their third wedding anniversary. And only a few months earlier, they had moved into a spacious home they hoped to fill with their life's treasures.

"She was buying drapes, filling up the empty new house," Jones told the *Oregon Journal*.

Shooting sprees like this one have sadly become all too common, with cities like Dayton, Ohio; Parkland, Florida; Santa Fe, Texas; Virginia Beach, Virginia; Thousand Oaks, California; Pittsburgh, Pennsylvania; Annapolis, Maryland; Benton, Kentucky; Sutherland Springs, Texas; Las Vegas, Nevada; Orlando, Florida; and hundreds of others becoming synonymous with mass death. In virtually every case the seemingly senseless outbursts of violence are accompanied by a full-throated clamor for gun restrictions and an equally full-throated defense of the Second Amendment. After the twin shootings in Dayton and Santa Fe in 2019, a hashtag movement grew up around the words "do something." Of course, "do something" often translates to "do nothing."

Gun control measures introduced in the Oregon legislature after the Portland shooting fell under the "do nothing" category. Just after the shooting, Portland Democratic Representative Gretchen Kafoury sponsored a bill calling for, among other provisions, a ten-day waiting period on gun purchases.[2] It went nowhere, and the ensuing four decades have not settled the debate over which gun limits are appropriate in a violent society. The shooting did produce one concrete outcome, however. Walk into any big-city courthouse today and you'll see airport-like security to protect those inside. The Portland shooting helped bring about those changes.

For the citizens of Portland, the safety upgrade was past due. A security audit of the Multnomah County Courthouse, where the shooting occurred, uncovered an alarming lapse in safety measures. No police officers were assigned to individual courtrooms, and no one was assigned to Deiz's courtroom that day. After the shooting started, her court clerk, Bob Frank, pushed an emergency buzzer on the bench that alerted county corrections officers in the jail, but they were four floors above, too far away to be of any immediate assistance. A circuit court administrator interviewed after the shooting said that a used metal detector was once put into the budget but later deleted. The reasoning: this was divorce court. But divorce court is often where the worst in a person can surface. Of the shootings that had occurred in the building up until that point, all had involved divorce cases.

Multnomah County now boasts a courthouse security system that rivals airport security. Magnetometers, or walk-through metal detectors, are used along with X-ray scanners and hand-held metal detectors. Those caught attempting to bring firearms into a court facility face a Class C felony. Banned are pocketknives, scissors—even knitting needles, no matter if Grandma can display the Christmas sweater she is knitting. If nothing else, Ernie's outburst that day led to changes that have saved innumerable lives.

"I smile every time I see one," Billie says of the now-ubiquitous metal detectors.

She spent just one night in the hospital, but for a long time, the shooting served as a ghostly presence, hovering in her thoughts and dictating her movements. She kept out of the public eye—and away from Ernie's son Michael—as much as possible. It was years before she allowed her son to meet Carolyn out of fear it would bring retribution from Carolyn's unhinged brother. She remarried and went about her life but even now is reticent to talk about what happened that day.

"I've spent most of my life trying to forget it," she explains.[3]

Michael's life after the shooting was marked by drug use, unemployment, criminal charges, and prison time. Just how much of that was tattooed on his forehead before February 1979 is difficult to say, though the moodiness, violence, and questionable mental health had been there for everyone to see both before and after Ernie took an innocent life along with his own. Michael wasn't Ernie. He was worse. But Ernie, for all his flaws and destructive psyche, might have been Michael's role model.

From the moment Michael leaned over the still body of his father, his life descended further into the maw of evil intent. No, it didn't start that day. Even Ernie, in all his rage toward Billie and the rest of the world, recognized his son's downward spiral when he told Carolyn her brother was "such a mess." But somewhere along the line Michael envisioned an exit plan that would mimic his father's grand gesture, an undertaking so complete that the whole world would know who he was and what he had done. Then he bungled the moment. Chalk it up to one more failure in a muddled life.

For years Michael McClain terrorized those around him, controlling them through intimidation and hatred. "My brother was a different character than my dad," Carolyn says. "He was more violent." And most of that violence, or the threatening power of it, was directed at his own family.

Carolyn can tick off Michael's many intimidations like she is compiling a list for grocery shopping. There was the night she and her then-husband Chris stopped at her mom's house after Nancy's death to see how she was doing. Michael mostly lived with his mother, even into his forties, having stripped from his life any alternate sanctuary. He worked some but could never seem to hold down a job for long. And unlike his dad, he didn't tend to pick up another one after the previous one was done. Michael was home that night and apparently not in the mood for family bonding. As they prepared to leave, Chris went out to the car and Carolyn held her son with one hand and the railing with the other as she descended the steps from the kitchen. Just then, Michael kicked her in the back with a force that nearly sent them both face-first down the stairs. She has no idea why he did it.

Michael's abusive nature was no secret to those around him. Joyce once bought a plane ticket to Hawaii for Mike and his girlfriend, though the trip was hardly paradise, particularly for the girlfriend. At one point, according to family members, Michael became so enraged that he hung her over the balcony of the hotel. That was a pattern with Michael: using fear to terrorize those closest to him. He once made her eat off the floor. He pulled a gun on her father. And, of course, he hit her. Eventually, and fortunately for her, she left him, along with their child.[4]

Someone who didn't leave Michael, no matter how much abuse he directed her way, was his mother Joyce. Psychopaths often tend to abuse those around them, and though Michael wasn't diagnosed during his life, he met most of the criteria. The psychopathic checklist widely in use today almost perfectly describes Michael: uncaring, emotionally shallow, irresponsible, insincere, overconfident, lacking perspective, selfish, unable to plan or look beyond the present, and a low tolerance for frustration that quickly lends itself to violence.[5] How violent was Michael? He once tied up his mother, poured gasoline over her body, and threw unlit matches at her in a mind game that appealed only to him. She left after that incident and lived at her boss's house for a time, but whenever Michael would see her, he would point his finger at her and use his thumb as a pretend trigger, reminding her who was in control. What thought was going through Michael's mind as his terrified mother shivered in fear while he emptied the contents of the gasoline can?

"I don't know what he thought," Carolyn says. "He thought of himself."

Michael was probably also thinking about himself when he pulled a butcher's knife on Carolyn. Or when he sat in a pickup truck across the street from her house with a rifle on his lap. Carolyn saw the weapon as she and a boyfriend drove by. What did Michael plan to do that night?

"I don't know," Carolyn says. "Kill us, I guess."

Like Herb Dockter, Carolyn warned against comparing her brother to her father. Ernie, she said, was "rational 99 percent of the time. People loved him."

Michael, on the other hand, was impossible to love.

"He tortured early on," Carolyn said, beginning with animals. "One night he cut off my sister's fingernails while she was sleeping. He tied up a friend of my sister to a tree in the woods. Chopped a wall down in my bedroom closet with a butcher knife to get to me. When he got through the wall and stuck his head in, I hit him with a shoe. I was about thirteen or fourteen at the time."[6]

None of it—the lack of respect, the intimidation, the guns, the drugs, the bizarre behavior—led Joyce to kick her son out of the house. In fact, Joyce never even called the police about Michael. Carolyn once asked her mother why she didn't reach out for help.

"My mom said she's already lost one child," Carolyn recounted from their conversation. "'I'm not going to lose another.'"

Eventually the police did catch up with Michael. In 1989, he was convicted on a drug charge: manufacture of a controlled substance.[7] The crime seems absurdly minor compared to what he had been doing, but it succeeded in getting him out of the house and, for a blissfully peaceful moment, out of their lives. Joyce could exhale knowing her troubled son wasn't lurking in the shadows. But although Michael was sentenced to up to five years in prison, he served only a little more than two.[8]

For those in the grip of fear from Michael, his incarceration was but a short respite, a pause before the real storm.

When Michael McClain was paroled in September 1991, it was subject to several conditions, including that he submit to periodic property searches and urine tests at the discretion of his probation officer. Unfortunately, the court-ordered supervision didn't staunch Michael's interest in drugs and guns. And somewhere along the way, he found another pursuit: making bombs.

The Pig 'n Pancake in Astoria packs 'em in, particularly for breakfast, when locals and tourists can gorge on Swedish pancakes, eggs Benedict, or a cheddar cheese omelet made with a healthy portion of Dungeness crab. The online reviews are mostly positive except when the parking lot is full and the waitstaff is too stressed to provide good service. Sunday morning brunch can be one of those times, as generations of family members pour out of church and head to the Pig. And as Michael McClain loaded his mom's car with the homemade bombs he planned on planting at the Dutch Cup and the Pig 'n Pancake restaurants on a Sunday in November 1996, he knew he could count on one thing: the parking lot would be full.

Michael knew something else as he prepared for his big splash: he would soon be returning to prison. A week or so before the bombings he was arrested after police found weapons and pot in his pickup truck during a traffic stop. How that played in his head, or even if it did, is difficult to determine. He probably left clues, but Michael McClain had been leaving clues for twenty years. Mike was Mike and the people who knew him well just hoped he wouldn't go too far off the rails. But those hopes were dashed on November 3, 1996, when Michael not only went off the rails, he envisioned taking a whole lot of people with him, leveling two restaurants full of those who had just soaked in a message of grace and hope from the pulpit.

Why Michael chose Sunday, the traditional day when Christians observe the Sabbath, is another one of those unknown mysteries. Maybe he just wanted a full house. But Michael always wanted to live in his father's shoes, and Sunday held no special significance to Ernie. Whether it was the nuns by whom he felt tortured or the cynical influences of his mother, Ernie rejected all that the church stood for. It's safe to say that whatever sustenance it provided the masses never reached him. Or Michael, for that matter. Seventeen years earlier Michael watched as his father left this world in a paroxysm of rage and senseless violence. The son adored the father and tried to emulate him in many ways. And on this day, a Sunday, he concocted his most elaborate imitation yet.

To get a sense of what Michael envisioned, you have to look at what happened three years after the Astoria bombings. On April 20, 1999, two teenage students attempted to blow up a suburban Denver high school at the precise moment when the casualty count would be highest. Although thirteen people died in Columbine High School that day, the bombs malfunctioned, sparing the world of more pain and grieving. Despite all his planning, preparation, and diabolical bent for mass murder, Michael's bombs did not detonate as he intended, either. It's hard to do a trial run when you're constructing an explosive device at your mom's farmhouse. Easy to miss a step or two. Or maybe Michael just chose the wrong day. Sometimes when Christians celebrate the Sabbath, the forces of evil get relegated to the back seat.

He planted the first bomb near the coatrack at the Dutch Cup and timed it to go off at 10:59 a.m. A second and much bigger bomb was placed beside the front door at the Pig 'n Pancake. Tick. Tick. Tock. Something went awry. Michael, standing near the Pig's cash register, couldn't have known the blast that he had intended for the Dutch Cup, a quarter mile away, had fizzled, a pop instead of a boom. But he had a front-row seat inside the Pig when his grand plan went up in smoke.

"They did not function as intended," a spokesman for the Oregon State Police Arson and Bomb Squad later said of the explosive material. "The quantity did have the possibility of substantial structural damage. We would have expected a lot of casualties."[9]

As it happened, only a few people were hurt by the bomb and none required even an overnight hospital stay. The combined forty pounds of bomb material could have leveled an entire block, killing dozens, perhaps even hundreds, of people. But just one person died that day: Michael McClain. A waitress named Linda Nichols told a local radio station that she heard an explosion, saw plaster fall from the ceiling, and then heard two pops. Michael's body went to the floor, just as his father's had seventeen years before.

"Apparently he had put a gun to his head," Nichols said.

The bomb team searched Joyce's farmhouse to see if Michael left behind any explosives or clues about a possible motive. U.S. Senate candidate Gordon Smith had been to the Pig earlier that morning, but no one thought it was a politically inspired act.

"We have received no warning calls about the explosions and we have received no calls subsequent to the explosions claiming responsibility or explaining any motive," Astoria Police Dispatcher Dick Lang said.

In the end, it may have been the simplest explanation of all. Asked what her brother's motivation was, Carolyn responded, "Go out like my dad. Make a big headline."

When Billie watched the news that night about an unidentified bomber who attempted to blow up two restaurants filled with people, she turned to her husband and said, "That sounds like a Michael McClain thing."

Michael didn't get the headline he sought, but the incident wasn't soon forgotten in Astoria. In June 2012, a man with a Middle Eastern accent made three 911 calls tipping police to some forty bombs planted in various locations in Astoria, including at the airport and at a McDonald's. In the next day's *Daily Astorian*, reporter Chelsea Gorrow wrote:

Monday's incident, although seemingly a hoax, was not the first such threat of its kind in the community's history. In November 1996, 42-year-old Michael McClain planted bombs at the Pig 'n Pancake restaurant and the old Dutch Cup coffee shop. A detonator cap explosion caused minor damage and shortly afterward McClain shot himself in the head. No one else was killed.[10]

No one else was killed. In a family where favors were few, that was one to be celebrated.

After returning to Minnesota following their dismal trip to Astoria, Oregon, Rose and her husband Bill lived the rest of their years in a small home in Fridley, Minnesota, a middle-class suburb of Minneapolis. Neither was in good health. Bill died at age fifty-seven in May 1969 and Rose the following January. She had turned sixty-eight just a few weeks earlier, a remarkable feat given the choices that she made in her life—and the choices that were made for her.

On her death certificate, the medical examiner wrote "liver failure," "cirrhosis of liver," and "chronic alcoholism" as the causes of death.[11] The real cause was probably more complicated. The truth is, Rose had a death sentence almost from the moment she was born. Her doctor could do nothing to extend her life but chose compassion toward the family in death. On her death certificate, in answer to a question about the duration of her alcoholism, he couldn't have been more charitable.

"Five years," he wrote.

Addiction can run in families—alcoholism has been linked to certain genetic factors, for example—but neither Ernie nor Millie felt the same ravenous tug as their mother. Perhaps both saw what it did to her, how even mundane tasks became impossible. When Millie was asked why she didn't go to live with her mother immediately after Rose got out of the institution, she said, "My mother didn't want me. I was a cripple."[12]

After Rose married Bill Saastamoinen, she did ask Millie to come live with her and her new husband. This time Millie refused.

"She only wanted a maid," she explained years later.

The life of Rose DeChaine is both maddening and tragic. Had she been treated for her real disease—alcoholism—she might have carved out a more productive existence or at the very least she might have lived a happier life. Addicts have to want to be treated; they have to possess the deep desire to do the work, and even that may not be enough. It's highly likely that Rose would have failed at recovery. But no one gave her that chance. She was written off as damaged goods, broken and beyond repair. Remember those immortal words of Charles Dight: "A good house cannot be built from rotten lumber."[13]

There is even scant evidence that Rose was, to use the state's word for it, feebleminded. Her letters to the warden when Ernie was in prison were thoughtful and intelligent, not the ramblings of an incoherent mind. True, she did poorly on her IQ tests at the Faribault institution, but she was given the first test just four days after her admission and her second one—used to justify her sterilization—two weeks later. She wasn't an inmate. She was a lab rat. And when you think about it, the score on that test—a rating roughly equivalent to that of a nine- or ten-year-old—isn't the least bit surprising. After all, she'd had about the same amount of schooling as a nine- or ten-year-old.

Rose wasn't a great mother—Millie freely admits that—and if so inclined, eugenicists could well point to Ernie's behavior and that of his son Michael as justification for their conviction that apples don't fall far from trees or—and this was their real fear—that one bad apple contaminates the whole bushel.

But even those isolated examples fall apart under close scrutiny. Many people have described Ernie as brilliant. Doesn't sound like someone with a feeble mind. And although Michael was deeply disturbed, no one else in the family appears to have inherited that particular condition. Carrying it one step further: if Rose was tainted through blood, where did that come from? Mary? Joseph? Their parents? How far back did it go? Henry Goddard was convinced the so-called Kallikak family had been tainted all the way back to the Revolutionary War.[14] "No amount of education or good environment can change a feebleminded individual into a normal one," he wrote.

Yet if the DeChaines were so inflicted, why is it that so many of Rose's brothers and sisters were what we think of as normal? Why was she singled out? Put another way, if Rose inherited her alleged immorality and mental illness as part of her birthright, wouldn't many other people from that line have intellectual disabilities? Both of her parents came from big families, as did their parents and their parents before them. Remember, one of the DeChaines had fourteen children. Another in the line had fifteen offspring. The law of averages indicates that at least one of them had a mental impairment. The height of absurdity—not to mention bigotry—would hold that most or all of them did.

Rose was a complex woman whose mental struggles were seen as an incendiary threat. That she survived at all is probably due to her own personal grit, a desire to do things on her own terms, and an unwillingness to succumb to the harsh judgment of others. Despite all her flaws, she was one tough cookie. She was sterilized to protect society, while little thought was given to protecting her. She was a pariah, an outcast who forfeited her right to freedom based on an assumption of guilt and a healthy dose of hatred. But she was also a survivor. The eugenicists were so certain that mental illness and morality are inherited traits that they missed the one quality that was as much a part of her as her heart and lungs. Her ancestors fought for independence, for the right to govern themselves. Rose fought, too, and was just as outnumbered. Yet she

Michael 115

persevered just as they did, carving out a life her handlers at the Faribault institution didn't believe was possible. "Is immoral," one wrote on her chart.[15] It's too bad the mirrors in the state's institutions faced only one direction.

In the late 1960s, Rose legally changed her first name to Maxine.[16] Maybe it was a clever attempt to dodge a creditor but in a way it fit. After all, Rose is a symbol of beauty, and that's a word that could never be attached to her life.

As Rose lay in her hospital bed during her final hours, her labored breaths sounding like a fireplace bellows with a hole in it, Millie brought her four boys to see their grandmother one last time. Rose was in incredible pain, yet she extended her arthritic and bony hand in a gesture of tenderness, love, and deep regret. To outsiders, Rose always carried the look of someone who doesn't want to be bothered, a looking glass into the abyss of her cynical life view. But to her grandchildren, the embodiment of a future pure and unblemished, she wore only smiles. And she smiled that day, smiled as if her life was nothing but sweetness and joy. In a world where she was shunned and abused and where cruelty abounded, Rose's smile was her last parting gift.

NOTES

1. "Attorney, Gunman Killed before Terrorized Court," *Oregonian*, February 14, 1979.

2. "Lawyer Shot to Death in Murder, Suicide," *Walla Walla Union-Bulletin*, February 14, 1979.

3. Author interview with Billie McClain.

4. Author interview with Carolyn Phillips.

5. Ibid.

6. "The Hare Psychopathy Checklist: The Test That Will Tell You If Someone Is a Sociopath," *Business Insider*, November 24, 2016.

7. Clatsop County Circuit Court Sentence Order, March 1, 1989. The actual charge was Manufacture of Controlled Substance.

8. Oregon Board of Parole, September 1, 1991.

9. "Bombs Planted in Cafes Malfunctioned, Two Devices Had Potential for Substantial Damage," Associated Press, November 5, 1996.

10. "Terrorism Task Force, FBI Help Astoria Police with Bomb Threat," *Daily Astorian*, June 10, 2012.

11. Certificate of death, Minnesota Department of Health.

12. Author interview with Millie Sivanich.

13. Jessie A. Carlson, "Eugenic Sterilization: The Final Solution for America," *Undergraduate Research Journal at UCCS* 2, no. 1 (Spring 2009).

14. See Edwin Black, *War against the Weak* (Washington, DC: Dialog Press, 2012), 76–77.

15. Faribault School records.

16. Obituary for William Saastamoinen, *Minneapolis Tribune*, May 4, 1969.

Before he made national headlines in 1978, Ernie McClain was a charmer who never had trouble attracting young women. He went to prison, was married four times and had a mean streak that surfaced on that fateful day in Portland. But few knew about his troubled upbringing.

Rose on her wedding day, May 14, 1930. She had reason to smile. She had recently been released for the third and final time from the Faribault School for the Feeble-Minded, where she was sterilized as part of the eugenics movement.

Ernie and Millie in front of their grandmother's house in Brainerd sometime before both were sent to the orphanage in Duluth. Millie's bowed legs were the result of rickets, often caused by a nutritional deficiency.

Mary DeChaine was a stabilizing influence within her family and a chief reason Millie survived a very difficult childhood. Here, Mary poses for a photo in Brainerd with four of her children. From left to right: Clara, Mary, Bud, Mabel, and Rose.

Millie on her high school graduation day (right) with her mother Rose. The little girl with rickets not only survived, she became one of the first in her family to graduate from high school.

Lottie DeChaine (left) on her wedding day, April 29, 1913. Lottie died in a house explosion two years later, along with her baby, Irene.

Ernie, Joyce and their three children circa 1960: (from left to right) Ernie, Nancy, Joyce, Michael and Carolyn. Nancy's death in August 1978 would rock the family to its very foundation. Less than six months later, Ernie shot up a courtroom in Portland, killing an attorney before shooting himself.

Ernie during his reunion with his father, Leo Jerred. Nancy is directly behind Ernie and Michael, who would later set off two bombs in a pair of restaurants, is playing near the car.

Nancy McClain. Some believe it was her death that caused Ernie to succumb to his demons.

Millie examines the records for her brother Robert at the former Woodland Hills residential treatment center in Duluth, the site of the former St. James Catholic Orphanage where she and her two brothers were placed.

This photograph was likely taken at the St. James Catholic Orphanage in Duluth and may have been the last time Millie and her two brothers saw each other.

Millie sees her great-granddaughter for the first time: Riley Rose Martin.

9

Robert

The St. James Catholic Orphanage sat on a hill overlooking the grand city of Duluth, whose beauty and location once led to an exalted nickname: Zenith City of the Unsalted Seas.[11] In the halcyon days of American expansionism, Duluth achieved national prominence as the largest port on the greatest of the Great Lakes—a stopping-off point for great men on their quest to discover the world.

For Rose's two sons, however, it wasn't nearly so grand. It was there that Ernie saw his world shrink—and where Robert entered a new world altogether.

At the St. James, as one article states, children from "broken homes" were given a new beginning: "At the end of the Woodland trolley line sat a pot of gold for those children—St. James Orphanage."[2]

For some, this new beginning was indeed a pot of gold, exposing them to the best the world had to offer; for others, as we've seen, a slide into the dark tunnel of abuse in its most venal form.

Robert Conradson was three years old when he entered the St. James. What he knew about life you could fit in a shoebox: a mother he rarely saw; a brother and sister who teased him but who also held his hand when he screamed into the night; a familiar cast of interwoven characters that included aunts, uncles, grandma, and the boy next door, the one who kept tripping on his shoes because he could never keep his laces tied.

Robert was too young to know his home was "broken"—and too innocent to know that all this was about to change.

July 8, 1928: The two strangers sit on the opposite side of the table in a room next to where the priests have their morning coffee. On Robert's side, directly to his left, is a representative of the St. Louis County Child Welfare Board. On his right, a nun, the one who brought him down from the activity room. Robert considers her to be one of the nice ones.

"Robert, you don't know us, but my name is Gloria and this is Raymond," says the woman sitting directly across from him. Robert can't help but notice how short she is, shorter than Ernie even. The man seems tall, even sitting down, but is as skinny as a stick figure, the kind his friend Stephen likes to draw in his notebook.

Robert grabs a pen that is sitting on the table next to the nun and is about to draw a stick figure himself when she snatches it out of his hand. "Is that how we behave when someone is talking?" she scolds, and then, turning to face the woman, says: "Continue, Mrs. Anderson. Robert's just a little nervous."

Robert doesn't know what nervous means, but if it has anything to do with wanting to draw stick figures, he would agree with her.

The Anderson woman leans forward. "Robert, honey, we're going to take you home with us."

Robert looks back at the nun, who is staring at the far wall where a stack of books is piled on a couple of small desks. What was so interesting about a stack of books? He wishes they had left him in the activity room. A couple of boys there were playing jacks. He doesn't know much about the game, but he likes rolling the pointy things. He thinks they look like stars. Stephen once let him take one of them into his bed, where he hid it under the sheets so the night nunner couldn't see it.

He turns back to the woman and then looks at the man, who seems reluctant to talk. Maybe he can't talk. Robert is thinking about that when the man says, "Robbie, I think you'll like where we live. It's far away from here, but you'll have your own room."

Robbie. Nobody ever calls him that. His sister calls him Bobby, and Ganny did, too, but Robbie? He isn't at all sure he likes it. On the other hand, he's never had his own room before. At the orphanage, he shares a room with eleven other boys. Well, sometimes there are ten. The nunners always count them off before turning out the lights. One. Two. Three. Four. Last night, she counted to twelve, but that wasn't normal. His bed is just to the left of the door, so he is always one of the first ones counted, either one or two. Last night he was number one. "Here," he called out.

"Here?" the nun says sternly, a direct giveaway that you better say something else and quick.

"Here, ma'am."

His mind is anywhere but at the table where the two strangers are when the child welfare lady says, "Robert, these are your new parents. They are going to take care of you much better than we can. You're very lucky."

He doesn't feel lucky. Why is it that grownups are always telling you stuff that isn't true? He doesn't even know these people. Do they even know what jacks are? No, he doesn't feel lucky. He doesn't feel lucky at all.

"Now, now, dear, there's nothing to be afraid of," she continues, perhaps seeing the tear running down Robert's left cheek. "You're going to love it with the Andersons. There's a playground three blocks from their home and

Mrs. Anderson will read you bedtime stories every night. Won't you, Mrs. Anderson?"

"Absolutely," the Anderson lady says. "Robert, we bought some brand-new books for you that look like a lot of fun. We've been waiting for you for a long time."

Waiting for him. That sounds strange. It's not like he was lost or anything. The tears come in torrents now—"gushers" Ernie calls them. All four of the adults are talking now, trying their best to make him stop crying. Robert doesn't hear any of it. Well, he does hear the Anderson lady say, "Is it OK if I offer him some candy?"

"I think that would be OK," the nun says, dabbing her eyes with a tissue.

The woman unwraps the hard candy, sticks her hand forward and says, "I've got a sweet tooth, too, Robert. Welcome to the family."

Welcome to the family. Robert looks over to the nun again to see if it is OK. Why is she crying, he wonders? It's only a piece of candy. He quickly grabs it out of the Anderson lady's hand before anybody can change their mind. His own room and candy. He can get used to this. When the short lady comes over to his side of the table and kisses his forehead, he forgets about his tears. Forgets about everything. As he runs his tongue over the candy, hard and sweet, the sugar sends an urgent message to the rest of his body that all is right with the world.

His own room and candy. Yes, he can get used to this.

From that day forward, Robert was no more than a hologram to the DeChaine family, his willowy image as faint as a patch of light on a screen. To Millie, he's that three-year-old boy she remembers running across the bridge to the park, stopping to toss a stick into the stream on one side and running to the opposite edge to watch it float away, eventually disappearing altogether.

Millie never lost that memory, but other moments were taken from her: Robert at her high school graduation, Robert at her wedding, Robert at her kids' baptisms, Robert at their birthday parties, Robert showing up in a snowstorm because he knew her pipes were frozen, Robert displaying the ring he planned to give his girlfriend on the anniversary of their first date. The bonds of siblings are unbreakable, strong enough to withstand hurricane-like gales. But they are no match for a nuclear warhead, and that's what this was. The two of them running over the bridge was real. The rest of it was light on a screen, a trick of photography that only intensifies the longing.

Robert vanished from the DeChaine family the way so many family members before him had done. But he didn't die in a home explosion or get hit by a car. There was no funeral service at which his loved ones could gaze one last time into his heart and soul and feel a connection that lives on through eternity. They didn't even get to say good-bye. It was like a movie in which someone pulled the plug. Except that the rest of the film was shipped off to points unknown, without a single clue about where to find it. Millie knew the beginning of Robert's life. What happened after that was like that stick floating down the river, hurtling toward a destiny of uncertainty and peril.

Robert's sister Millie has had a remarkable life, not just because of her longevity—she reached her 100th birthday in November 2021—but because of her innate goodness and grace. Turns out, the hand she was dealt was no match for the cards she was determined to play. But a full life isn't necessarily a complete one, and one question always nagged at her. It's the kind of question that can surface when you least expect it. It may go away for a while but never completely leaves you. Millie never knew what happened to that beautiful boy running over that bridge, never knew what happened to Robert.

Bonds between siblings are unbreakable. Until they're not.

Throughout this book I've referred to Millie by her given name, but it's not the one I've used my whole life. Millie is my mother, so to me she has always been Mom. Which, of course, means Rose is my grandmother. I saw my grandma on many occasions as a kid—visits I hated because I thought they were so boring—but I knew nothing about my mom's childhood or Rose's awful treatment by individuals who should have known better. I didn't know about Robert until my mom was well into her eighties, and even that came by accident.

Though we live several states apart, my mother and I have always been close. I don't keep many secrets from her and she's straightforward with me. At least I thought so. I was in town one day, probably drinking a cup of coffee—the pot at my mom's is always full with either Maxwell House or Folgers, depending on which one is on sale—when I casually mentioned an internet search I had done for my mother-in-law's father. Both my mom and Ginny, my wife's mom, were abandoned by their fathers when they were very young. Ginny had picked up bits and pieces about her father through the years, at one point sending a letter to an address she found. When the letter was returned unopened, she felt rejected and gave up. But as she entered her late sixties, she wanted to try again and asked for my help. She had a name, a possible location, and the name of a son. Thanks to the internet, it took me less than an hour to determine that her father, who had died two years earlier, had two surviving sons. I found their phone numbers and gave them to Ginny who, bless her heart, acted as if I'd just performed quantum physics.

She waited a day before calling, nervously practicing each word of her speech. Then she got their answering machines. On each machine, she left the same message: "I don't want to alarm you, but I have reason to believe we have the same father."

Both called back. One was a minister, the other a truck driver. Patiently they filled in some of the blanks about their father—*her* father—sharing intimate details about his life. One small detail rose above the others: he liked to write poetry. For years Ginny had done the mailings for her husband Ron's customers at the Merit Chevrolet dealership in St. Paul, reminding them to buy their next car from Ron. With each mailing, she wrote a poem.

He liked to write poetry. Of course.

When I told my mom about Ginny's quest, she said she too would like to find out more about her father. And, she said, she'd like to find her brother Robert.

"Your what?" I asked.

"Bobby. I've told you about him."

"No, Mom, you haven't. Are you telling me I have an uncle I didn't know about?"

She shrugged. "I guess so."

Just as I did with Ginny's brothers, I went to look for him—but this time even quantum physics wouldn't have been much help. I had no last name, no names of relatives, not even the name of the adoption agency where he and my mother were separated more than seven decades earlier. All I had was a photograph my mom gave me showing Robert when he was three years old. It is the photo in the front of this book, my mom flanked by her older brother Ernie on her right and her younger brother Robert on her left. Mom has no memory of the photo being taken, but it quite possibly was the last time the three of them were together, and the last time Mom and Ernie saw their brother.

My mother has no memory of her father. She knew his last name was Conradson but wasn't sure about his first name. Everybody called him "England," so she figured his name was England Conradson. Figured he was British. A clerk at the Crow Wing County Clerk's office in Brainerd uncovered his real name for me. It was Ingram. And he was Norwegian, not British. My father was a full-blooded Norwegian, and I knew my grandmother, Rose DeChaine, was French Canadian, but I always thought I had English blood, too. That's the great part about exploring your roots. Sometimes you find out who you are.

Using Census records, old newspaper clippings, and the archives of local historical societies, I discovered that Ingram Conradson moved from Minnesota to North Dakota, remarried, and lived most of his adult life in Oregon.[3] He died in 1977. I found a phone number for a son and rehearsed my speech, just as Ginny did. Except in my case, an answering machine would have been more welcoming.

"I've been doing some research on your father," I said when the son answered the phone.

"My father? My father's dead."

"Yes, I know, but I've discovered that he was my mother's father, too."

Silence.

"Are you still there?"

"Yes."

"Did you know he was married before he married your mother?"

"Yes."

"Can you tell me something about him?"

"No."

Eventually the conversation warmed, and I learned a few nuggets about my grandfather. He was a World War I veteran, a farmer, and a fisherman.

A fisherman, of course. My mother has always loved to fish.

Every family has its secrets, and unearthing them can cause unnecessary hurt. But it can also bring about understanding and what psychologists like to refer to as closure. If Robert wasn't a hologram, then who was he? I didn't want my mother going to her grave not knowing the answer to that question. And the more I learned about my grandmother's sojourn into the sordid world of eugenics, the more I wanted to find out for myself. The words of William Hodson echo: "Children of defective parents are almost certain to carry the defective gene." *Almost certain.* I knew this was pure nonsense when it came to my mother and I had my doubts about Ernie. But what about Robert? He might have been adopted at the age of three, but his biological mother was one of those "defectives" the state was so convinced were tainting the human stream. I wanted to find Robert to give my mother closure. But I also wanted to find him to prove these people wrong.

My search for Robert became an obsession, one that lasted the better part of twenty years. Each question I answered led to another question, which led to another, and so on. The effort had mostly ground to a halt, stymied by a lack of information about any bread crumb of his life history, including his name. *I didn't even know his name.* I knew his first name was once Robert, but adoptive parents often change that, too. Robert easily could have become a Joseph or a Steven or a Matthew. He looked to be about three in the photo I had of him, whereas Ernie was maybe nine or ten. My mom's growth was stunted, so it was hard to tell how old she was, but I figured the photograph was taken sometime around 1928. And since they were all together, it likely was taken at an orphanage. I knew they were all sent to one sometime in the 1920s. But which orphanage? A process of elimination took me . . . nowhere.

The cholera epidemic of the mid-1800s drove the need for the first orphanages in Minnesota, followed by the Civil War.[4] They were mostly unregulated until the 1890s, and even then, they were only loosely monitored with visits and reports made to the State Board of Charities. In 1917, roughly ten years before my mother and her two brothers were sent to the St. James Catholic Orphanage in Duluth, the Board of Control assumed full authority over the orphanages in Minnesota—one of the many reforms included in the

Children's Code, which revolutionized child protection in Minnesota. The law called for annual inspections and benchmark standards that were strictly enforced. Minnesota was considered a leader in the childcare industry for its efforts to bolster safeguards for parental rights and standards for ensuring the safe upbringing of children. As previously mentioned, much of this reputation was richly deserved. Unfortunately, there are exceptions.

By 1926, 1,304 children were housed in orphanages in Minnesota, and fewer than half of them were there because of a death in the family.[5] The biggest category was the one represented by Robert's family: both parents were living (or so it was assumed) but were not able to adequately care for their children. The Roaring Twenties were not so spectacular for those on poverty's edge, and as I searched for Robert, I knew the circumstances must have been dire to land all three children in an orphanage somewhere in Minnesota. Determining what those circumstances were turned out to be the easy part. Finding out which orphanage housed the children was decidedly more difficult.

A lot of reporting involves turning over rocks, and if I had turned over the right one sooner, I would have come across the name of the orphanage years earlier. But my mom didn't know which orphanage it was, and most of those familiar with what happened had long since passed away. Without much additional guidance, I tried to approach the task logically: discover which orphanages existed at the time and see if they kept logs of who was living there in the late 1920s. I found the list of orphanages thanks to a 1938 study done with money from the Works Progress Administration project, the same Depression-era put-people-to-work effort that produced the interviews with various members of my family in Brainerd that I mined for this book.

Even before I got the list, I knew the orphanage couldn't be in Brainerd. The Crow Wing County Poor Farm took in the poor and helpless, and there were children there, but the place housed mostly adults, like seventy-two-year-old W. F. Gilpatrick, who was said to be "feeble-minded" in the logs, or twenty-one-year-old Mrs. E. Hughswish, whose husband was in jail. The few children living there were with their mothers, whose plight in life had left them homeless or financially unsteady. And anyway, that particular poorhouse—and there were many in Minnesota—closed around 1912, years before my uncle, my mom, and their brother would have landed there.[6]

The most complete study of orphanages from that period was authored by Sister Claire Lynch, a professor of history and academic dean of the College of St. Benedict in St. Joseph, Minnesota, the nation's only Benedictine college for women. Sister Claire, who died in 1995, was a legendary figure at St. Benedict and is credited with spurring admission of the school's first black students. She did so much for the school that a building is named after her. But for my purposes, she performed another service: compiling information on each and every orphanage operating during the time when my mother and her two brothers landed in one of the orphanages on that list. The question was, which one?

The closest orphanage to Brainerd at the time was the St. Cloud Children's Home, which had relocated from Little Falls and was run by the Franciscan Sisters of the Immaculate Conception and later by the Catholic Charities of St. Cloud. Catholic Charities are known for their record keeping, and the material I received from the St. Cloud chapter indicated a willingness to work with families seeking information about adoptions. They have a form you can fill out requesting "postadoption services." I began to get excited.

I knew from my research that the orphanage had a first-rate reputation. Located on the banks of the Mississippi just south of St. Cloud, the place is considered cutting-edge, and it advertises throughout the United States. I still have the notarized form that I had my mother fill out requesting information. Here is what she wrote:

> I was in an orphanage with my brother Robert and I'm trying to locate him. Robert Conradson, DOB unknown. My date of birth is 11/19/21. He is about two years younger.

Genealogical research can get pricey, so I made the plunge with fingers crossed. Since the arm of the St. Cloud diocese that keeps genealogical information is entirely self-supporting, fees are assessed every step of the way. The organization charged $25 as a file-opening fee, and the price went up from there. Non-identifying birth family history documents were $100. The charge for a full search was based on a sliding scale depending on income, maxing out at $550. Charges of $65 an hour were assessed for information not contained in the file. It began to dawn on me that I better guess right or risk draining my entire bank account.

I sent in my $25 to get the process started and hoped for the best. It's been my experience that good causes are often rewarded, and this was a good cause. My mother had her brother snatched away from her as if she didn't matter. She deserved to find him or at least find out what happened to him. But no notarized form to the Catholic Charities of St. Cloud would be able to do that. The orphanage might have been cutting-edge in the day, but neither my mom, Ernie, nor Robert was ever there.

I kept looking. I knew Rose had moved to Minneapolis sometime during the 1930s, so it made sense that the orphanage would be in the Twin Cities. It also made sense that it would be Catholic, the religion practiced by many of her family members, although I requested information from Lutheran Social Services as well. In her research, Sister Claire discovered that ten Minnesota orphanages were founded by Lutherans and nine by Catholics.

That encompassed most of the orphanages that existed in the state from the late 1800s through the 1930s. My mom eventually joined the Lutheran Church, but that came after she married my father. Given the history of faith in her family—excluding Rose, of course—the orphanage she was in was almost certain to have been run by the Catholic Church. And if it wasn't in St. Cloud, I became convinced, it had to be in the Twin Cities, the state's dominant metropolitan area. That's where Rose lived beginning in the 1930s and where both my mom and her brother Ernie lived after Rose was released from the Faribault institution. In my letter to the Catholic Charities of St. Paul and Minneapolis, I emphasized the injustice of my mom's situation:

Dear Sir or Madam:

I am searching for information on my mother and her brother, both of whom lived in an orphanage in St. Paul during the 1920s. My mother, Mildred Conradson, was placed in the orphanage for a short time, probably around 1923–1924. My uncle, Ernest Jerred, was there for a longer period, perhaps as late as 1930. A third sibling, named Robert, was placed there in the mid-to-late 1920s. I do not know his last name, but it was most likely Conradson at the time he was placed in the orphanage.

At the time I wrote this letter—December 2003—I was off a little on my dates. The three children were placed in the orphanage in Duluth on the same date: March 3, 1928.[7] Of course, they weren't placed in the orphanage in St. Paul, either. That was a guess and, as it turned out, I guessed wrong. But I was accurate on a couple of other things. Robert's name when he went to the orphanage was Conradson. And although I didn't know it at the time, a search on Ernie's last name during the 1920s—Jerred—would lead to my eureka moment when random stars miraculously aligned. But that moment was impossible to imagine after the response to my letter to the Catholic Charities of St. Paul and Minneapolis, which included this plea: "My mom is now eighty-two years old and is very interested in finding out this essential information about her childhood."

The licensed social worker who responded, Judy Dow Sikorra, couldn't have been nicer. But you can't produce records that don't exist, and the hunch that the three children were sent to an orphanage near where their mother lived in the 1930s did not bear fruit.

I began contacting any group I could think of, including the International Soundex Reunion Registry, which specializes in reuniting families displaced by adoption, divorce, and other means of separation. The nonprofit uses "adoption angels" to help novices navigate the system as they search for a loved one.

"Since 1975, many thousands had their dreams come true," the group's literature boasts.[8]

I have no doubt many dreams have come true this way. As adoption records become unsealed in state after state, news outlets have recorded many of these reunions, which can bring joy and also heartbreak. But in my case, it brought nothing at all. If Robert was ever placed in an adoption registry, the adoption angels at Soundex couldn't find any record of it. Years later, after I discovered which orphanage the three children were taken to, I pulled out Sister Claire's research on orphanages in Minnesota. Listed on page eight of her report on file at the Minnesota History Center in St. Paul is the St. James Catholic Orphanage at Woodland Hills in Duluth. I guess my true adoption angel was trying to point me in the right direction all along.

My breakthrough moment came courtesy of Ancestry.com, the world's largest for-profit genealogy company. Like much genealogy research, it isn't cheap. But it puts at your fingertips an astounding amount of information that you can access twenty-four hours a day. Yes, the searches can be maddening, and its web crawlers at times seem not to know how to filter out nonresponsive information. But if it wasn't for Ancestry.com, I wouldn't have found the orphanage where my mom and her two brothers were sent. And, of course, my search for Robert would have been a complete failure.

My wife Lynda typically goes to bed before I do, and when I'm not reading or watching television, I search for stuff online. Sometimes it's useless sports trivia, like how many points per game NBA star Kevin Durant tallied in his one year of college at the University of Texas (answer: 25.8). But on this night, I went on Ancestry.com and trolled around for information about my uncles. The 1930 Census, accessible through Ancestry and other online services, has provided a treasure trove of information about my family, including the whereabouts of my vagabond grandmother Rose, who was an "inmate" in the clubhouse on Harmon Place in Minneapolis when the 1930 Census was taken. It was an apt description—she did not have freedom to come and go—but for a long time I thought that was false labeling on the part of the census taker.

This time I searched not for my grandmother but for Ernie, and I used a name I don't think I had tried before: Jerred. I knew Ernie's father was Leo Jerred, and at some point, I must have done searches using that full name. But I don't think I ever tried running the name through the archives of the Census Bureau, and when I did, my heart leapt. Because when the 1930 Census was taken, on April 3, 1930, ten-year-old Ernie was living in the St. James Catholic Orphanage in Duluth.[9] There was little other information provided, other than that ominous word "inmate" describing his relationship to the head of the household. The information provided was small but its importance couldn't be measured. Because if Ernie was housed at the St. James, that almost certainly meant my mother and her brother Robert were, too.

In gathering research on the St. James, I quickly discovered that it ceased being an orphanage in 1971, when it was converted into a residential treatment center for at-risk youth under the name Woodland Hills. Although just up the road from St. John's Catholic School, it was no longer affiliated with the Catholic Diocese of Duluth and had an independent board that was represented by the best the community has to offer: a retired judge, a retired neurosurgeon, various distinguished corporate citizens, and representatives of community-based organizations such as the National Association for the Advancement of Colored People, otherwise known as the NAACP. The center's motto—"We're in this together"—encompassed its general philosophy that all children can be rescued if provided the right support and guidance. How's that for irony? In Rose's day, there was a completely opposite belief about the potential of children, particularly if they had a parent identified as feebleminded.

Years later I would spend a full day at the Woodland Hills treatment center, which closed in July 2021. Although I am by no means an expert, I caught a distinct vibe of camaraderie and purpose among the residents, who arrived there from throughout the state, including the violent streets of North Minneapolis. Unfortunately, kids from troubled backgrounds don't always catch a break, even now. The facility, which underwent another name change since my visit—becoming the Hills Youth and Family Services—was sued in 2018 on allegations of sexual abuse involving boys in its care. The suit was eventually settled, though the terms were not disclosed.

Upon its closing, which put at risk the type of programming that children like Rose never received, Leslie Chaplin, the Hills' chief operating officer, told the *Duluth News Tribune*: "This is an unfortunate outcome that no one wanted, and a devastating blow to children's mental health services in Minnesota."[10]

Eugenics might be in our rear window, but those with mental deficiencies still struggle to get the treatment they need.

When I first heard about Woodland Hills—or, rather, the precursor to Woodland Hills—I went to the website and saw a photograph of the St. James taken, it looked like, around the time it was rescued from the "awfullest fire horror in state's history." That got me thinking: does the treatment center operate out of the same building as the orphanage where my mom lived for a short time in 1928?

When I called Woodland Hills, I was told yes—and no. Very little of the old building is recognizable. Much of the facility had been added onto, adapted, and remodeled. But some of the vestiges were still there, along with the signature woods that gave it its name. I knew I had to go, but would my mom want to walk those same halls again? After all, we're not talking about pleasant memories. The orphanage may have been Judge Kinder's only option for the children who were wards of his court, but for my mom it led to a lifetime separation from her younger brother. Still, I had to ask. I spent years trying to find the orphanage, and just to walk those grounds with my mom would provide a sense of accomplishment, maybe even closure.

As it turned out, it provided much more.

Mom didn't need much convincing. After I told her about the St. James and asked if she wanted to see it, she said simply: "OK." The officials at Woodland were happy to accommodate us but warned against high expectations. "There isn't too much that's the same from when your mother was here," one told me.

We scheduled the visit for July 17, 2015, thirteen years after my mom first asked me to help her find her brother. To be honest, I didn't expect much. The little information I had about the place was that all three children were sent there. And how could I even be sure of that? Maybe Ernie had been transferred before the 1930 Census was taken, and the other two children were placed in some other orphanage. It could easily have been a wasted exercise, and after all this time I knew my mom didn't need that. But we went anyway and made arrangements to meet my brother Mike and his wife Margaret at the former orphanage. As we circled the place looking for a parking spot, I asked Mom if she recognized anything. "No," she said, adding, "That was a long time ago."

Every researcher needs a Sister Claire, whether a sympathetic bureaucrat or just someone wired to help. Our angel at the Woodland was Breanna Schueller, a development associate who was intrigued by my mom's story. Instead of just taking us on a tour of the facility and its grounds, as I had asked, Schueller went into the basement of the building and found something totally unexpected: the records of Ernie, Robert, and my mom's stay at the St. James. When she greeted us, Schueller asked what would become music to my ears: "How much time do you have?"[11]

The church had kept a "child history record" on each resident who crossed through the front doors. Schueller was careful not to reveal anybody else's records but gave us open access to the pages devoted to Ernie, Robert, and my mom. Each was a form that in today's world would be kept on a computer spreadsheet: child's name, date admitted, place of birth, religion, mother and father, and so on. It was through these records that I discovered that each child had been admitted on the same day, who admitted them, and why. Much of the information I knew, such as the fathers of my mom and Ernie and the hospital my mom was sent to not long after she was admitted because of what the records said was a leg deformity. But even what I thought I knew was slightly off. I had assumed all three were there in the mid-1920s, not at the tail end of the decade. Under name of employer for Rose was listed "Feeble-minded Ins" in Faribault. It put some clarity to that word "inmate" used to describe my grandmother in the 1930 Census and led me to another avenue that would fill in pieces to the puzzle. Whoever wrote the words "Feeble-minded Ins" on the child history record wasn't being insensitive. That was the name of the place.

As Mike, Margaret, my wife Lynda, and I pored through the record books, eureka grabbed us by the throat. Because in Robert's record under "name of person receiving child" was listed: Mr. and Mrs. Ray Anderson, 407 Shackleton Street, Eveleth, Minnesota.[12]

Sure, these could have been social workers who transported Robert to Eveleth, but *married* social workers? Not likely. Based on these records, there was a 95 percent certainty, maybe more, that Mr. and Mrs. Ray Anderson were Robert's adoptive parents. Thanks to Breanna Schueller, who became curious after hearing my mom's story, we now had the names of the couple who adopted Robert and, perhaps, a clue as to what happened to him after he left the orphanage. The fact that the last name was Anderson, which is as common in Minnesota as the mosquito, was only a slight letdown. Robert was adopted by a family in Eveleth. After thirteen years of searching, my quest to find him took a giant leap forward.

Eveleth, like so many of the towns throughout the Iron Range of Minnesota, owes its existence to mining. The original town site was even moved to make way for another mine. And like all mining towns, one of its earliest commercial ventures was a tavern. But Eveleth became more than just an ore town, though the open-pit mines nearby were the sole reason for its existence. It was natural to assume, as we all did, that whoever this Ray Anderson was, he was a miner who raised Robert in the backdrop of the nation's most abundant provider of iron ore, the key ingredient needed to manufacture steel. After the enormity of our find at Woodland Hills began to settle in, Lynda put her arm around my mom and said, "This is so cool. Robert was a miner on the Iron Range."

But like so many of our assumptions throughout this process, this one turned out to be faulty. If Robert ever was a miner, there is no record of it that I could find. And when I did get a hit, as I did many times searching property records and the like for a Ray or Robert Anderson, there were few clues indicating that I had the right one. I finally found the first name of "Mrs. Ray Anderson," but this too involved roadblocks. There were so many spellings of her name that the path led mostly to dead ends. In Minnesota, Ray Anderson couldn't be more generic.

Then, slowly, doors started to crack open.

I tracked the property for Ray Anderson in Eveleth but didn't find much. I later discovered why: the house, which is no longer standing, was owned by Ray's wife's father, who was a miner. Ray and his wife Santa (her family was Italian) lived with Santa's parents for a time after they were married in 1925, and likely even for a short time after returning from the orphanage with their new child. They shuttled back and forth between Illinois and Minnesota before spending the rest of their years in Chicago, where Ray worked for the Wrigley Chewing Gum Company. What impact Robert's difficult early childhood had on him is not known, but there are indications he struggled in life and, in the end, suffered a painful death. We never know what our influences are, but Rose didn't make it easy for any of her children. If Robert carried that with him when he became an Anderson, it was a gaping wound that most assuredly didn't disappear with a name or address change. When I finally found his death certificate, it was so depressing that I hesitated even telling my mother. By this time Rose was well into her grave, and the reason given by the medical examiner was "chronic alcoholism."[13] I suppose it's no surprise that Robert—the person my mother and I had been searching for, the brother she spent a lifetime wondering about—died the same way Rose did, his body unable to tolerate even one more minute of self-abuse.

Robert's death certificate was relatively easy to find. The orphanage records gave his date of birth as April 20, 1925. Like other internet genealogy services, Ancestry.com has death indexes from each state that are searchable with a date of birth. The first name that popped up when I did my search for Robert—typing in his name, date of birth, and Minnesota as a place where he lived—was "Robert C. Anderson, DOB April 20, 1925, DOD September 12, 1993." His mother's maiden name was listed as Donsfrio, one of the many ways her first and last name were spelled in various records I've come across in my searches. I couldn't be positive, but I was pretty sure this was my uncle. Raymond's father, and thus Robert's grandfather, was named Carl, so the middle initial made sense. They kept Robert's first name but gave him his grandfather's name for a middle name and Anderson for a last name. They were Swedish and probably thought Robert was Norwegian, with a last name like Conradson. Whether they were ever told the truth—that his mother was French Canadian and his father was of unknown origin—is unlikely. But since this was Minnesota, the father could well have been Swedish, too. His last name might even have been Anderson.

I ordered the death certificate from the Minnesota Department of Health, which confirmed the unmistakable: my mom's brother—the guy I had been searching with the faint hope that he might still be alive—died in 1993.[14] It gave his birthplace as Eveleth, which of course wasn't accurate but was where his life after the orphanage—and with the Andersons—began.

Other clues in the death certificate said something about who he was. He worked for a painting contractor, was divorced, and was a veteran. The cause of death was multiple organ failure, but spontaneous esophageal rupture— or Boerhaave syndrome—was listed as a contributing factor. Boerhaave syndrome results from a tear of the lower esophagus and often occurs because of violent vomiting due to excess eating or drinking. I was pretty sure which one of those two indulgences it was. Robert may not have remembered his biological mother, but he carried her curse to his grave.

In addition to his parents' names listed on his death certificate, another name caught my eye: Kathryn A. Esaw. She was listed as the "informant," and since she obviously knew a lot about him—his date of birth, parents' names, and so on—I wondered who she was. Was she a daughter? A friend? Maybe she could tell me more about him. Once again, I got excited. Robert was gone, but someone who knew him—someone obviously close to him— might be able to fill in more pieces to the puzzle. I couldn't find a current listing for her, but I discovered that the last address where Robert was living when he died—588 Van Buren Avenue in St. Paul—was owned by Kathryn Esaw, or at least it used to be. Then, as I dug deeper, I found something that made my heart sink: her obituary. Kathryn Esaw outlived Robert by just five years.[15]

As anyone who does this sort of work knows, nothing goes in a straight line. The dead sometimes leave bread crumbs to follow, and sometimes they don't. What should be easy is often frustratingly difficult. Then something happens to crack open a window, if only a little. The death certificate said Robert was buried in Riverview Cemetery in St. Paul, one of those small, tucked-back-into-the-neighborhood cemeteries that you'd never find if you didn't know it was there. I called the caretaker to make sure Robert was indeed buried there. If nothing else, I thought I could take my mom to see her brother's gravesite.

"He's here all right," the caretaker told me, and then gave me the identifying plot number.

"Just out of curiosity," I said. "Do you also have a Kathryn Esaw?"

"Sure do," he said. "She's right next to him."[16]

Now that was interesting. Kathryn Esaw had to be more than just a casual friend. Maybe even a lover. I went back to her obituary. Throughout the course of my research, I have searched hundreds of obituaries. They can be an incredible font of information on birth dates, marriages, work histories, and family members. Some are more informative than others, but sometimes even small details lead to something much more substantial. In the case of Kathryn Esaw, her obituary led me to the one person I needed: her son Gary.

Gary Peppard, as it turned out, lives just a few blocks from my mother-in-law. He was guarded—talking to strangers about family members doesn't come naturally for most people—and I was tongue-tied myself. After all, Gary was the first person I had come across who actually knew Robert as an adult.

He called him Bob. Gary said he thinks his mother met him at an adult day center in St. Paul where she volunteered. Perhaps she was his adoption angel. Whatever they were, they lived together at the house on Van Buren for several years. After his initial reluctance, Gary talked about Robert's demons.

"You never like to say anything bad about someone," Gary said in true Minnesota-nice fashion. "He had his issues. He had alcoholic issues. He was in and out of rehab. In and out of trouble. I don't think he went to jail or anything.

"He went from job to job," Gary continued. "I think painting was his biggest thing. He painted houses or painted rooms or something like that."[17]

Gary didn't know his mother was buried next to Robert. He had visited her grave many times but never noticed the name on the modest stone beside hers.

"My mom was a real caring person, but she had her needs as any single woman would have," Gary said almost apologetically.

I asked him to describe Robert's physical appearance. All I had was the photo of Robert taken when he was three. Gary said he didn't think he had a photograph but said Robert was of slight build with thinning hair, almost bald. He was maybe five foot eleven or six feet tall—my height—but it was hard to tell, Gary said, because he was hunched over a lot.

"What do you mean?" I asked.

"I just think it was the wear and tear on his body."

The alcoholism, Gary said, was a constant. "He was trying to stay straight but would fall off the wagon. My mom would find bottles of booze all over the house." He'd disappear and she wouldn't hear from him for days. Then he would reappear. "He always came back."

"He was battling alcohol all the time," Gary said. "He was trying to get help, but it wouldn't work for him."

A few years after his mom lost her companion, Gary put her into an assisted living facility in St. Paul, the kind of place that helps people who can no longer live independently. My mom and my mother-in-law are both in similar facilities, and my wife and I continually marvel at the full life they've provided our parents. But from what I know of Robert, I don't think assisted living, with its daily check-ins, would have worked for him. Those powerful demons would have surfaced again and again.

Gary did see a tender side to Robert. "He was nice and friendly, always helped my mom," he said. "I thought this was a good thing. He wasn't ambitious, but he was good to my mom."

Given all that Robert had been through, that wasn't a bad epitaph—much better than "chronic alcoholic."

My quest to find Robert was always a pipe dream of sorts. The odds of finding him at all were astronomical, much less finding him alive. By the time I started looking, Robert would have been around eighty years old, well past the life expectancy for men. Add to that a pattern of hard living, and you get what you get. I should have been satisfied with getting this far, but now that I knew something about him—could visualize the balding, slightly stooped gauntness of the man in my head—I wanted to know more. Everybody has a story. What was his? I knew the only source for those answers lay within the family histories of the two people who drove the same road I did along a spectacular vista in Duluth looking for something that would give their life more meaning. Rose may have brought Robert into the world, but it was in the Zenith City of the Unsalted Seas where Mr. and Mrs. Raymond Anderson gave him his new beginning.

I assumed none of the immediate family was alive (not true, as I would later discover), but I was desperate to find something, anything, that would help me piece together the outlines of Robert's life. Initially I couldn't find Ray Anderson and his family in the 1930 Census, which would have told me where they had moved after leaving Eveleth. Then I hit on the record in a place I hadn't bothered to check: the 1930 Census for Illinois. It had never occurred to me that the family might have moved to Chicago. The haystack was big enough searching just Minnesota records for a Ray Anderson. And even the name "Ray" was a bit of a guess. The records at Woodland Hills were handwritten, and though most of it was legible, the "a" in Ray could easily have been an "o," making him Roy Anderson. I discovered there are quite a few of those in Minnesota as well.

Fortunately, the death certificate was typed and under the father's name on the form, someone had typed Raymond Anderson. The mother's name was listed as Sana Gloria Donsfrio. The Donsfrio matched the death index from Ancestry.com, but this first name "Sana" was a mystery to me. As it turns out, her real name was *Santa*, and she often used Gloria, which is the name listed on her marriage certificate.[18] Donsfrio was a variation of the name Donfris, which is what the family used after emigrating from Italy. Robert's adoptive parents were Swedish and Italian, part of the melting pot that was a big part of Minnesota's heritage.

The 1930 Illinois Census was an eye-opener. Raymond, Santa, and Robert—age four-and-a-half and listed as the "adopted son" on the form—were living in a rented house for $25 a month at 1617 Roosevelt Road in Chicago. Seven people were living in the home, including two of Raymond's brothers: Anard, who was twenty-three at the time, and Harry, who was twenty-one. Raymond was twenty-seven and Santa was listed as twenty-five. She was born in Italy, according to the document, came to the United States at the age of one in 1906, and spoke Italian during her early years in the United States.

I later found the alien registration papers for Santa and her father, James Donfris, which are kept on file at the Iron Range Research Center in

Chisholm, Minnesota. The papers for Santa and her father are both dated January 16, 1918, when Santa was fourteen years old. The form says James arrived in the United States in May 1904—the same month and year that Santa was born—and that she came in 1909.[19] I've seen other records, though, that indicate that she came over when she was an infant. Immigrants don't pack interpreters along with their luggage when they cross the Atlantic, so misinformation is an occupational hazard in this line of inquiry.

Both forms—for Santa and for her father—say they departed by ship from Naples and had lived in the small village of Montefalcone in the province of Benevento before immigrating to the United States. I've looked up photographs of Montefalcone, and its beauty makes you wonder why they wanted to leave it behind. But nobody at the turn of the century went to Eveleth, Minnesota, for the scenery. They were there for the jobs, and during mining's heyday, there were plenty of them.

Santa was the third of six children of James and Antonia Donfris, who followed that invisible pipeline of Europeans to the Iron Range of Minnesota. James got work at the Oliver Mining Company in Eveleth as a "blaster." Santa and her husband, Raymond, lived with Santa's parents for a time before moving to Chicago. On the immigration form, James answered "no" to a question asking whether he spoke or wrote English, but Santa answered the opposite. She also said she was attending school, which is something Robert's biological mother never did, or certainly didn't do at the age of fourteen.

The sixth and seventh members of the house on Roosevelt Road were Santa's nineteen-year-old brother Albert and his eighteen-year-old sister Helen. The last names for both were listed as "Dunfris" on the census form, yet another of the many spellings of the immigrant family. Both were born in Minnesota and had not attended school in the last year, according to the records. Raymond's job was listed as a "brander" in a meatpacking plant. In fact, the three brothers all worked in the meatpacking industry. Anard was a meat hanger and Harry a laborer. Santa didn't work—Robert was four-and-a-half at the time—but Helen was a packer in a bakery, and Albert worked as a bank janitor.

Their neighbors, too, were immigrants, and they came from all over the world: Yugoslavia, Lithuania, Sweden, Italy, Mexico. Many neighborhoods in Chicago today have a similar makeup. The Andersons traded one melting pot for another, and the industry they chose—the famed Chicago slaughterhouses—was an international magnet for the working class.

Today, Chicago barely resembles the city in 1930, particularly the one square mile on the south side that was home to the Union Stock Yards. Tens of thousands of animal pens housed cattle, hogs, sheep, and calves—until they were paraded along viaducts to the kill floors and packinghouses in what came to be known as Packingtown. During World War I, 50,000 people worked in the stockyards, including women and children who earned mere pennies doing some of the more unpleasant tasks in an environment that frequently saw workers standing in rivers of blood from the butchered livestock and breathing the pungent air of mass animal slaughter.[20] The odor wafted over the entire city and nearby neighborhoods that to this day are called Back of the Yards. And if the stench was nose-pinching outdoors, think about the workers who toiled in dark rooms with little ventilation and few sanitary regulations. It was dirty, difficult, dangerous work, but above all, it was *work* and people flocked to Chicago from Europe and throughout North America, including from the house in Eveleth where Robert was taken after leaving the orphanage in Duluth.

From their rented home on Roosevelt Road, Raymond and his two brothers—Anard and Harry—would have taken a streetcar down maybe two miles to the front entrance on Exchange Avenue, where the stone gate is preserved in postcards as a monument to historical relevance. In addition to a workplace for thousands, the stockyards were a tourist attraction, and thousands of people paraded through each year to watch the spectacle of living things turned into raw meat. Numerous authors, including Rudyard Kipling, described the sea of cattle pens and chutes and hanging carcasses in unflattering terms, but Sarah Bernhardt may have said it the most vividly, writing of the "almost human cries of the pigs" as they were brought to slaughter.[21]

The stockyards were already in an accelerated state of decline when Raymond and his brothers worked there. There were numerous reasons for the downturn, but one of the big ones had to do with the growth of another industry—trucking—that allowed producers to deal with more local markets. Shipments to Chicago declined, as did the size of the labor force. But another factor also did in the stockyards, and it is something for which Chicago is forever known: fire. Virtually everything in the yards was constructed with wood: the buildings, the pens, the viaducts, even the floors. Fire was a frequent occurrence in the stockyards, but an inferno in May 1934 wiped out nearly the entire cattle operation, about a dozen structures, and fifty nearby houses.[22] Only one person died in the fire, but some 150 firefighters were injured. One of the destroyed buildings was a gambling house and bar owned by the son of Mrs. O'Leary—owner of the famous cow—proving again that some families carry around fate in their pockets.

The fire wasn't the end of the stockyards—much of it was rebuilt, this time using concrete on the bridges and runways—but Raymond wasn't around to see it. Records show he was back in Eveleth by 1935, living again with Santa's parents. Whether it was the fire, the Great Depression—companies like Swift and Armour either laid people off or cut their wages dramatically—or that he just grew tired of the daily blood and guts, Raymond packed up his family and left Chicago. He would eventually return to the city but leaving the slaughterhouse when he did turned out to be a wise career move. By the late 1950s, the Chicago stockyards had become a relic of the past.

Raymond didn't stay long in northern Minnesota. The 1938 Minneapolis City Directory shows he and Santa were living at 4528 41st Avenue South in the state's biggest city. That raises a tantalizing prospect: the neighborhood was not far from where my mother was living at the time. In other words, her brother—who was just thirteen then—was living just a few miles from the sister he knew for only a short time before they were separated forever.

Raymond's occupation was listed as a shipper, but this would be a fleeting thing, too. The 1941 city directory—the last listing I could find for him— shows him working in the garment industry. Depression-era jobs were hard to find, and Raymond apparently took what he could get.

Before we leave the 1930s, I should tell you about one other big development that came into Robert's life: He got a sister.[23] I learned about her from the 1940 Census. Ray and Santa were both thirty-six years old in 1940, according to the Census (apparently Santa had gained a few years on her husband since the 1930 Census), and Robert was listed as fourteen. The fourth member of the family—Patricia—was eight. She was adopted, too, as was another sister, Sheila, who was born in 1946 but came into the family at the age of three in 1949. In other words, Robert had two sisters from his adoptive family and a brother and sister from his biological family. I can't help but think that some of the tumult that occurred in the family—with Robert and maybe even with Ernie—could have been avoided, or at least lessened, if they could have been reunited somewhere along the way. But maybe that's just wishful thinking.

Public records are a researcher's crack cocaine, but they can also lead you astray. Raymond's wife, listed as Gloria S. Anderson in the 1938 Minneapolis City Directory, is written as Alovia Anderson in the 1940 Census. Before I knew her real name, I spent hours searching on the name "Alovia." I'm not sure why she used Gloria on some records and Santa on others, but when I finally tracked down Sheila Fletcher—Robert's adoptive sister—she told me an amusing anecdote. Raymond's actual name was Rudolph, but somehow it got changed on his birth certificate to Randolph.

"I don't know how he became Ray," Sheila said.[24] If not for that name change, however, Sheila and Robert's parents would have been Santa and Rudolph. The fact that Rose—Robert's mother—was born on Christmas Eve (and her mother on Christmas Day) is proof that the stuff we believe as kids may be more real than we think.

James and Antonia Donfris, Santa's parents, arrived in the United States just as Rose's ancestors had—with little in their pockets but with a burning resolve to carve out a better life than what they had. That they picked that part of the country was no accident: Eveleth and the nearby towns of Hibbing, Virginia, and Chisholm were the base of a steel empire that had attracted the likes of John D. Rockefeller, Andrew Carnegie, and the industrialist whose company would employ James for thirty-five years: Henry Oliver.

Oliver was like a lot of the Iron Range entrepreneurs: opportunistic, visionary, and adept at rounding up other people's money. He grew up with Carnegie in Pittsburgh, but they weren't close, and Carnegie once referred to his boyhood friend as a poor manager, offering faint praise with the words "good fellow that he is."[25] But Carnegie agreed to bankroll Oliver's venture out of fear that Rockefeller would step away with all the profits. It would prove to be a mutually beneficial arrangement. The Oliver Iron Mining Co. became the leading supplier of iron ore from the Mesabi Range in Minnesota, and the company would eventually become a subsidiary of the U.S. Steel Corporation.

In Italy, James's name was Vicenzo and various members of the family are listed as D'Onfrio, Sondrio, or Donfris. Immigration clerks tended to go with the simplest translation, or maybe James simply wanted to have a name that blended better in the American melting pot. He needn't have worried. Most workers in the Iron Range came from European countries.

A study of the employees of the Oliver Mining Company in 1907—when James was clearly working there—shows 84.4 percent of the 12,018 employees were foreign-born, and nearly half of them had been in the United States for less than two years. Some were recruited through the *padrone* system, essentially a labor agent who contracted with companies for groups of employees, usually from Slavic countries. This system proved useful when huge numbers of workers were needed, such as during strikes.

In Minnesota, the family added two more members: Albert, who was born in 1912, and Helen, who was born a year later. Like so many of the Iron Range families, the flock would scatter in search of something else, as the boom-and-bust of the region became one of the state's ongoing soap operas. A few stayed behind, including Santa's older brother John, who lived much of his life in Duluth, where he worked until 1970 at the Diamond Tool and Horseshoe Company. When he died in 1983, his obituary mentioned that he was a member of the St. James Catholic Church in Duluth, which isn't far from the former orphanage where my mother and her two brothers stayed and where Ray and Santa Anderson picked up John's nephew Robert in 1928. If only he knew the secrets the ghosts inside that orphanage concealed.

Santa was sixteen in 1920, living on a street called North Side Park in Eveleth, and attending school. The street may have been mislabeled in the census because the street number—407—was the same as the number on the address where Ray and Santa lived after adopting Robert. That suggests the couple was living with Santa's parents after they were married in 1925. That wasn't unusual for early-twentieth-century immigrants whose families tended to be large and whose breadwinners typically toiled for meager wages.

Raymond and Santa were married on January 10, 1925, in Duluth.[26] I wondered what had happened to cause them to adopt Robert three years later, and I also wondered if their second child, Patricia, was adopted. Sheila, the third child, solved that mystery for me.

"We were all adopted," she said. "Dad couldn't have children." Sheila died in 2017, a victim of chronic obstructive pulmonary disease, a serious lung ailment that makes breathing difficult. When I talked to her, about a year before her death, she said she lacked the strength to rummage around in old boxes looking for photographs or carry out long conversations. But in a few words, she described her parents for me: "My dad was tall with blue eyes and my mom was a short Italian lady."[27]

The tall guy and the short Italian lady—along with their adopted children, Robert and Patricia—returned to Chicago sometime in the early 1940s. America was at war, and there was scarcely a family that wasn't affected. The Andersons were no exception. Raymond was never in the service—he was too young for the first war and too old for the second, he liked to tell folks—but I knew from Robert's death record that he had served. On the form under "military veteran," Kathryn Esaw had answered yes. That meant Robert was in the service but when? And which branch? Answering those questions should have been easy. Unfortunately, fate would intervene. Remember that explosion and fire that killed Rose's sister Lottie and her baby in 1915? Well, fifty-eight years later, another fire would touch the DeChaine family. Only this time it was a part of Robert's past that was destroyed.

Since 1956, the National Personnel Records Center in Overland, Missouri, has housed the nation's military archive, a centralized stockpile of individual service records that was seen at the time as a model for innovation and efficiency. But on July 12, 1973, that model took a serious hit. A mysterious fire broke out on the building's sixth floor and destroyed anywhere from sixteen to eighteen million records, about a third of the entire archive. Gone were about 75 percent of the records for certain air force personnel—those individuals discharged between September 25, 1947, and January 1, 1964, with last names that landed alphabetically after Hubbard—and 80 percent of all army personnel discharged between November 1, 1912, and January 1, 1960. No cause was ever determined for the fire—cigarette butts found in trash cans led to speculation about a staff member smoking—but whatever caused it, the loss was and is heartbreaking. No duplicate or backup records exist.[28]

Heroic efforts were made to salvage the fire- and water-damaged records, and in the end 6.5 million records were reconstructed and preserved. But the National Archives website probably says it best: "In terms of loss to the cultural heritage of our nation, the 1973 NPRC Fire was an unparalleled disaster."

I knew nothing about the fire when I made my first request to the NPRC for Robert's service records. On the form under "branch of service" I wrote, "Army, we believe." It's bad enough that Robert had the same name as five zillion other people in the country, but I chose a branch of service whose records had been all but obliterated.

I made the request under my mom's name hoping a sympathetic bureaucrat would be taken in by her story of wanting to find her long-lost brother. Anyone can request records from the NPRC, but I suspect that those with a close family tie get preferential treatment. At least I hoped so. I filled out the form, had my mom sign it, and attached this note:

> When I was a little girl, I was in an orphanage in Duluth, Minnesota, with my brother Robert. He was adopted by a couple in Eveleth, Minnesota, and I never saw him again. I am now ninety-four years old and want to know what happened to him.

As anyone who has ever made a service record request knows, it can take months. After my initial request, I received an email that said I would receive an official response by April 4, 2016, roughly six months after my mom's letter. It was a long time to wait, but at least I was in the system and overdue for some luck to come my way. This is probably a terrible analogy, but this type of research is like raising a child. At times, it can drive you crazy, but at the precise moment when you are about to tear your hair out, something happens that makes it all worthwhile. Well, I needed that moment, and I needed it now.

It didn't happen on April 4. I gave it a few more weeks and then called the center in Missouri and inquired about my request. It's a good thing I did, because a customer service representative told me the correspondence had been misplaced. So much for finding a sympathetic bureaucrat. She was nice, though, and said she would put the request on a fast track. She also gave me a piece of advice: "Don't limit yourself to the army."

On May 11, I got a form letter: "Thank you for contacting the National Personnel Records Center. The record needed to answer your inquiry is not in our files."[29] The letter went on to describe the fire and the extensive damage done to service records for the time period I was requesting. "We must have a service/serial number," the letter stated.

How was I supposed to get a service number? I had Robert's Social Security number from his death certificate, but none of the services during World War II used Social Security numbers as identifiers, instead assigning separate service numbers to each individual. *Great.* I was already searching for a needle in a haystack. Now the haystack got decidedly bigger. I logged on to Ancestry.com and this time searched the site's archive of military records. Under the heading "Army enlistment records 1938 to 1946," there were plenty of Robert Andersons, including those with ties to Minnesota, but none of them seemed to match his circumstances. A Department of Veterans Affairs database of fourteen million veterans and VA beneficiaries similarly came up empty. Then I remembered what the customer service rep at the NPRC told me: "Don't limit yourself to the army." I tried a file labeled "U.S. World War II Navy muster files, 1938–1946," hoping to find something that would give me more ammunition in my search for Robert's service record. I soon discovered that the muster files—quarterly lists of enlisted navy personnel attached to ships—contained individual service numbers. That was the very thing I needed, but there didn't seem to be any pattern. And even when I hit on a Robert Carl Anderson, there was no way of determining whether it was *my* Robert Carl Anderson. Next to a name on some of them was a service number, rank, and date of enlistment. I knew none of those things about my uncle.

I began searching ships for any records that had shipmates whose original enlistment was Minnesota. If all Minnesotans had the same first two numbers, for example, I could isolate those and request the service records from the NPRC. It was a long shot, for sure, but what choice did I have?

The USS *Pennsylvania* included hometowns on its muster records, and I found a service number for a sailor from Chicago: 299 89 58. There was also one from Minneapolis: 318 51 97. All I had to do now was to find other sailors from there and see if any number sequences matched up. If they did, there was a chance I could narrow the number of Robert Andersons in the records.

I soon found another sailor from Minneapolis with the service number 328 52 02 and one whose number was 328 53 29. Two more Chicagoans had 299 as their first numbers. Maybe there was a pattern: 299 for Chicago and 318 or 328 for Minnesota. A nice thought, but that turned out not to be the case. The USS *Reno* had a couple of Chicago sailors, but the numbers weren't even close to what I saw on the *Pennsylvania*. Their numbers appeared to be random. The same was true for the other ships that had sailors' hometowns listed. The ones from Minneapolis and Chicago were all over the map. Whatever system was used to distribute numbers to service members did not appear to have anything to do with where those service members came from. If only they had used Social Security numbers to identify people during World War II. I had that number for Robert, but when it came to tracking his military service, it was about as useful as a pair of glasses on a blind person.

I did another search for just the Robert Carl Andersons and hit on one from Minneapolis who was aboard an aircraft carrier called the USS *Essex*. His rank was listed as AMM3c, otherwise known as a machinist mate third class.[30] The *Essex* had been in some serious combat, I discovered, participating in numerous battles in the southern Pacific. In November 1944, fifteen sailors onboard the *Essex* were killed and forty-four wounded when a kamikaze struck the flight deck as planes were refueling for takeoff in the Philippines. The dates weren't perfect—Robert would have had to be seventeen when he enlisted to match this record—but I knew that wasn't unusual for World War II. Lots of boys enlisted at that age, particularly in the months after Pearl Harbor, when Robert would have turned seventeen. I sent off my request to the NPRC with my mother's signature and the reason for the request: she's ninety-four and running out of time.

In truth, I didn't expect much. The navy was a sheer guess on my part, a shot in the dark. I got my reply within ten days of sending the form, and after reading the first few words, I said to my wife Lynda, "It's a rejection letter." Except it wasn't. The June 14, 2016, letter started out like a typical rejection letter: "Thank you for contacting the National Personnel Records Center." Then it veered. "In response to your request for personnel and medical records for the veteran cited above, we have located an archival Official Military Personnel Folder."

What? I had to read the sentence twice to make sure I wasn't seeing things. I wasn't. My shot in the dark with the tiniest of weapon had somehow found its mark. Or so it appeared. I still had doubts. The service number—639 01 59—was the same one I had listed on the form. I clearly stated that I wasn't sure about it, but it's possible someone saw the number, checked to see if there was a record corresponding to it, and fired off the letter I was now holding in my hands. The cost to see the record was $70, which I quickly paid. I knew this could fill in a lot of the blanks about my uncle and stick a giant needle in the eugenics' balloon. *Children of defective parents are almost certain to carry the defective gene.* "Oh yeah? How does a war hero fit into your warped calculation?"

I knew, too, that whatever I found would give a more complete answer to the question that had long haunted my mother. And maybe give her some peace. All she really knew about her brother was what I had told her, which wasn't much. And I didn't shield her from what I found: he was an alcoholic. After dealing with her own mother all those years, the information wasn't much of a surprise to her. But he had to be more than that. If he was a mechanic on an aircraft carrier that engaged in serious combat, which this Robert Carl Anderson appeared to be, he may have possessed the same mechanical aptitude as his brother Ernie. Ernie liked to make things. Maybe Robert did too. Rose's brother Elmer saw some serious combat during World War I. I couldn't help but feel proud that Robert—the boy who was snatched from the family and never heard from again—did his part to fight for his country at a time when bravery was sorely needed.

The phone call I received next tore the gut.

"I don't think this is your guy," an archivist for the NPRC told me. Nothing matched, including the parents. This was a Robert Carl Anderson, all right, just not the *right* Robert Carl Anderson. The archivist said he would keep looking and refund my money if he couldn't find anything. And that's what happened.

"The information provided by you does not match the information in the archival record," wrote archives technician Joe L. Wise on June 30, 2016. "The service number 639 01 59 does not match with the person you are seeking."[31]

Turns out obsessions are like that mole in the middle of your back: you can forget about it from time to time, but it never goes away. I kept digging.

In 1949, the state of Minnesota sold $84 million in bonds to provide "adjusted compensation" for those who served honorably between December 7, 1941—Pearl Harbor Day—and September 2, 1945, when Japan's surrender became official. The dollar amount wasn't much—awards were capped at $400 for those who went overseas—but it was meant as a token of appreciation by the good people of Minnesota to the brave souls who made the sacrifice for their country, some of them the ultimate sacrifice. The records, stored on microfilm by the Minnesota Historical Society, show that thousands of Minnesota veterans or their beneficiaries applied for and received the bonus payments.

Unfortunately, if Robert was one of them, I couldn't find any mention of it. The records are mostly a listing of names that include only middle initials. There were a few Robert C. Andersons, but there was no way of telling whether the C stood for Carl or Charles or Clarence. Hell, it could have been Cornelius for all I knew. An address was listed along with a series of digits, some with eight numbers and some with seven. I wrote down three Robert C. Andersons in my notebook, checked the addresses with the city directories in Minneapolis and St. Paul from the 1940s, 1950s, and 1960s, and saw that they too used only middle initials if they used initials at all. The trouble with haystacks is that once in a while you get lost in them.

Weeks later, I pulled out the notebook with the three names I had written down along with their service numbers. Two of them had eight digits and each began with 37. That didn't correspond with any of the navy numbers I had looked at, so I began researching army service numbers, and sure enough those all had eight numbers and the soldiers from Minnesota were in the group beginning with 37.

Service numbers date to World War I and weren't discontinued until the Vietnam War.[32] As World War II approached, the numbering system greatly expanded, and the two records I was looking at were in the thirty million series, which was reserved for enlisted draftees. The fact that so many army records from that period have been wiped out is disheartening to say the least, but archivists have managed to recover millions of army records, including the honorable discharge papers of the late actor Burt Lancaster. His October 14, 1945, discharge form can be found on any number of internet sites and has burn marks along its left edge, on the top right corner, and in the middle. But the military history is mostly intact and shows that he was a rifle expert who received a European–African–Middle Eastern Service Medal and a Good Conduct Medal. His occupation was listed as "entertainer." In other words, if Burt Lancaster's record was preserved, maybe Robert's was, too. I fired off a letter to the NPRC and hoped for the best.

I had to laugh when I went back to the third number I had written down as I pored over the microfilm records at the Minnesota History Center looking at bonus payments to World War II veterans. It had a familiar ring: 639 01 59. Yep, this was the Robert Carl Anderson who had served as a machinist mate third class aboard the *Essex* in the South Pacific. We weren't related, it turns out, but I knew more about his service than I did my own uncle's. My Robert survived the war, but the record of his service appears to be gone for good, erased most likely by a worker who thought lighting a cigarette amid a repository of millions of Americans' life stories was a good idea. Or maybe he just didn't care. That one selfish decision, though, had enormous consequences. We all lost something on July 12, 1973, and it's something that can't ever be replaced. We lost our history.

By the time Raymond Anderson began working for the Wrigley Chewing Gum Company, the famous business giant for which the company was named had long since departed to his custom-designed sarcophagus in California, leaving his fortune to his son, Philip, along with the legacy of a worldwide icon. William Wrigley supposedly had $32 in his pocket when he founded his first company, which sold soap, not gum. The whole gum thing came about because Wrigley knew he'd have more satisfied customers if he gave them a premium when they purchased a product. If you bought soap, you received baking powder. If you bought baking powder, you got a few packages of chewing gun. The gum became more popular than the soap or the baking powder, and that flicked on a light bulb of entrepreneurial inspiration: give the people what they want.[33]

Before World War I, packages of Wrigley's gum sold for five cents—a penny a stick. The war led to a shortage of raw materials such as sugar, but Wrigley knew that if he raised the price, he'd lose his market share. Desperate to hold on to every customer he could, he kept the price at five cents, distributed boxes of the stuff to the troops overseas, and fired up his advertising engines to make the Wrigley name synonymous with patriotism. After the war, he engineered the ad slogan: Five cents before the war, five cents during the war, five cents now. Gum sales soared, aided in no small part by the company's public nod toward patriotic philanthropy.

The plant where Raymond worked, at Thirty-Fifth Street and Ashland Avenue in Chicago, was the result of another of Wrigley's ingenious business ploys. For years the company contracted with a Chicago manufacturer, Zeno

Manufacturing Co., to supply chewing gum under its various labels, including Wrigley's Spearmint, which became the most popular gum brand in the
world. But as close an association as Wrigley had with Zeno and its chief
principal, A. G. Cox, he didn't own the company, and in Wrigley's world,
that wouldn't do. After Zeno's stockholders initially balked at a merger,
assuming they could squeeze Wrigley enough so that he'd overpay, he called
their bluff and threatened to build his own manufacturing plant. The merger
went through just as Wrigley knew it would, but he built his own factory
anyway, a sprawling plant that stood for nearly one hundred years. When the
long-dormant structure was demolished in 2013, some of the city's manufacturing history went with it. A period ad from Wrigley shows the giant Chicago
factory along with a pack of Spearmint and the boastful but true statement:
"The brand that is sold all over the world."

By the time William Wrigley Jr. died in 1932, his son Philip was already in
charge of the company, famously vowing, "Everything will go on as usual."
But although Philip would never have the autocratic voice of his father, he
was a transformative visionary who brought the company to new heights, at
least as far as chewing gum was concerned. The Chicago Cubs, which his
father purchased in 1925, remained lovable losers who would win a pen-
nant occasionally and then sink to their more familiar spot in the National
League's second division. (As we all know, that changed in 2016.)

Philip Wrigley was known for his taciturn ways, particularly in public. In
a tribute to him some seventeen years after his death, the *Chicago Tribune*
sportswriter Jerome Holtzman in 1994 recalled Wrigley's reluctance for public speaking. One year, while accepting an award handed out by the Chicago
baseball writers, Wrigley leaned into the microphone and said, "Thank you."
A few years later, after winning the award again, he was asked to speak longer. "Thank you very much," he said.[34]

I wasn't able to learn much about Raymond's years at the Wrigley Chewing
Gum Company. The company doesn't keep files on former employees, even
those long deceased. The Chicago History Museum also has no archive of
employment records on the company. Sheila Fletcher, Raymond's youngest daughter, said he was an engineer for the company, but another family
member—the former husband of Robert's niece—said Raymond worked on
boilers, which seems likely given his manufacturing background. He was
a jack-of-all-trades and probably had many duties in keeping the massive
plant running.

Raymond was born in Michigan, worked in the Chicago stockyards, had
a job in the garment industry in Minneapolis, and then manned the boilers
for one of the nation's most iconic companies. Santa was an immigrant from
Italy whose father worked as a blast man in a Minnesota strip mine. The outlines of their lives are preserved in records and frozen in time, but they are

mere footnotes in a personal history that shaped the lives of countless people, including my uncle. To what degree he benefitted from their parenthood I will never know. Every family has its secrets, boxes that will forever be unopened. But this much I do know: Raymond and Santa Anderson had big hearts. No one adopts three children, providing a home for a child who might not otherwise have one, unless they are wired to do good in the world. In his later years Raymond had children and grandchildren living under his roof, just as my great-grandmother Mary did when she took in my mom and various other members of the extended family. She was wired to do good in the world, too.

Santa's father, James Donfris, died in 1950 in the St. Anne's nursing home in Duluth. Her mother, Antonia Vichollo Donfris, had passed eight years earlier, so James's death must have closed the Minnesota chapter of her life or at least minimized it a great deal. Her brother John still lived in Duluth, but her brother Albert, who had shared a house with the young family in the early 1930s, lived near their home in Chicago. In 1949, Raymond and Santa adopted their third child, Sheila, some twenty-one years after they had adopted Robert and seventeen years after adopting Patricia. When I found her phone number, approximately one year after learning who Robert's adoptive parents were, I stumbled through the conversation like a ten-year-old who lost his lunch money. Finally, I apologized.

"You have to understand. You're only the second person I've met who knew Robert."

Unfortunately, Sheila didn't know Robert. Not really. He wasn't around much if at all when she was a young girl, and she completely lost contact with him as an adult, which in her mind was no big loss. The last time she saw him was in the 1960s or 1970s, she told me.

"He came to see us," she said. "He was with a lady and he was an alcoholic."[35]

Sheila said Robert was found dead in front of the mission where he was staying. I didn't think that was accurate because of the address on his death certificate, which was the address where he had been living with Kathryn Esaw, but then I looked at the paperwork more closely. Robert died of multiple organ failure and spontaneous esophageal rupture.[36] He had the first condition for two weeks and the second for four, according to the death certificate. I had assumed that meant he had been in the hospital for that length of time, but maybe the medical examiner had written that down postmortem as a guess. There was no hospital listed, and I later learned that Kathryn had worked or volunteered for years at the Hallie Q. Brown Community Center in St. Paul. I called there, but no one was around who remembered her or Robert. Still, it made sense. Robert probably met Kathryn at the center—that was her son's recollection, anyway—and he couldn't have been a picnic to live with. He may have left at various times and ended up on the steps exhaling his final breath.

"He was found dead in front of the mission," Sheila had told me. Whether it is true or not, it is an image I can't quite exorcise.

Sheila said her father worked at the Wrigley Chewing Gum factory for thirty-five years, which means he retired around 1970. Santa died in December 1976, and it was her obituary that gave me a jolt. Listed among the many surviving family members were two of her grandchildren: Robert and Patricia Anderson.[37] I can't be certain, but in all likelihood, these are Robert's kids. *My* Robert's kids. To that point, the scant information I had been able to uncover about him could be summed up in four words: he was an alcoholic. But at least now I knew there had been some joy in his life, at least for a minute and maybe more. Perhaps they hated him and maybe they do still. He might have been a worse parent than my grandmother, who at least took in her daughter, if for no other reason than she was forced to by her new husband. Or maybe, just maybe, he gave them a chance at enjoying life, went to their band concerts, and took an active role in helping them mature. Only they would know.

Unfortunately, I wasn't able to find them. The problem, of course, is their names. When the creators of the 1950s TV show *Father Knows Best* wanted to portray a generic family, they knew to give it an ultra-popular name: Anderson. I discovered the contours of Raymond and Santa's lives, but that was because they were living in a small Minnesota town nearly a century ago, sufficiently in the past that I could use public census enumerations that document which family members are living under one roof, their ages, where they are working or whether they are going to school, if they own their home or are renting, what their nationality is, and even how much money they made in the last year. I used the 1920, 1930, and 1940 Census to follow the movements of the Andersons, almost like a stalker on today's Facebook. But the trail mostly ended there, well before Robert's children would have been born.

I pored over Minnesota and Illinois birth records using every tool I knew, narrowing the date window to sometime between 1943—when Robert was eighteen—and 1965, when he was forty. Even then, the possibilities seemed endless. On my spreadsheet, I typed the words "can't be him" after each false hit, and there were a lot of false hits. For a birthday present a friend bought me a DNA kit to track potential relatives. You ship off your saliva and they do a scientific match with others that share some of the same identifiers. From the hundreds of names there were a few Andersons, along with a Patricia or two, but the only response I got when I reached out was from a nice woman who said she married into the Anderson family, changed her name, and did not have a father named Robert. In other words: "can't be him."

This was beyond depressing. Not only had I failed my mother, but my effort to hold a middle finger up to the Henry Goddards of the world was a bust as well. It was Goddard who believed that 40 percent of immigrants were feebleminded, a condition he said could be diagnosed with "just a glance." *Just a glance.* The sheer number of people persecuted by the spread of this nonsense is mind-boggling. I wanted Robert to be, if not a war hero, at least a contributing member of society, a good person. Yet who's to say he wasn't at least that? Even with the little I was able to unearth about him, I knew he was more than a skid row derelict whose body was found on the front steps of a sanctuary for lost souls. He served his country and comforted a lonely woman toward the end of her life. The words of Kathryn Esaw's son suggest that beneath all the demons there was good in the man.

"He was nice and friendly, always helped my mom," Gary Peppard had said. "I thought this was a good thing. He wasn't ambitious, but he was good to my mom."

He was good to my mom. In the absence of any further testimonial, that one will have to do.

Robert was still living when his father, Raymond Anderson, died. Raymond had lived deep into his eighties and touched the lives of his children, grandchildren, and "fond friend Bandit," all of whom were listed in the obituary that ran in the *Chicago Tribune* in January 1992. But one of his children wasn't mentioned in that obituary, and apparently had been erased from his life entirely. Robert must have disappointed Raymond enough that any mention of him was verboten. And in a way, that's how his life began, as a whispered thing that had to be wiped from the books. Robert made his own choices as an adult and whatever self-destruction he engaged in was his and his alone. But his identity was taken from him by people who placed confidence in a system that assumed that a clean break from the past was in the best interest of everyone involved. And it wasn't. Raymond and Santa Anderson may have rescued Robert from an awful fate, probably gave him his only chance at a normal life. But not all fate is preordained. We'll never know what would have happened if Robert had stayed in Rose's household, if he would have been raised by an alcoholic who could never summon the three words all kids need to hear: "I love you." Yet I can't help but think that when Robert's first family was airbrushed away by a system of limited compassion, my mother wasn't the only one who suffered. Ernie and Robert also lost something. And maybe Raymond, Santa, and their extended family did, too.

In May 2017 two records I had requested through the federal Freedom of Information Act arrived on the same day. One was Robert's application for a Social Security number on December 17, 1941.[38] On it he listed his place of birth as Duluth, Minnesota—which wasn't true but might have been what his father had told him—and gave his current address as 3411 East 45th Street in Minneapolis. My mom by then had moved to the Minneapolis suburb of Columbia Heights, but she wouldn't have been far away, another irony. The most interesting part of the application was the signature. I have a photograph of Robert when he was three years old and had talked to a few people who knew him, but this was the first document I'd found showing his handwriting. And that carried with it enormous possibilities. I now knew how he signed his name.

The second record was a response to my request from the National Personnel Records Center for Robert's service records. After my earlier failed venture, I made another request using one of the service numbers I'd found in a batch of records on bonus payments made to returning soldiers following World War II and got a hit. In my hands was a service record from a Robert Anderson from Minnesota.[39] The cover letter from the NPRC apologized for the quality of the photocopy, but I didn't care. It was the quality of the information I was after. On a single sheet of paper were two words: honorable discharge. The serviceman's grade (private first class), date of induction (May 26, 1943), and marital status (single) were all on the form along with his decorations. He received a Good Conduct Medal for his service in the "European–African–Middle Eastern Theater." Could this possibly be my Robert? No middle name was listed, only the initial C. But the form had something else that suddenly became important: a signature.

My wife is better at these things than I am, so I had her compare the signature on the Social Security application to the honorable discharge papers. One I knew was Robert, the other one I wasn't so sure. Lynda put the two photocopies next to each other and studied each letter for identifying markers. Tick. Tick. Tock. After what seemed like forever, she looked up: "It's not him." As I looked at the form more closely, other information also didn't match, including the birth date. This Robert was born on September 22, 1924, about seven months before my Robert was born in a prison hospital in Faribault, Minnesota. This clinched it. If my uncle served honorably, or even if he didn't, the records most likely went up in smoke.

Robert was gone, and the proof of that is in one of those small, tucked-back-into-the neighborhood cemeteries that you'd never find if you didn't know it was there.

There was one thing left for me to do.

In September 2015 my mom, my wife Lynda, my brother Mike, and I visited Robert's gravesite. As my mom looked down at that modest stone with Robert's name on it, I couldn't help but reflect that it was the closest she'd been to her brother in nearly ninety years. Afterward we went to the house where he had lived in St. Paul with Kathryn Esaw. When I walked to the side of the house, trying to imagine what Robert's life was like in that two-story home with plastic siding and a slightly worn look, a small girl came outside followed by her mother. They were renters who had no idea how significant a glimpse of their home was to the person standing in front of them. And in the end, that's what I got of Robert's life: a glimpse. My search for him uncovered things I never imagined, but it didn't get me any closer to him and didn't, unfortunately, give my mother what she desperately wanted and deserved: a chance to see Robert one last time. She got a few answers, but the questions are endless, and some, I suspect, are completely unanswerable. If Rose were alive, I'd love to ask her this one: who was Robert's biological father? Then I would tell her something about the son who got away, how he fought for his country and comforted a lonely woman in the late stages of his life. I'd tell her what a wonderful person her daughter turned out to be, how her family cherishes each minute they get to spend with her. As for Ernie, I wouldn't sugarcoat anything that he did, except to tell her it wasn't her fault.

None of it was her fault.

NOTES

1. From http://zenithcity.com/thisday/july-4-1868-thomas-foster-coins-duluths-nickname-the-zenith-city-of-the-unsalted-seas/.

2. From John Hatcher, "Belief in Duluth Children Stands Strong," *Statesman* archives, University of Minnesota–Duluth.

3. Ingram Conradson's father, Louis Conradson, was a county commissioner in Mott, North Dakota. A birth certificate for Ingram's son Dean also shows he was born in May 1938 in Taylor, North Dakota. The obituary for Louis, who died in 1943, said that Ingram and his wife Elizabeth were living in Portland, Oregon, at the time of his father's death.

4. Minnesota Historical Society, Adoption Research, Owatonna State Public School.

5. From Sister Claire Lynch, *Orphanages of Minnesota* (St. Paul: Minnesota Historical Society Library, 1938).

6. *Brainerd Daily Dispatch*, October 15, 1981, heritage edition. For a history of poorhouses in Minnesota, see Ethel McClure, "Unlamented Era: County Poor Farms in Minnesota," Minnesota Historical Society, www.collections.mnhs.org.

7. St. James Catholic Orphanage records.

8. International Soundex Reunion Registry website: www.isrr.org/index.htm.

9. 1930 U.S. Census, Duluth, Minnesota.

10. "After 112 Years of Operation, Youth Treatment Facility in Duluth Closing," *Duluth News Tribune*, June 14, 2021.

11. The six magical words spoken by Breanna Schueller at the Woodland Hills treatment center, which opened the door to discovering the names of Robert's adoptive parents.

12. St. James Catholic Orphanage records.

13. Certificate of Death, Minnesota Department of Health.

14. Ibid.

15. Kathryn Esaw's obituary appeared in the *St. Paul Pioneer Press* on May 24, 1998.

16. Author interview.

17. Author interview with Gary Peppard.

18. Marriage records, St. Louis County, Minnesota, May 17, 1925.

19. Alien Registration and Declaration of Holdings, Minnesota Commission of Public Safety, February 16, 1918.

20. Dominic A. Pacyga, *Slaughterhouse: Chicago's Union Stock Yard and the World It Made* (Chicago: University of Chicago Press, 2015), xi.

21. From "The Bloodiest Blocks in Chicago," *Wall Street Journal*, October 2, 2015.

22. Ibid.

23. Author interview with Sheila Fletcher.

24. Ibid.

25. David A. Walker, *Iron Frontier: The Discovery and Early Development of Minnesota's Three Ranges* (St. Paul: Minnesota Historical Society Press, 1979), 206–7.

26. Marriage certificate, St. Louis County Board of Health.

27. Author interview with Sheila Fletcher.

28. See Walter W. Stender and Evans Walker, "The National Personnel Records Center Fire: A Study in Disaster," *The American Archivist*, October 1974.

29. Letter to author from the National Personnel Records Center, May 11, 2016.

30. Numerous sites contain information on Navy rank abbreviations. See airandspace.si.edu.

31. Letter to author from the National Personnel Records Center, June 30, 2016.

32. See Archives.gov, National Personnel Records Center, Service Numbers and Social Security Numbers.

33. Paul M. Angle, *Philip K. Wrigley: A Memoir of a Modest Man* (Chicago: Rand McNally, 1975), 12.

34. Jerome Holtzman, "Cubs' 'Mr. Wrigley' Made a Difference but Not Noise," *Chicago Tribune*, December 6, 1994.

35. Author interview with Sheila Fletcher.

36. Certificate of Death, Minnesota Department of Health.

37. "Death Notices," Chicago Tribune, December 21, 1976.

38 Robert's December 17, 1941, application for a Social Security number. It is the only record I have that shows his signature.

39 Honorable Discharge papers for Robert C. Anderson, who served from June 3, 1943, to February 1, 1946. The signature did not match the one on the Social Security number application. This was not my uncle.

10

Questions

I was an editor for my college newspaper, the *Minnesota Daily*, in 1979 when our wire editor, Bill Norton, said, "Hey, some guy just went crazy and began shooting people in a courtroom in Portland."

Bill wanted to know if we should include the story in our digest of news around the world.

"Who was he?" I asked.

"Ernest McClain," Bill read off the Associated Press copy.

"Ernie McClain? I think I know him."

I read the story Bill handed me and knew immediately. This was my uncle. I knew he didn't live in Portland, but Astoria isn't that far away and the AP story said his son Michael was with him in the courtroom.[1] I knew Michael. He even lived with us for a time when I was a kid.

"Some guy just went crazy," Bill had said.

Of course, that wasn't the half of it.

Ernie's courtroom madness has lingered over the family like a perpetual black cloud. We will likely never fully understand why Ernie did what he did, but new research is providing insights into the thought processes of mass shooters whose actions, unfortunately, are popping up on our phones on a regular basis.

Technically, Ernie wasn't a mass shooter. The FBI definition, developed not long after he started firing inside that Portland courtroom, classifies mass shootings as having four or more deaths in a single setting, excluding the shooter.[2] Ernie killed one person in addition to himself, putting him in the category of someone who murders a spouse and then turns the gun on himself. But although his wife Billie may have been Ernie's intended victim that day, he easily could have killed more, and at one point it seemed as if he was aiming his weapon at Judge Mercedes Deiz. Had Ernie's attorney, Ronald Miller, not grabbed him and wrestled for the gun, there's no telling how many people would have died that day. His gun was fully loaded, and he had more rounds in his coat pocket if he needed them. If not a mass shooter, he had potential to be one.

We know a lot more about the tendencies of this class of murderer than we did a generation ago—sadly, because we now have so many examples to draw from. In the fall of 2019, the U.S. Department of Justice released the results of a massive study on mass shooters, advertised as the largest study of its kind ever funded by the federal government.

The Violence Project was headed by psychologists Jillian K. Peterson, a professor of criminology and criminal justice at Hamline University in St. Paul, and James Densley, a professor of criminal justice at Metropolitan State University, which has campuses throughout the Twin Cities. The two later turned their research into a book published in 2021: *The Violence Project: How to Stop a Mass Shooting Epidemic.* I'm citing their work because I saw so many similarities between Ernie's background and the 171 shooters the researchers profiled as part of their study. Most of the shooters endured multiple traumas as children and carried around a wide-ranging set of perceived grievances as adults. Most of them, too, died as Ernie did, either by taking their own life or giving law enforcement little alternative, a classification popularly referred to as "suicide by cop."

The study, which covered a period of more than fifty years, found four main correlations among mass shooters:

1. They were exposed to early childhood trauma or violence.
2. They could identify a personal grievance or crisis point pushing them to violence.
3. They studied the actions of past shooters and sought validation for their methods and motives.
4. They had the means to carry out an attack.[3]

Ernie certainly matches the criteria for numbers one, two, and four. On number three, I'm not so sure. I have no doubt that Ernie planned the attack. You don't carry a handgun into a courtroom without some forethought. But I can't see him hoping to go out in a blaze of glory. That fit his son Michael better than it did Ernie. Michael timed two bombs to go off in a pair of crowded restaurants on a Sunday morning. He wanted his name in lights. But that wasn't Ernie. He had a short fuse and could carry a grudge. Carolyn can vouch for that. But she is adamant that her father didn't have the same unstable mindset of her brother, who was incapable of any type of empathy or compassion. As she points out, Ernie was rational 99 percent of the time. Unfortunately for Candise Jones and her family, that proved to be not nearly enough.

In August 2019, after thirty-one people were killed in back-to-back shootings in El Paso, Texas, and Dayton, Ohio, President Donald Trump declared that the nation had "a big mental illness problem."[4] To the authors of the Violence Project, such rhetoric not only stigmatizes millions of Americans who are affected by mental illness—the vast majority of whom are not violent—but is overly simplistic and may even be completely wrong. The mass shooters in the Violence Project database who had a history of mental health concerns isn't too far off from the percentage meeting that same criteria among the general population. And most of the shooters in the database shared other risk factors beyond mental illness, such as unemployment, substance abuse, and past trauma. It's convenient to blame mental health—and often politically advantageous—but the authors say little is known about the role that mental health plays in motivating mass shooters. In fact, the percentage of killers in the study known to use psychotropic medications—roughly one in five—is almost identical to the percentage in the general population.

In a finding that would likely surprise those who jump to conclusions about mass shootings, very few of the shooters had a history of delusions or hallucinations either before or during the act, and even in those cases, it played a minor role at best.[5] Saying the nation has a mental health problem may be accurate on some level, but it is of little help in finding answers to why people do what they do.

Most of the shooters in the database had experience with childhood trauma, something I wrote about earlier in this book. It doesn't track that all kids who endure difficult childhoods encounter such problems later on—my mother is certainly an example of that—but the reverse does hold up much more convincingly. Those who do have troubles as adults, including a propensity toward violence, normally had negative experiences as children.

The Violence Project researchers examined some of these experiences, which included parental suicide, physical or sexual abuse, neglect, domestic violence, and severe bullying. There was little understanding of bullying in Ernie's day, but we now know that it can cause severe and long-lasting consequences. One of the shooters in the database was lit on fire by his classmates. Another one brought a screwdriver with him every day to "feel safe."[6] Depression, anxiety, hallucinations, delusions, and suicidal tendencies can all be triggered by severe childhood trauma that may include bullying.

Was Ernie bullied? By the nuns, almost assuredly. By others, in all likelihood. He was a skinny kid who had no siblings to protect him or to offer him sanctuary during his two years in the orphanage—years about which he later told stories of being beaten by the nuns and of trying to run away. I keep thinking about what Eugene Saumer said when I asked him if he told anybody about what Father Manning had done to him: "I didn't say nothing to nobody," he said.[7] Eugene, at least, had three brothers in the same building he was in. If Ernie was bullied or worse, who was he supposed to tell? The priests? The nuns?

His mother?

Almost all shooters have a crisis point or grievance that preceded their actions, and that was certainly true for Ernie. His youngest daughter had died in a boating accident, his wife had left him and was seeking a court order for child support, which he no doubt thought was unfair, and he was broke. The Violence Project researchers found that more than 80 percent of mass shooters were in crisis just prior to their crime, which was communicated to the people around them through a marked change in behavior. About 30 percent were "actively" suicidal before the attack, and 40 percent planned to die during the violence.[8] Was that the case for Ernie? If so, he shared it with the one person who was in a position to do something for him: his son Michael. Nothing about what he did that day was spur of the moment, right down to transferring his car into Michael's name a short time before the shooting. If Ernie hadn't been suicidal before that point, he certainly was during the days leading up to the shooting.

The theory about Ernie having a brain tumor sounds like a family trying to spin a terrible tragedy. But several shooters in the database had brain damage, in some cases severe. The authors used as the starting point for their research the 1966 clocktower shooting at the University of Texas. There were, of course, mass shooters before Charles Whitman, but when the former Eagle Scout and Marine killed his wife and mother and then positioned himself in the observation deck some twenty-eight floors above ground on the campus in Austin, a threshold had been crossed. Television and radio broadcasts did what they now do routinely: inform the public in real time. For ninety-six minutes—surely an eternity for the helpless souls who Whitman targeted at random from his perch high in the sky—the media kept a nation riveted to their electronic devices (back then, televisions and radios), just as they have done many times since. As I write this, a fifty-one-year-old electrician just shot and killed five coworkers at the Molson Coors Brewing Co. in Milwaukee.[9] Within a week in March 2021, one gunman killed eight people at three spas in Atlanta and another killed ten people at a supermarket in Boulder, Colorado.[10] The list goes on and on, triggering numbness, and, unfortunately, paralysis.

Whitman's body count numbered sixteen (he was killed by a police sharpshooter, making him the seventeenth death that day). No, he wasn't the first mass shooter in the United States, but his crime is seen as a watershed moment in America's tilt toward mass violence. Not only are these shootings becoming more numerous, the number of victims is spiraling upward. During the 1970s, when Ernie committed his crime, mass shootings claimed an average of eight lives per year. By 2019, it was fifty-one.[11]

Unlike Ernie, who left no note that might explain his behavior, Whitman wanted people to know what was roiling around in his head.

"I do not really understand myself these days," he wrote. "I am supposed to be an average, reasonable and intelligent young man. However, lately (I cannot recall when it started) I have been a victim of many unusual and irrational thoughts."

Many unusual and irrational thoughts. Chilling.

Whitman started his note at 6:45 p.m. on July 31, 1966, and finished it early the next morning after stabbing both his mother and his wife and then covering each of their bodies with a white sheet. Of his mother, he wrote, "I am very upset over having done it. However, I feel that if there is a heaven she is definitely there now."

He had similar words for his wife, Louise, professing his love for her and adding, "I cannot rationally pinpoint any specific reason for doing this. I don't know if it is selfishness, or if I don't want her to have to face the embarrassment my actions would surely cause her. At this time, though, the prominent reason in my mind is that I truly do not consider this world worth living in, and am prepared to die, and I do not want to leave her to suffer alone in it."[12]

He didn't bother to ask his wife, but there is a good chance that she might have preferred taking her chances in this world that he didn't think was worth living in.

If Ernie had turned and began spraying the courtroom with bullets, he would have landed in the Violence Project database. Something stopped him from joining that particular club. (Quite possibly Ronald Miller, who wrestled him for the gun, causing a bullet to lodge harmlessly in the ceiling.) But there are similarities that can't be dismissed. Whitman was extremely intelligent, as was Ernie, and was the product of a marriage defined by domestic abuse. (I don't know if that was true of Rose's marriages, but the traumatic factors were almost too numerous to mention.) Whitman's work history also resembled Ernie's in that he never settled down in any one job for very long, and he had a few run-ins with the law. Although he received an honorable discharge from the service, he was once court-martialed for gambling and threatening another Marine.[13] He confessed to friends that he was abusive toward his own wife on a couple of occasions but resolved to do better and not turn into his father. After explaining his reasons for taking her life in his note to the world, Whitman said, "I intend to kill her as painlessly as possible."

There are many reasons that people kill—painlessly or otherwise—and for Ernie it may have been a simple act of revenge. But beneath that one layer of twisted thought was a landfill of brokenness that began filling almost the minute he was born. My mother survived a rough childhood, and in a way Ernie did, too, but what he carried with him into adulthood was a scar no one could see. In the immediate aftermath of the shooting, his ex-wife Joyce told reporters that Ernie was depressed after his daughter's death. Ernie, she said, "maybe blamed himself and regretted things he should have done for our three kids."

That's plausible, of course. Ernie was a deep thinker. But unlike Charles Whitman, who wanted the world to know what was bouncing around in his head, Ernie chose to let his actions speak for themselves. Except they couldn't do that, at least not completely, and the tragedy of his life became the tragedy of his death. Ernie did a horrible thing, and for that he will be remembered. But no single act, no matter how heinous, defines who you are. Did Ernie think of the pain he would cause others as he drove to the hearing that day? Did he think about what impact the shooting might have on Michael, who he knew was having problems? Did he think about his other children, including Ernest Jr., who came close to having to grow up without a mother or a father?

Ernie was deprived of a normal childhood. Was he so selfish as to want that for his own children? Did he care at all what happened to them?

There are no answers to any of these questions. But that's probably too simple. We don't know the mindset of someone like Ernie any more than Henry Goddard could detect feeblemindedness with a single glance.

As I was sifting through files recently, I came across the original story that Bill Norton had yanked from the wire service's teletype machine the day Ernie began firing away in Portland. I'd forgotten I kept it, but it chills me today just as it did forty-some years ago.

> Portland, Ore. AP—A man who had just been cited with contempt for non-payment of child support shot and killed an attorney in a courtroom Tuesday, then turned the gun on himself and committed suicide, a sheriff's office spokesman said.[14]

It's the kind of impersonal, just-the-facts-ma'am lead that I've written many times. But this story wasn't impersonal. There was a set of facts, but it wasn't the whole story. Perhaps Ernie didn't belong in the database after all. The researchers wanted to probe the minds of murderers, hoping to give us clues about what makes them tick. But the road map in Ernie's brain was cluttered with too many squiggly lines and zigzags for that to happen. He may have acted alone, but as he lifted his arm and pointed that gun to his head, he brought all of us into his darkness.

NOTES

1. From the Associated Press, February 13, 1979.

2. Numerous sources carry the FBI's definition of a mass shooter. For one such source, see Richard Berk, "What Is a Mass Shooting? What Can Be Done?" crim.sas.upenn.edu.

3. See Jillian K. Peterson and James Densley, The Violence Project, www.theviolenceproject.org.

4. Spencer Kimball, "Trump Says Mass Shootings in El Paso and Dayton Are a 'Mental Illness Problem,'" MSNBC, August 4, 2019.

5. Jillian K. Peterson and James Densley, *The Violence Project: How to Stop a Mass Shooting Epidemic* (New York: Abrams Press, 2021), 60–62.

6. Ibid., 178.

7. Author interview with Eugene Saumer.

8. Peterson and Densley, *The Violence Project*, 25.

9. From "Milwaukee Brewery Employees Return to Work after Shooting," *Milwaukee Journal*, March 2, 2020.

10. See "First Atlanta, Then Boulder: Two Mass Shootings in a Week," *New York Times*, April 16, 2021.

11. Peterson and Densley, *The Violence Project*, 5.

12. Numerous publications have reproduced Charles Whitman's suicide note, including David Eagleman, "The Brain on Trial," *The Atlantic*, July/August 2011.

13. Ibid.

14. The Associated Press, February 13, 1979.

11

Survivors

The saga of the DeChaine family is riddled with tragedy and of course heart-break. But what is most remarkable is not how abnormal they were, but how resilient they continue to be. Those touched by Ernie and Michael—and Rose, too—bear scars no surgery can remove. But at the same time, and within this same family, there emerged true survivors. The wanton cruelty baked into the eugenics movement is exposed by those who came before us and those who could never be. But its true colors are illuminated by those who are still here, people whose lives are not marked by hatred or resentment but who instead are a symbol of redemption and hope.

Ernie's daughter Carolyn is one of those people. Her sister was nineteen when she was lost at sea, her body swallowed up by a fate that robbed her family even of touching her hand or kissing her cheek one final time. Her father, Ernie McClain, left her with a scar near her eye and a horrible memory of hatred and malice. Her brother Michael was a gangster wannabe who didn't have the courage to deal with the mess he created.

Her personal life has had its own disappointments. A first husband was abusive and sunk into a fog of alcoholism, eventually dying because of it. He might have taken Carolyn with him, but she said she heeded the advice of a police officer who told her to leave or end up in a coffin. She took the kids and left.[1]

A second marriage ended as well, but it has hardly defined her. Quite the contrary. Her personality is beyond pleasant, almost bubbly. She is one of those people who is so at home with the sweep of social media she could have invented it. Her posts reflect who she is: opinionated, reflective, comfortable. They are full of funny and inspirational sayings and railings against political correctness. Pull up her page and you're likely to read something like "You don't stop dancing because you grow old. You grow old because you stop dancing." Or, as she wrote recently, "Love being retired! Have the freedom and time to do whatever I want. Travel, visit friends, work on my properties. Threw my alarm clock away!"

Like most of us, Carolyn is very proud of her children and has photos of them and her grandkids posted all over her Facebook page. Her son Brian manages a furniture store nearby. Erik, her other son, is the chief operations officer for a biopharmaceutical company in Portland and a part-time faculty member at Oregon Health and Science University. The work he does, finding new ways to treat blood clots that could result in a stroke or a heart attack, couldn't be more removed from what his uncle and grandfather did. He wants to preserve life, not destroy it.

I once asked Carolyn how she managed to stay so upbeat after all that her family has endured—after what *she* has endured. There was no great revelation. I suspect it's simply who she is. No matter what happens to her, she doesn't stop dancing. In another post on Facebook, she wrote: "There are moments in life when you wish you could bring someone down from heaven. To spend the day with them just one more time, give them one more hug. Kiss them good-bye. Or hear their voice again."

Carolyn deserves that hug, as do so many others who refuse to let misfortune spoil their life story.

Like Carolyn, my mother Millie shares this same trait of determined perseverance. She never knew her biological father, who left when she was an infant, struggled with a crippling disease called rickets as a child, and was scarred by an alcoholic mother whose concern for her daughter seemed low on her priority list. Yet in photographs from the era, she is always smiling, enjoying life, and seemingly oblivious to the hardship that was everywhere around her. How could such pain lead to such joy?

Turns out, it's not all that complicated. She thrived because just enough people cared about her—her aunts and uncles, her stepfather, and, after she became an adult, my father. But the person perhaps most responsible for her survival, at least during those early years, is her grandmother. Mary Melvina Forcier stayed behind after virtually her entire family, including her parents, moved to the West Coast. We now know her reasons. She was needed by too many people in Brainerd, none more so than a little girl with rickets.

Mary's life was one of service—not to her country, but to her family. Well, maybe both. There's no telling how many people found cover under those giant wings.

After her second marriage ended, Mary Forcier–turned–Mary DeChaine–turned–Mary Lorbecki became Mary Lease. It was an easy transition. After John Lorbecki, Archie Lease was a breath of fresh air. Gary Peppard once said of Rose's son Robert: "He wasn't ambitious, but he was good to my mom." That was Archie. He was good for Mary, even if he lacked Joe's work ethic. My mom remembers how Archie would shake the couch cushions of each home he entered, looking for spare change.

"Any kind of sale, he would go looking for bargains," she said. "I don't remember him ever working."[2]

Perhaps Archie understood that the most important work isn't necessarily what you do for a paycheck.

As Mary got older and the kids moved on, there was an emptiness to her house that didn't dissipate no matter how many pictures she put on the walls. She no longer needed someone in her bed—good heavens, those days were gone—but she did need someone to talk to, to help her move a chair when her sewing thread rolled underneath it, or to rub liniment on her back when the pain became unbearable. Archie would do things like put his pants on over his pajamas, but he was there for Mary when it mattered, including when it mattered most.

On the night of March 7, 1946, Mary sat up in bed and asked her husband to get her a clean nightgown. He did as she asked. She asked him to comb her hair. Again, he did what she asked. Then she said good-bye to the world and died peacefully in her sleep.

"What a way to go," my mother once remarked.

Death had always been a somber occasion in the DeChaine household, but when Mary went to bed that night, it was more of a celebration. She knew there was a place for people like her. She didn't know what it would look like when she got there. She just knew that was where she belonged. *Mary always knew.* That's why she had Archie fetch her best nightie and comb her hair. After all, where she was going, you always want to look your best.

I know my mom will make that same journey someday, but we're all hoping to delay the inevitable as long as possible. She serves as a daily reminder of the wrongheadedness of eugenics, once described by the author Edwin Black as a "pernicious white-gloved war prosecuted by esteemed professors, elite universities, wealthy industrialists and government officials colluding in a racist, pseudoscientific movement."[3] William Hodson likely wasn't thinking of my mother when he wrote, "Children of defective parents are almost certain to carry the defective gene." It is now clear that he should have been.

Her apartment at times has resembled a museum, packed with oddly shaped figurines and Popeye-like miniature wall statues of grumpy sailors, nineteenth-century police officers, and cartoonish pirates wearing devilish grins, faded cappy hats, and the obligatory eye patch. Photographs of her sons and grandkids are scattered about—you can't have too many of those—but to get the full measure of her life, now a century old, you need to look in the shoebox she keeps at the rear of an upper shelf in her closet. There, in black and white, is a portrait of a family.

There's Lottie in a glamour portrait of the era, staring to the side, lips bright red, her left hand brushing a pageboy haircut and proudly displaying her wedding ring. It's a mesmerizing photo and not just because Lottie was a beautiful woman. The picture had to have been taken just months before her death.

There's Elmer, Rose's brother, who was a spitting image of Ernie: mysterious, handsome, and eye-catching. He died when he was hit by a car crossing a highway with a gasoline can in his hand.[4]

There's Ernie's daughter Nancy, who died at sea, and Clara's daughter Violet, shot on the back steps of her home by her estranged husband.

And then there is Ernie. Lots and lots of pictures of Ernie. In one, he and Millie are posing in front of their grandmother's home, most likely just after their mother was first sent to the institution. Millie is in a white dress, her hair unbrushed and looking like she just woke up. Her legs are bent and her shoes so worn the soles must have been as thin as sandpaper. To the rear you can see the house, torn tarpaper covering the sides, its wood frame exposed as if just waiting for a match. Looking at the picture, you can almost smell the dust.

Standing next to Millie in the photograph and dressed in his Sunday best is Ernie, his white shirt neatly tucked, his hair combed into uneven bangs. His shoes are old and scuffed and he is wearing knickers. But that's not what stands out in the photo. His left hand is clasping Millie's right hand as if to say, "I'm here for you." He was being a chivalrous Don Quixote protecting his little sister. Only it wouldn't be Ernie who would protect Millie. And as events would unfold, there was no one to protect him, either.

The photographs and mementos in Millie's apartment attest to a life fully lived: fishing at her Aunt Mabel's cabin, proudly posing with her mother on the day of her high-school graduation, striking a pose on the hood of a car as if she was Rita Hayworth. It's all there, a century of memories, both the good and the bad. Still, there are some photographs she displays more prominently than others. Mom has always loved dogs, and in one of the pictures, her adoptive father Orvel—shirtsleeves rolled up, collar unbuttoned, and a grin stretching from ear to ear—holds their dog Wimpy. Looking at the photo, you'd think her life had always been perfect. And as remarkable as it might seem, given the circumstances of her upbringing, maybe it was.

Orvel and Rose must have had a strange relationship. Rose's favoritism toward Ernie was such that Orvel took my mom under his wing. They did yardwork together, went fishing, and attended professional wrestling matches. Football legend Bronko Nagurski was a big name in the ring back then, and during the war years, wrestling promotions were a common tactic for drawing crowds. Boxer Jack Dempsey fought and beat wrestler Bill Curry in one of those promotions, and after his baseball career Babe Ruth—the "Big Lug" in Joseph's eyes—took to the ring as a referee. In Minnesota, wrestlers with assumed stage monikers like "Killer Kowalski," "Mad Dog Vachon," and "Gorgeous George" were household names. Mom introduced wrestling to me

and my three brothers and also pushed us to read an author who wrote westerns: Zane Grey. I later discovered that Zane Grey was Orvel's favorite writer.

Mom's favorite aunt growing up was Rose's sister Mabel. (We called her
Aunt May-me.) Mabel married a man named Warren Beckley, who damaged his hearing working in the Northern Pacific roundhouse. After that, he
wouldn't let his son work for the railroad—near sacrilege in a rail town like
Brainerd—out of fear that the same thing would happen to him.

Mabel and Warren lived near the railroad shops but also bought a cabin
outside of town on Long Lake. Rose, Orvel, and Mom hung out there during the summer months, and Ernie spent time there as well. Mabel once told
my mom that the cabin would be hers after she died, but Mabel died before
Warren, and he ended up selling it to a former coworker. Later, he apologized
to my mother for not following through on the promise from his late wife.

Why Orvel adopted my mother—she was essentially an adult then—is still
a bit of a mystery. Mom says Orvel wanted to protect the family's money
from one of his relatives, but when I asked her what money there was, she
said, "Not much."[5] The adoption named Orvel and Rose as her legal guardians, though they were in the process of splitting up at the time. Those
consenting to the adoption included Rose, my mom, and the state's director
of social welfare. The paperwork for the adoption says Ingram Conradson
deserted his daughter and that she had been cared for since then by Rose and
Orvel: "The home of the petitioner is a fit and proper place and home for said
minor child and petitioner is in a position to provide the necessities of life for
said minor child," the adoption petition says.[6]

Obviously, the judge didn't know the whole story. Not long after he signed
the adoption paperwork—or maybe even before—Rose left. She told Mom
that Orvel was boring, so maybe she wasn't quite as enamored with Zane
Grey as he was. In reality, they had little in common, the biggest disconnect
being her drinking. Rose's third husband went the way of the first two, except
Orvel didn't turn his back on the children like those other men did.

During the mid-1940s, Mom took several trips West with Orvel, who
towed a trailer through Oregon, California, Nevada, Arizona, New Mexico,
and Texas. Whatever bond existed between father and daughter before was
cemented in the prairies, mountains, and deserts of the great West. Orvel was
her equalizer, a sanctuary amid the upheaval sown by her mother. But he
had heart problems, and in 1956—the year I was born—he died at the age
of fifty-one. I never got to meet him, but I know him, just as I know Mary,
Louise, and the other members of the DeChaine clan who left a legacy of
goodness that survived long after their deaths.

My mom met my dad while working in Minneapolis for the Commodity
Credit Corporation, a government agency created during the Depression to
stabilize farm income and prices. My dad grew up in a farm community deep

in Republican country in western Minnesota, where his grandfather served in the Minnesota legislature and where his father was elected numerous times as the county auditor. When he was a kid, the area was best known for the "Bloody Fifth," an epic congressional battle in which Charles F. Kindred and Knute Nelson unveiled the type of gutter campaign tactics—bribery, payoffs, and the like—reminiscent of Boss Tweed and Tammany Hall.[7]

Ellsworth—or Al, as Mom called my dad—never ran for political office, but politics ran deep in his blood, dialed up perhaps during the Depression, when he shared an efficiency apartment with a roommate he almost never saw because they worked opposite shifts. Of course, politics is writ large in Minnesota, often played before a national stage. Harold Stassen, a former Minnesota governor, ran for president ten times. Eugene McCarthy served in Congress for a couple of decades but is best known for his antiwar platform in the 1968 presidential election. Walter Mondale was Jimmy Carter's running mate in 1976 and 1980 and was the Democratic nominee—and the party's sacrificial lamb—in 1984 when Ronald Reagan won forty-nine states, leaving Mondale to pick up just one: Minnesota.

But the Minnesota politician who most resonated with my father was the same one Ernie wouldn't cross the street to see: Hubert Horatio Humphrey. My dad adored Hubie. My baseball coach as a kid was Fred Gates, who was the son of one of Humphrey's chief political lieutenants and was so close to the Humphrey family that he was in the room when the famous senator died. Fred, who died just before Christmas 2017, became close to my family, too, probably aided by my father's pride in his connection to his dad's boss. You might say Fred represented the three things my dad cherished: family, politics, and sports. Dad was a sports nut and would often tell the story about how he got a scholarship to play baseball in college but threw out his arm. Baseball also was responsible in a way for a big insurance claim my father had to make. After he came home one day, the family Buick rolled down the street and crashed into a neighbor's car because Dad—dashing into the house so he could get the Minnesota Twins game on his transistor—forgot to put the vehicle into park.

He married my mom after serving in World War II, during which he was stationed in northern Africa and Italy. He didn't talk about the war much, but in a box of memorabilia that he kept from those years is a postcard of Mussolini hanging by his feet in Milan, Italy, where he'd been shot along with his mistress on April 28, 1945. Two days later, with the war in Europe no longer in doubt, Hitler committed suicide.

After the war, Dad returned to his old job as an accountant and did what just about everyone did during the postwar boom: began raising a family. Although I was picked on by my older siblings—constantly it seemed—I realize now what an idyllic life I had. My parents had four children in seven years, but I never felt like it was a chaotic household. We didn't have a lot of rules, but there was one I dared cross just once: showing disrespect to my mom. I never saw my father so angry.

My mother went back to work around the time I hit my teens. It was a part-time job, but it meant Dad had to cook supper, and that wasn't his strong suit. I remember eating a lot of fish sticks and potpies. Mom was no gourmet cook—we wouldn't have appreciated it if she was—but I always felt better when she was the one doing the cooking.

A lot of us put our aging or deceased parents on a pedestal, and I don't doubt that I've overlooked some of my dad's failings, but I don't know a single soul who knew him and doesn't say he was a good man. He wasn't the loudest person in the room, but I suspect on most occasions, he was the smartest. He was quirky, told the same stories over and over, but led by example and his example was to model decent behavior. He and mom must have fought on occasion, but they somehow kept it from their children, or at least from me.

My dad was fourteen years older than my mom and died in 1991 at the age of eighty-two. He had Alzheimer's for many years, and it was in the nursing home where he was housed during the last year of his life where my mom met her second husband, Art Sivanich. Mom was taking care of Dad while Art was doing the caregiving for his wife. They saw each other every day, became fast friends and—years after their spouses had died—husband and wife. Art, like my dad, was a good man. He was in the Coast Guard in World War II and served aboard *LST-793*, which earned two battle stars during the war.[8] Art organized the first reunion of the shipmates in Minneapolis in 1983, and for each year afterward, the group met in a different state: Arizona, Virginia, Kentucky, Ohio, Florida, New York, Georgia, Missouri. They would get together and socialize—OK, drink—renew acquaintances, and pay tribute to a replica of the ship's bell that they would treat like the Heisman Trophy. As the years wore on, the group got a little thinner, its ranks shrunken by Father Time. In 2005, the shipmates held their twenty-third and last reunion in New Orleans, postponing the original date because of Hurricane Katrina. The next year, Father Time caught up to Art as well.[9]

He was a former Minneapolis police officer who used to do safety programs at my elementary school, where I knew him as Officer Sivanich. He was a big, garrulous guy whose prize possession hung on his wall: the five cards that mark the night he had a perfect twenty-nine hand in cribbage. Art liked to celebrate his victories. No, not the one in World War II. That was nothing compared to the day he and my mom scored a Swarovski crystal figurine at a garage sale for twenty-five cents. My kids like to joke about the time he took us through side streets so he could point out where cops used to live. Perhaps his most memorable quality, though, is that he treated my mom well.

If life is a roller coaster, my mom started at its most perilous point. But she survived because of those around her and her own quiet grace, a strength of character that is the reason she attracts so many "good men." In the independent living complex where she used to live, she met Dean Christofferson, a former mortician who lived down the hall until Father Time caught up with him as well. For nine years, Dean was my mom's best friend, card-playing buddy, and significant other. When I couldn't get my mom on the phone, I would call Dean and she was usually there. They were on different floors when she first moved there, but she was shifted to his floor after a remodeling.

"It takes me forty-six steps to get to Dean's now," she announced after the move.

During a recent trip home Mom showed me a journal from one of the trips West she took with Orvel. It's titled "My Trip to California" and dated May 30, 1946, which would have made her twenty-four years old at the time. Each day is chronicled in the journal along with her musings and commentary about what she saw. I cracked up when she talked about Orvel's nervousness about her driving—"Dad's hair is two shades whiter," she wrote. "For some reason, he doesn't approve of the way I take curves at sixty miles per hour."[10]

I remember well—how could I forget?—how she used to hang on for dear life whenever I got behind the wheel with her when I was that age.

There were other amusing anecdotes in the day-by-day synopsis—"Beef cattle (in Oklahoma) are plentiful and look different than Minnesota cattle"— but what comes across is the enduring bond she had with her father. If they fought on the trip, it wasn't recorded, and it seems that she recorded most everything else: the times the car would overheat, the $2 fishing license she bought in California, her first-ever glimpse of the Pacific Ocean. "What a wonderful sight," she wrote. "If I lived there, I am sure most of my time would be spent out there fishing."

In Los Angeles, they parked the car at Hollywood and Vine and took a three-hour sightseeing bus, marveling at the actress Marion Davies's mansion, which she had just purchased for $120,000—a sum unimaginable to a girl from Brainerd. San Francisco held the same allure for Mom, and she was fascinated as people jumped onto moving streetcars, hanging on for dear life as the vehicles chugged up the seemingly endless hills. As she and Orvel drove through Northern California and the redwood forests, she wrote, "I kept thinking how ideal it would be to have a cabin in among the redwoods close to the ocean." In her scrapbook, the parking ticket they got in Portland was mounted next to postcards from Laurelhurst Lake and St. Johns Bridge. After traveling through Oregon and reaching Seattle they started on the journey back, stopping at one of my favorite places in America: Glacier National Park. Forty years later, my mouth would be similarly agape as I too drove on the Going-to-the-Sun Road and witnessed the same awesome vista along St. Mary Lake.

Travelogues can be boring, but as I read my mom's descriptions of a bear climbing on their car in Glacier National Park—"When he started to take the pipe out of Dad's mouth, we decided to roll the window up"—I realized that despite all the chaos, her life was a scrapbook, too. She refused to be defined by rejection or dysfunction, though those were certainly options laid out at her feet. Instead, she took curves at sixty miles per hour and kept her foot on the gas as her dad's hair turned white.

At the beginning of her journal, she pasted "A Cowboy's Prayer," written by an anonymous author who describes nature as his church. It must have resonated, because as Orvel drove through the redwoods of Northern California, she repeated one of the author's lines: "Where else can man be a man but out west of the Great Divide."

Ernie couldn't protect her as he held her hand outside their grandmother's tarpaper shack in Brainerd. But somebody did. Perhaps the author of "A Cowboy's Prayer" is right. Nature is a church. And as those doors opened for my mom after a rough childhood, more than a little sunlight began to pour through.[11]

My mother turned one hundred years old on November 19, 2021. She's outlived two husbands and all of her closest friends through the years, but she is content, passing the time with her books, puzzles, Minnesota Twins games (my dad would be proud), black-and-white movies—she loves TCM, the Turner Classic Movies channel—and her adoring family, which constantly marvels over her strength and endurance. And for her, that is enough. She never seems to dwell on what she doesn't have. For years she has struggled with her hearing, and I often find myself screaming into the telephone, hoping she can catch what I'm saying. Sometimes I think she's guessing, maybe hearing one or two words and piecing together the rest of the sentence the way I do when I try to decipher something in French using an internet translator. A few years ago, her eyesight was failing her, and we all worried when her eye doctor recommended a cornea transplant. She was ninety-four at the time, and any operation at that age seemed ill-advised, even dangerous. But she insisted and when the doctor pulled off her bandages, her first words were, "That wasn't pain free." But within a few hours she was saying something else in answer to the question of whether she could see better: "yes." She was soon back to reading books, cross-stitching rugs, and playing the dice game 15,000, at which she excels. Years ago, when I asked her what she was doing one day, she said, "I'm teaching a class." My mom has never been a teacher, so I asked what class she was talking about. "Dice," she answered as if the question was completely ridiculous.

In her new independent living complex, she plays bingo—stopping only briefly during the coronavirus pandemic—and when she first moved in, she taught a cross-stitching class. Makes sense. After all, what is the point of getting old if you keep all that wisdom to yourself?

When my mom first asked me to find her brother, I had no idea what direction that search would take. Some of the people I met along the way were reluctant to talk, hesitant to reopen old scars. That's understandable. This isn't exactly a story of triumph. Or maybe it is. I set out to find Robert, to see what happened to the boy who disappeared from my mother's life at a time when she could have used someone who loved her. Robert's life—what little I learned about it—was nothing to write home about, but he had two loving, adoptive parents who did what they could to surround him with family. My mom had none of that, at least from her parents, yet she has lived a wonderful life. I wanted to find inspiration in Robert's story, but the true inspirational figure was next to me the whole time.

"That wasn't without pain," my mom had said. Yet when the bandages came off, she could see. Kind of a metaphor for her life.

In the spring of 2017 my wife Lynda, our daughter Nicole, her daughter Riley, and I went to see my mother in Minnesota. It was Mom's first chance to see her great-granddaughter, who was seven months old at the time. As my mom got down on her hands and knees to play with Riley, the bond was unmistakable. Riley knows when people care about her, and though she couldn't talk intelligibly, she communicated with smiles, laughter, and that sound she used to make in the presence of someone who she knows loves her: "*aaaaaaaaaaaah.*"

Ninety-five years separated the two people on the carpet, and it struck me how different their lives are. When my mom was born, Warren Harding was the twenty-ninth consecutive white man to hold the job of president. When Riley was born, a mixed-race man, Barack Obama, was the nation's forty-fourth president—and the first African American to hold the job. My mother grew up in crippling, Depression-era poverty and endured severe neglect from her mother. Riley, meanwhile, has complete confidence that she will be well taken care of at all times, and someone will always respond when she says, "I'm hungry." Mom doesn't hear well, whereas Riley perks up whenever music comes on, particularly if it's a song from the movie *Frozen* or her favorite TV show, *Daniel Tiger's Neighborhood.* On the other hand, both have an easygoing nature that is intoxicating to those around them.

Like all moms, my daughter Nicole chose the names for her daughter carefully. The name Riley has no family significance, but Nicole liked it and knew it was one that she would never grow tired of. Riley's middle name, however, runs deep into family lore. It was also the middle name of Lynda's sister Sharon—Nicole's aunt—who died way too young and suffered from chronic obstructive pulmonary disease, the same disease that afflicted Robert's sister, Sheila Fletcher. Sharon's death was not without pain for all of us—a lot of pain, in fact—but it is at least some comfort that her memory lives on through the niece she never met.

Though unintended, the name has another meaningful connection for me, and it has to do with the ninety-something woman playing on the floor with her great-granddaughter. Names don't have to have meaning. We chose the ones for our kids for the same reason Nicole picked Riley: because we liked them. But middle names are funny. Parents agonize over them, yet they often become forgotten appendages, like a Christmas gift that gets left in the box. Maybe Riley's will, too, but I doubt it. We didn't choose the names of our children because of legacy, but Riley's middle name is one that conjures pain, sorrow, and enduring love. Mostly love. Not all names have meaning, but this one does.

My mom rocks back and forth on hands and knees, coaxing another impish grin from the infant child who instantly adores her. They are at opposite ends of life but have joined in the middle for this one glorious moment of mutual admiration. And as my mom places a plastic toy tantalizingly close but just out of reach of the girl who has not yet learned to crawl, Riley Rose Martin drags herself forward using first one arm and then another, determined to overcome any obstacle that might get in her way.

NOTES

1. Author interview with Carolyn Phillips.
2. Interview with Millie Sivanich.
3. Edwin Black, *War against the Weak* (Washington, DC: Dialog Press, 2012), xv.
4. From "Struck by Car, Killed," *Brainerd Daily Dispatch*, October 20, 1939.
5. Author interview with Millie Sivanich.
6. Adoption record from Anoka County, Minnesota, March 21, 1942.
7. See Carl Zapffre, *Brainerd* (Minneapolis, MN: Colwell Press, 1946), 27.
8. Stories about the reunions of the crew of the *LST 793* can be found on the website http://lst793.com.
9. Art's obituary ran in the *Minneapolis Tribune* on March 1, 2006.
10. From Millie's journal, "My Trip to California."
11. Ibid. My mom pasted it onto the opening page of her journal "My Trip to California" on May 30, 1946.

Dates

June 12, 1838: Antoine DeChaine, Joseph's father, is born in Saint-Paulin, Quebec, Canada.

May 8, 1839: Louise Marineau, Joseph's mother, is born ten miles away in Saint-Leon-le-Grand, Quebec.

1861: Antoine and Louise are married in Saint-Paulin.

May 8, 1863: Joseph DeChaine, first son of Antoine DeChaine and Louise Marineau, is born in Saint-Paulin.

December 25, 1865: Melvina Forcier, Joseph's future bride, is born in Brandon, Vermont. The family eventually settles in Brainerd, Minnesota.

Spring 1881: Antoine, Louise, their eight children, and Antoine's mother, Celeste LaJoie, set out for Brainerd, Minnesota. They arrive there later that year.

July 4, 1887: Joseph marries Melvina "Mary" Forcier in Brainerd.

December 24, 1901: Rose DeChaine, daughter of Joseph DeChaine and Mary Forcier, is born in Brainerd.

July 27, 1914: Lottie DeChaine, Rose's sister, marries John Verkennes.

February 26, 1915: Lottie dies along with her fifteen-month-old daughter, Irene, after pouring kerosene on a dying fire in their heat stove. She survives long enough for John to arrive from his worksite in the Northern Pacific Railroad roundhouse.

April 12, 1915: Antoine DeChaine, Joseph's father, dies in Brainerd.

September 16, 1916: John Verkennes, Lottie's widower, marries her sister Dora.

December 9, 1916: The first of John and Dora's four children is born. They name her Irene after John and Lottie's daughter who died in the house explosion.

February 15, 1918: Rose, just sixteen years of age, marries Leo Jerred in Todd County, Minnesota.

December 22, 1919: Ernie (Jerred) McClain is born in St. Cloud, Minnesota.

June 2, 1920: Rose and Leo divorce.

August 7, 1920: Joseph DeChaine, Rose's father, dies of throat cancer.

May 21, 1921: Rose marries Ingram Conradson in Bemidji, Minnesota.

November 19, 1921: Mildred Melvina Conradson (now Millie Sivanich) is born in Brainerd to Rose DeChaine and Ingram Conradson.

July 1, 1922: Railroad shopmen stage a national strike. John Verkennes and his brothers walk off the job and are not welcomed back. Most of the Verkennes family members move to Flint, Michigan. The strike financially cripples many families in Brainerd, including the DeChaine family.

September 1922: Ingram Conradson abandons Rose and her two children.

August 12, 1924: Rose is admitted to the Faribault School for the Feeble-Minded for the first time. Two unnamed individuals testify that she is "immoral."

January 10, 1925: Ray Anderson and Santa "Gloria" Donfris, who become the adoptive parents to Robert, marry in Duluth, Minnesota.

April 8, 1925: Minnesota's Republican governor, Theodore Christianson, signs the state's eugenics sterilization bill into law. It takes effect the following January.

April 20, 1925: Robert Conradson is born inside the Faribault institution.

April 23, 1926: Rose is sterilized at Faribault, the state's leading testing ground for eugenic sterilizations; less than one month later, she is released for the first time.

May 19, 1926: Mary DeChaine marries John Lorbecki in Brainerd, Minnesota.

December 11, 1927: Rose is readmitted to Faribault after she, her three children, and her mother's estranged husband, John Lorbecki, are picked up in International Falls, Minnesota.

December 13, 1927: John Lorbecki is jailed on a charge of desertion. The charges are later dropped.

March 3, 1928: Rose's three children—Ernie, Millie, and Robert—are admitted to the St. James Catholic Orphanage in Duluth, Minnesota.

July 2, 1928: Rose is released from Faribault for the second time and placed at the Harmon Place in Minneapolis, a "clubhouse" operated by the state and used to transition feebleminded—and sterilized—women to life outside the institution.

July 8, 1928: Robert leaves the St. James after he is adopted by Ray and Santa (Donfris) Anderson of Eveleth, Minnesota.

August 13, 1928: Millie is released from the St. James and taken to her grandmother's house because of what is described as a leg deformity. Two weeks later, she is transported to the Gillette Hospital for Crippled Children in St. Paul, which specializes in cases involving indigent children. She undergoes several operations and is returned to her grandmother's home in Brainerd after her discharge on December 8, 1928.

March 30, 1929: Rose is readmitted for the third time to the Faribault School for the Feeble-Minded.

December 24, 1929: Rose is discharged from Faribault and placed at a second clubhouse, the Lynnhurst Girls Club in St. Paul.

May 14, 1930: Rose marries her third husband, Orvel McClain, following her release from the Lynnhurst Club.

June 2, 1930: Ernie is released after spending more than two years in the St. James Catholic Orphanage. He is taken to his grandmother's home in Brainerd but soon goes to live with his mother and her new husband in Minneapolis. His sister Millie follows after Rose reveals to Orvel that she also has a daughter.

June 8, 1931: Patricia Anderson is born in Chicago, Illinois. She is adopted by Ray and Santa Anderson and becomes a sister to Robert.

February 24, 1941: Ernie is sent to prison on a charge of third-degree burglary. He serves almost four years.

March 21, 1943: Orvel McClain formally adopts Millie. The petition says her biological father, Ingram Conradson, deserted the family.

April 12, 1943: Louise (Marineau) DeChaine, Joseph's mother, dies in Brainerd at the age of 103.

October 11, 1944: Ernie is released from prison.

March 7, 1946: Mary, Rose's mother, dies in Brainerd at the age of seventy-nine.

1949: Sheila Fletcher is adopted at age three by Ray and Santa Anderson, becoming a sister to Robert and Patricia Anderson.

June 29, 1954: Michael McClain, Ernie's son, is born in Astoria, Oregon.

December 15, 1956: Orvel McClain, Millie's adoptive father, dies.

May 2, 1969: William Saastamoinen, Rose's fourth husband, dies.

January 12, 1970: Rose dies. Her death certificate gives the cause as chronic alcoholism.

July 12, 1973: Fire destroys millions of service records at the National Personnel Records Center in Overland, Missouri. Robert's military record is among those destroyed.

December 20, 1976: Santa Anderson, Robert's adoptive mother, dies in Illinois.

February 27, 1977: Ingram Conradson, Rose's second husband and the biological father to Millie, dies in Portland, Oregon.

August 23, 1978: Nancy McClain, Ernie's nineteen-year-old daughter, dies at sea.

February 13, 1979: Ernie takes a .357 Magnum revolver into a courtroom in Portland, Oregon, and kills an attorney, Candise Jones, before turning the gun on himself.

June 14, 1991: Ellsworth Erickson, Millie's first husband and the father of her four children, dies in Minneapolis.

January 1992: Raymond Anderson dies in Chicago.

September 12, 1993: Robert Anderson, Ernie and Millie's brother, dies in St. Paul, Minnesota.

November 3, 1996: Michael McClain, Ernie's son, plants bombs in two restaurants in Astoria, Oregon. Both fail to ignite properly and Michael kills himself inside the Pig 'n Pancake restaurant.

February 27, 2006: Art Sivanich, Millie's second husband, dies.

September 12, 2016: Four former residents of the St. James Catholic Orphanage file separate lawsuits against the Diocese of Duluth alleging that they were molested by clergy members at the St. James Catholic Orphanage between 1948 and 1969. It is the same orphanage where Ernie was housed from March 1928 until June 1930.

January 11, 2017: Sheila Fletcher, Robert's sister and the third child adopted by Ray and Santa Anderson, dies in Chicago.

October 21, 2019: A bankruptcy judge approves a $39.2 million settlement of 125 claims of sexual abuse filed by plaintiffs against the Diocese of Duluth. Included in the settlement are the four lawsuits alleging clergy sexual abuse at the St. James.

Bibliography

Books

Angle, Paul M. *Philip K. Wrigley: A Memoir of a Modest Man.* New York: Rand McNally, 1975.

Berton, Pierre. *The Last Spike: The Great Railway 1881–1885.* Toronto: Anchor Canada, 1971.

———. *The National Dream: The Great Railway, 1871–1881.* Toronto: Anchor Canada, 2001.

Black, Edwin. *War against the Weak: Eugenics and America's Campaign to Create a Master Race.* Washington, DC: Dialog Press, 2012.

Brown, Craig. *The Illustrated History of Canada.* Toronto: Key Porter, 1987.

Davis, Colin J. *Power at Odds: The 1922 National Railroad Shopmen's Strike.* Urbana: University of Illinois Press, 1997.

Folwell, William Watts. *A History of Minnesota.* St. Paul: Minnesota Historical Society, 1969.

Humphrey, Hubert H. *Education of a Public Man: My Life and Politics.* Minneapolis: University of Minnesota Press, 1991.

Josephson, Matthew. *The Robber Barons: The Classic Account of the Influential Capitalists Who Transformed America's Future.* Boston: Mariner Books, 1962.

Ladd-Taylor, Molly. *Fixing the Poor: Eugenic Sterilization and Child Welfare in the Twentieth Century.* Baltimore: Johns Hopkins University Press, 2017.

Larson, Agnes M. *The White Pine Industry in Minnesota.* Minneapolis: Regents of the University of Minnesota Press, 1939.

Lass, William E. *Minnesota: A History.* New York: Norton, 1998.

Lombardo, Paul. *A Century of Eugenics in America.* Bloomington: Indiana University Press, 2011.

Lubetkin, M. John. *Jay Cooke's Gamble: The Northern Pacific Railroad, the Sioux, and the Panic of 1873.* Norman: University of Oklahoma Press, 2006.

Luecke, John C. *The Northern Pacific in Minnesota.* St. Paul: Grenadier, 2005.

Lynch, Claire. *Orphanages of Minnesota.* St. Paul: Minnesota Historical Society Library, 1938.

MacKay, Donald. *The Lumberjacks*. Toronto: Natural Heritage/Natural History, 1998.

Malone, Michael P. *James J. Hill: Empire Builder of the Northwest*. Norman: University of Oklahoma Press, 1996.

Merrill, Maud, and A. C. Rogers. *Dwellers in the Vale of Siddem: A True Story of the Social Aspect of Feeble-mindedness*. Boston: Gorham Press, 1919.

Morgan, Robert. *Lions of the West: Heroes and Villains of the Westward Expansion*. Chapel Hill, NC: Algonquin, 2011.

Myers, Gustavus. *A History of Canadian Wealth*. Toronto: Lewis & Samuel, 1972.

Pacyga, Dominic A. *Slaughterhouse: Chicago's Union Stock Yard and the World It Made*. Chicago: University of Chicago Press, 2015.

Parkman, Francis. *Montcalm and Wolfe: The French & Indian War*. Cambridge, MA: Da Capo Press, 1984.

Peterson, Jillian, and James Densley. *The Violence Project: How to Stop a Mass Shooting Epidemic*. New York: Abrams Press, 2021.

Raiter, Franklin R., and Francis M. Carroll. *The Fires of Autumn: The Cloquet–Moose Lake Disaster of 1918*. St. Paul: Minnesota Historical Society Press, 1990.

Thomson, Mildred. *Prologue: A Minnesota Story of Mental Retardation Showing Changing Attitudes and Philosophies prior to September 1, 1959*. Minneapolis, MN: Gilbert Publishing, 1963.

Walker, David A. *Iron Frontier: The Discovery and Early Development of Minnesota's Three Ranges*. St. Paul: Minnesota Historical Society, 1979.

Walz, Thomas. *The Unlikely Celebrity: Bill Sackter's Triumph over Disability*. Carbondale: Southern Illinois University, 1998.

White, Richard. *Railroaded: The Transcontinentals and the Making of Modern America*. New York: W. W. Norton, 2011.

Zapffe, Carl. *Brainerd*. Minneapolis, MN: Colwell Press, 1946.

———. *Indian Days in Minnesota's Lake Region*. Brainerd, MN: Historic Heartland Association, 1990.

Zimmerman, William Jr. *William Wrigley, Jr.: The Man and His Business, 1861–1932*. New York: R. R. Donnelley, 1935.

Other Sources

Ancestry, www.ancestry.com

Bishop Accountability, www.bishop-accountability.org

Clatsop County Circuit Court, www.co.clatsop.or.us

Crow Wing County Historical Society, www.crowwinghistory.org

Family Search International, www.familysearch.org

Federal Bureau of Investigation, www.fbi.gov

International Soundex Reunion Registry, www.isrr.org

Kaiser Permanente, www.healthy.kaiserpermanente.org

Library of Congress, www.loc.gov

Minnesota Department of Health, www.state.mn.us

Minnesota Department of Human Services, https://mn.gov/dhs

Minnesota Historical Society, www.mnhs.org

Minnesota House of Representatives, www.house.leg.state.mn.us
Minnesota Official Marriage System, www.moms.mn.gov
National Park Service, www.nps.gov
National Personnel Records Center, www.gsa.gov
Oregon Board of Parole, www.oregon.gov
St. Louis County (MN) Board of Health, www.stlouiscounty.mn.gov
U.S. Census, www.census.gov
U.S. Centers for Disease Control, www.cdc.gov
U.S. District Court, Sixth Judicial District, www.mncourts.gov

Newspapers, Other Media

Associated Press, www.ap.org
Atlantic, www.theatlantic.com
Baltimore Sun, www.baltimoresun.com
Brainerd Dispatch, www.brainerddispatch.com
Catholic News Service, www.catholicnews.com
Chicago Sun-Times, www.chicago.suntimes.com
Chicago Tribune, www.chicagotribune.com
Daily Astorian, www.dailyastorian.com
Duluth News Tribune, www.duluthnewstribune.com
Milwaukee Journal Sentinel, www.jsonline.com
Minneapolis Star Tribune, www.startribune.com
Minnesota Public Radio, www.mpr.org
National Catholic Reporter, www.ncronline.org
Natural History Magazine, www.naturalhistorymag.com
New York Times, www.nytimes.com
Newsletter of the Benedictine Sisters, www.duluthbenedictines.org
Oregonian, www.oregonlive.com
Scientific American, www.scientificamerican.com
Wall Street Journal, www.wsj.com
Walla Walla Union-Bulletin, www.union-bulletin.com

Index

Anderson and Associates, 71, 72
angels, adoption, 126, 128, 132
apologies, Minnesota with, xvii,
xix, 81–82
Associated Press, 106n19
Astoria bombings, 111, 112
Atlanta spa, mass shooting, 154
Austin, Horace, 5

"baby farms," 43–44
Becken, Joyce Frances. *See* McClain,
Joyce Frances Becken
Beckley, Mabel DeChaine (sister):
childhood, 14, 15, 16, 18, 21, 22;
with family, 23, 25, 30, 31, 33, 94,
162, 163, *p2*
Beckley, Warren (brother-in-
law), 23, 163
Benedictine sisters' community, 70
Bernhardt, Sarah, 135
Bernstein, Charles, 83
Binet, Alfred, 42
Binet-Simon IQ test: cultural bias and,
42–43; of DeChaine, Rose, 26n3,
43, 50–51, 61, 114; of feebleminded
with sterilization, xviii, 42, 50–51; of
McClain, Ernest Jerred, 97. *See also*
intelligence, of women
Black, Edwin, xvii, 46, 161
Black Hills, 6
Blueberry War, 5
Board of Control. *See* State Board of
Control, Minnesota
bombings, xviii, 98, 111, 112–13, 152
Boom Lake plant, 8–9, 10
Brackett, Alfred B., 4
Brainerd, 11; Boom Lake plant, 8–9;
as boomtown, 4–6; education in,
16–18; founding of, 3; lumber
industry, 7–10; NP Railway strike,
35–36; on Ojibwe territory, 4–5; U.S.
Census for, 26n3
Brainerd Baseball Club, 5
Brainerd Dispatch (newspaper), 3, 10,
19–20, 25, 36, 61, 62, 64–65

Brainerd International Raceway, 7
Brainerd Lumber Company, 9
Brainerd Tribune (newspaper), 5, 8, 10
brains: damage in mass shooters, 102–3,
154; frontal lobotomies, 82
Bridgeman, H. L., 6
Buchtel, Quin, 73
Buck, Carrie, ix–x, 46–49, 57n14
Buck, Emma, 46–47
Buck, Vivian, 47, 48, 49
Buckman, Jean. *See* Dockter, Jean
Buckman McClain
Buck v. Bell, ix, 46, 49, 57n14
bullying, 153
Bureau for the Feebleminded and
Epileptic, Board of Control, 82
Burquist, Joseph A. A., xxiii–xxiv

California, 46, 76, 107, 143, 163,
166–67, 169n11
Canada, ix, 1, 2, 7, 11n2, 13, 17
Carlton County Vidette
(newspaper), xxiii
Carnegie, Andrew, 137
Carter, Jimmy, 164
Cartier, Sharon, 168–69
Carver, George Washington, 46
Cassell, Rebecca, 85
Catholic Charities of St. Cloud, 124
Catholic Charities of St. Paul, 125
Catholic Church, xxiv, 46, 57n21, 137;
Benedictine sisters' community,
70; Catholic Charities of St. Cloud,
124; Catholic Charities of St. Paul,
125; College of St. Benedictine,
123–24; Diocese of Duluth, 70,
71–72, 73; nuns, 70, 74–75, 77,
78, 94, 117–19, 123–25, 126, 128,
153; with pedophile priests and
sexual abuse, 71–76, 153; St. Cloud
Children's Home, 124; St. Cloud
Reformatory, 95–97; St. John the
Evangelist Church, 72, 73, 75; with
sexual abuse lawsuits, 71–73, 75;

Fox, Frederick (Father), 72, 73
Frank, Bob, 108
Freedom of Information Act, 148
frontal lobotomies, 82
Frost, Robert, 90
Fulghum, Robert, 78

Gable, Clark, 7
Galton, Francis, x
Gates, Fred, 164
Germany, ix, xviii, 25
Gillette Hospital for Crippled Children, 67, 81, 82, 85, 86
Gilpatrick, W. F., 123
Goddard, Henry H., 44, 114, 147, 156
Goodhue, James Madison, 10
Gormly, Charles J. (Reverend), 73
Gorrow, Chelsea, 112–13
Gould, Stephen Jay, 48–49
government, with reproductive organs, 46
Grant, Ulysses S., 3
Great Depression, 86, 93–94, 135–36, 164, 168
Grey, Zane, 163
guardianship, 43, 44, 63, 84, 89
guards, at Faribault School for the Feeble-Minded, 52
gun control, 108
Gurrell, John, 5

Hall, Charles, 84
Hanna, Guy C., 84–85
Harding, Warren, 36, 168
Harmon Place, Club House for Girls, 82, 83, 84, 88, 126
Hart, Richard, xxiii–xxiv
hatred, of women, 46, 50, 85
Hill, James J., 10
Hills Youth and Family Services, 127
Hitler, Adolf, xviii, 164
Hodson, William, 49–50, 122, 161
Holmes, Oliver Wendell, 48, 49
Holtzman, Jerome, 144
homosexuality, 83, 88

housekeeping, 50, 53, 54, 84, 85, 89, 93
House of the Good Shepherd, 83–84
Howe, Jeremiah J. "Jerry," 8–9, 10
Hughswish, E., 123
Humphrey, Hubert Horatio, 93–94, 164

immigrants, 2, 10, 11, 138, 145; abuse of, xi; with education, 17; eugenics and, 44; forced sterilization of, x; intelligence of, 42, 147; slaughterhouses and, 134–35; WPA interviews with, 26n1, 86, 123
immorality, x, xi, 17, 39, 39n1, 41, 83, 86, 114, 115; of Buck, Carrie, 47; coupling, 44; of DeChaine, Rose, 50, 51, 56n2; degeneracy and, 43; morality and, ix, 43, 47, 49, 85; sterilization and, xvii
Indiana, with eugenic sterilization, 46
indigenous people, x, xi, 4–5
infant homes, 44
infidelity, women and, 47
inherited, feebleminded as, 44, 47, 48, 49–51, 114, 122, 141, 161
insanity, ix, xxi, 44, 49, 82, 83, 85
institutionalization: as public policy, 41; of targeted populations, x
intelligence, of women: eugenics and, x, xvii–xviii, 42; IQ tests, xviii, 26n3, 42–43, 50–51, 61, 97, 114; reproduction, morality and, 43, 47, 85
International Soundex Reunion Registry, 125–26, 149n8
interracial marriage, x
Iowa City, 52
IQ test. *See* Binet-Simon IQ test
Iron Range, Minnesota, xxiii–xxiv, 129, 134, 137
Iron Range Research Center, 133–34

Japan, ix, 142
Jefferson, Thomas, 1, 11n2
Jerred, Ernest "Ernie" (son). *See* McClain, Ernest "Ernie" Jerred

About the Author

John Erickson spent more than thirty years in journalism at daily newspapers in Illinois and Ohio. At the *Dayton* (Ohio) *Daily News*, he led the coverage on three stories that were finalists for the Pulitzer Prize, including a series that won the Pulitzer for National Reporting in 1998. In 2019, he was inducted into the Ohio Associated Press Media Editors' Hall of Fame. John grew up in Minneapolis, Minnesota, and graduated from the University of Minnesota with a degree in journalism. He and his wife Lynda live in Ohio with their two children, Travis and Nicole, and their grandchild, Riley.

CPSIA information can be obtained
at www.ICGtesting.com
Printed in the USA
BVHW031047210622
640104BV00003B/3